Amen & Amen

Sermons of the
Reverend Kristian R. Davidson

Compiled and Edited
by

Carol J. Garvin

Copyright © 2016 by Carol J. Garvin

All rights reserved, including the right of reproduction in whole or in part in any form.

LIBRARY AND CATALOGUES CANADA CATALOGUING IN PUBLICATION
Garvin, Carol J., 1939 –
Amen & Amen:
      Sermons of the Reverend Kristian R. Davidson
252GAR
I. Sermons, II. Presbyterian, III. Davidson, Kristian R.

ISBN: 978-0-9917652-2-5

Cover photo and design by Carol J. Garvin

These sermons are transcribed here as they were found on Mr. Davidson's computer, unaltered except for minor changes in spelling, grammar, punctuation, and layout for publication purposes.

The Reverend Kristian Robert Davidson

Table of Contents

Title	Date	Page
Free to Go Fishing	2004-02-08	6
Still Cheering for the Underdog	2004-03-21	13
A Fragrant Offering	2004-03-28	21
What's Riding on It?	2004-04-04	30
It Is Finished	2004-04-09	38
No Nonsense	2004-04-11	45
Beyond the Shadow of Doubt	2004-04-18	51
"Follow Me"	2004-04-25	61
The Lamb is My Shepherd	2004-05-02	70
Commanding Love	2004-05-09	80
Remember the Future	2004-05-16	89
Opening an Open Mind	2004-05-23	99
Towering Achievements	2004-05-30	108
The Unwanted God	2004-06-06	119
Sharing a Meal with Sinners	2004-06-13	129
What Are You Doing Here?	2004-06-20	137
A Double Portion	2004-06-27	148
Sent Out as Lambs	2004-07-04	158
What Must I Do?	2004-07-11	168
Better Hospitality	2004-07-18	177
Don't Worry; Be Ready	2004-08-08	185
Kindling the Fire	2004-08-15	193
The Real Thing	2004-08-22	202
Claiming Expenses	2004-08-29	211
No Surrender	2004-09-05	220
Lost Causes	2004-09-12	229
God's Bottom Line	2004-09-19	238
Investing for the Future	2004-09-26	245
Mastering Faith	2004-10-03	255
Food for Life	2004-10-10	263
Praying for Faith	2004-10-17	272
Seeing Through the Crowd	2004-10-24	281
Honest to God	2004-10-31	290
Remember the Way	2004-11-07	298
Can You See It?	2004-11-14	306
The Last Word	2004-11-21	314
Resting Secure	2004-11-28	322
Nothing to Lose	2004-12-05	330
What Are You Looking For?	2004-12-12	339
Appendix A: Memorial Minute		348

Preface

The word of our God will stand forever.
(Isaiah 40:8b)

After a nine-month vacancy following the retirement of their former minister, the members of Haney Presbyterian Church, Maple Ridge, BC eagerly moved into a new phase under the leadership of The Reverend Kris Davidson. But after only nine more months his ministry abruptly ended. The congregation was devastated when he, his wife Sheryl, and older daughter Lauren died in a vehicle accident on January 7, 2005 as they returned home from a post-Christmas vacation in Alberta. Remarkably, their younger daughter, twenty-two-month old Katie, survived the accident.

Upheld by the prayers of the Haney congregation and surrounded by the love and care of her grandparents, aunts and uncles, Katie recovered. That she will have no memory of the accident is undoubtedly a blessing. What is a tragedy, however, is that she will also have no memory of her parents and sister, or of her father's significant ministry.

During the brief nine months between his ordination and his death, Kris made a huge impact on the lives of people in the church and community. His faith and humility witnessed to a deep love for God. His sermons rang with honesty and conviction.

By rescuing from the church computer and presenting here the sermons Kris preached during his nine months in Haney Church, it is my prayer that these words of her father will provide a permanent and tangible record for Katie of the Christian heritage that is hers as a child of God and the daughter of Kristian Robert Davidson.

Carol J. Garvin

Free to go Fishing

February 8, 2004

Luke 5:1-11

Last year when I was at the guidance conference for candidates preparing for ministry in the Presbyterian Church, I met a student who was attending Knox College. He told me a story about his attempt to find a larger apartment in Montreal shortly after the arrival of their newborn son. Apparently finding an apartment in Montreal is no easy task; so when one of his neighbours came to him saying she knew the perfect place, it seemed like a dream come true. The neighbour even arranged for someone to come by and take him and his wife to see the place.

And sure enough the time came and someone did come by and pick up my friend and his wife, but it wasn't long before he began to suspect that something wasn't quite right. They weren't going the right direction; in fact, they didn't go to an apartment building at all. The couple was taken instead to a meeting room in a church. Once inside, several people came in chanting, "Jesus, Jesus."

My friend recalls leaning over to his wife and saying, "I'm guessing there's no apartment."

Apparently this is what that church thought Jesus meant when he called the disciples to catch people. And they are by no means an exception. As churches throughout North America wrestle with the problem of church decline, the proposed solutions to the problem can range from discerning and thoughtful to aggressive and desperate.

So how are we to respond? What does it mean for us to be called by Jesus to a vocation of catching people? Let's take another look at our Gospel lesson for today.

We begin with Jesus standing by the lake of the Genesaret – another name for the Sea of Galilee – and the crowd is pressing in on him. Now for the most part this is not too difficult for us to imagine. Jesus has just finished performing healings and exorcisms; of course people would want to see him.

But the unusual part is that the people are pressing in on him not to see a deed of power, not to see an amazing trick. Luke tells us they were pressing in on Jesus to hear the word of God; but why? Couldn't they go to their local synagogue to hear the word of God? Why press in on Jesus?

Well, we need to remember something of the history of the people of Israel in order to get a sense of what the people are going through. Our Old Testament lesson is a good place to start. In an amazing vision, Isaiah finds himself standing in the midst of the holiness of God, but this is not a good thing. Isaiah himself knows the problem: he is a man of unclean lips living among a people of unclean lips, and here he is standing in the presence of God.

The people of Israel have fallen away from their calling to be a light to nations; they have forgotten the covenant and have followed after the idols of the nations around them. For Isaiah it must have seemed like this was going to be the end, but God will not abandon his people – he will not abandon the covenant. Instead, God sets in motion his plan to purify Israel. Isaiah is called to deliver the message to the people; and it is a message that will not win him any friends. Isaiah is called to proclaim a message that will stop the ears and shut the eyes of God's people. He is to make the people blind and deaf like the idols they worship. Isaiah is called to proclaim the beginning of the exile…but it would not be the end for the people Israel – God would be faithful to the covenant; a purified and faithful remnant of Israel would be restored.

Jeremiah spoke of this restoration as a second exodus – no longer would the people Israel be those who remember the Lord as the one who brought them out of Egypt. Instead, they would remember the living Lord who brought them up out of the lands where he had driven them. *(Jeremiah 16:15)* There would be a second exodus, a second temple, and a renewed covenant. Much of this came to pass. A number of the people returned from exile. They rebuilt the temple, but it wasn't long before they realized the promises of restoration were less than fulfilled; the people were in trouble again. Israel was living in the land, worshipping and sacrificing in the temple, but the presence of the Lord wasn't with them.

The prophet Malachi addressed the issue saying the half-hearted worship and the substandard sacrifices of the people had become an offense to the Lord and as such God had withdrawn his presence from the people. *(Malachi 2:3)* And if that were not enough, Israel was not being ruled by a descendent of David, but instead by a series of foreigners – Herod, Pilate and Caesar. Everyone knew something was wrong in Israel, but there was no agreement on how to make it right. Zealots, Sadducees, Pharisees, Essenes, each had their own solution to the problem, ranging from military force, to strict observance of the mosaic law, to isolation and asceticism.

The crowds – the people of Israel – are in the midst of an identity crisis; what does it mean to be God's people? Sure they are in the land. Sure, they have a rebuilt temple, but still there remains a very real sense of exile. Then along comes Jesus filled with the Spirit. He is doing amazing things –
    healing the lame and casting out demons,
        proclaiming the release of captives,
            proclaiming the end of their exile.

Is it any wonder the crowds are pressing in on him to hear the word of God?

So in order to teach the crowd, Jesus jumps into a nearby fishing boat and tells the captain whose name is Simon to put out a little way from the shore and then he sits down and teaches. But what does he teach? Luke doesn't tell us, not because it isn't important, but because here the teaching is not so much about what Jesus says, but about who Jesus is.

Remember in the synagogue at Nazareth how Jesus taught? He read from the scroll of Isaiah, then sat down and proclaimed it. Here in the boat there is no scroll. The people are not crowding in on Jesus because he is a great biblical interpreter. The people are beginning to realize that Jesus has an authority all his own; when he teaches they are hearing the Word of God. But then who is this Jesus?

We are about to find out. Jesus asks Simon to put out into the deep water and let the nets down for a catch. It's important here to understand that the type of fishing Simon and his partners were engaged in was not done with a casting net; that kind of fishing is done closer to shore. Deep water fishing was done by lowering a net into the water and dragging it behind the boat. The problem with this kind of fishing is that the nets are easily seen in the daylight; the fish could see the nets and get out of the way. So deep water fishing is done at night when the nets are not so easy to see. This is why the fishermen were cleaning their nets rather than fishing – they were preparing to go fishing again later that evening.

When Jesus asks them to lower their nets Simon responds by calling Jesus *master*. This is roughly the equivalent of saying that Jesus is now the captain of the fishing boat. Clearly Simon is impressed; he has heard Jesus teach and he has also witnessed Jesus cure his mother's fever. So Simon is showing Jesus as much respect as possible, but... Peter is an experienced fisherman; he knows what happens when you go deep water fishing in the daylight and he tries to warn Jesus. "We, the experienced fishermen, have been at this all night and have caught nothing, but if you say so I will let down the nets."

And indeed they do let down the nets... and catch so many fish that the nets begin to break, and even after calling their partners to come and help, the boats are so full they are in danger of sinking. These are not small boats – deep water fishing vessels had to hold a crew and all of their equipment. Imagine two large fishing boats so full they almost sank.

If you have a hard time imagining it, so did Simon. The impossible had just become possible right in front of his eyes, but more importantly, it was Jesus who was responsible for making it happen. Simon Peter suddenly becomes very aware of the fact that he is standing in the presence of the holiness of God in much the same way that Isaiah had gazed upon the King in the temple and cried out, "Woe is me, I am lost, for I am a man of unclean lips." Isaiah fully expected God to blot him out; but instead God blots his sins out. Here Simon Peter cries out, "Go away from me, Lord, for I am a sinful man." But the time has not yet come for his sins to be blotted out. There is work to be done first.

Notice that when Simon Peter cries out, he falls at Jesus' knees, and while this is to be expected in the presence of God's holiness, in that culture to sit at the knees of a teacher was an indication that you would teach what you had learned. So already there are hints here that Simon Peter will be sharing in the proclamation and ministry of Jesus. He, too, will teach the crowds the word of God that he was taught by Jesus.

And how does Jesus respond to Simon? He says, "Do not be afraid. From now on you will be catching people." Here Jesus is not simply saying, "Try not to be scared." Throughout the scriptures the phrase "do not be afraid" is used as an assurance that God will remain faithful to his promises and that God will be with his people during times of trial and persecution. The call to discipleship is accompanied by the assurance that the disciples will not be acting alone – God will be with them.

So with a little play on words Jesus assures these fishermen their new vocation will not be entirely foreign. They used to catch fish; now they will catch people. One of the unfortunate problems with this word play is that some have taken it to mean that catching people is just like catching fish – like the story I mentioned earlier – employing tactics that are roughly the equivalent of throwing a net over a person and dragging them off to church.

Clearly this is not what Jesus intended. The word that is used for "catching" in Greek does not mean set a trap – it doesn't mean to snare unsuspecting people – it means to capture alive, to prevent harm. But more than that, we need to keep in mind the image of fishing itself is used by the Prophets as a metaphor for gathering the people of God together; an image of a restoring Israel. Only this time in Jesus, God will fulfill not only his promise to Israel, but he will also fulfill his promise to Abraham – that all the nations of the earth would be blessed through him.

The call to discipleship, the call to catch people, is a call to participate in God's redemptive plan for the world.

And how do the fishermen respond? They leave everything and follow Jesus. I still remember the first time I read this. I remember thinking, "I have to leave my house, I have to leave my car, I have to leave my job." I could feel the weight of this phrase firmly on my shoulders. I admired the disciples for their immediate commitment but it sounded a little extreme – they left *everything*. When we try to image ourselves in this situation it can come across as a burden. We imagine leaving our homes, our possessions, even our careers, and it begins to feel too big – how could we possibly respond like that?

But is that really what the disciples left behind – boats and fish or, in our case, possessions and career? No. What they left

behind was their fear, their guilt, their worry, their anxiety. They are set free by Jesus. No longer will they be mastered by their possessions. No longer will they be mastered by their trade. Now their master will be the one
> who brings abundance out of scarcity,
>> who brings joy out of sorrow,
>>> who makes the impossible possible.

Now their master will be Jesus.

This is what is at the heart of the response of the disciples then and what remains at the heart of the response of disciples today. Jesus is Lord. We will not be mastered by any other –
> not by possessions,
>> not by wealth,
>>> not by career.

Everything we are and everything we have are placed in his service.

But what will it mean for us to be catchers of people? How are we to participate in God's redemptive plan? In our society when people have climbed the ladder of material success only to find themselves empty and alone and falling from the heights of ego – we will be nets that catch them. And when people have descended into the depths of despair – we will be the nets that draw them out. Not because we have the newest equipment, not because we have the best lake to fish in, but only because Jesus is there in the boat with us.

In Jesus Christ our exile is over. We are called out of the captivity of fear, called out of the captivity of sin. Even death itself can no longer hold us captive. We are free; free to sit at the knees of Jesus in the power of the Holy Spirit; free to hear his word of life; free to share in living and proclaiming that Word in a world that so desperately needs to hear it.

> Thanks be to God.
> Amen.

Still Cheering for the Underdog?

March 21, 2004

Luke 15:11-32

A few weeks ago I learned the final installment of the *Lord of the Rings* movies won eleven Academy Awards. I find that interesting. It is by no means a new story. Tolkien wrote this series of books decades ago and they have captivated readers and now moviegoers ever since. It is one of those stories with staying power – a cosmic battle between the forces of good and evil, one chance to defeat evil, and a hero who must overcome over-whelming obstacles if he is to succeed. And who is the hero entrusted with the fate of the free people of the world? A military genius? No, it's a farmer half the size of a normal human being, from a backwater town that most people have never heard of. He is by every definition an underdog, and people love to cheer for the underdog.

Maybe it's because we tend to see ourselves as someone who doesn't have all the know how, all the talent, all the finesse – but in the end there is still hope that everything will come out okay. If the underdogs can make it in the world then maybe there is hope for me, too.

Well, people were not all that different in Jesus' day. They had hopes and fears just like we do, so it is no wonder Jesus often taught by telling stories that struck at the heart of everyday life. One such story is the reading we heard this morning – the parable of the Prodigal Son.

Now the first thing that we need to remember is that Jesus wasn't the first or only person to use parables in his teaching. Parables were used as a kind of teaching tool that operated in much the same way as a joke does. It invites the hearers to become involved in a short story with a surprise or twist ending – in the case of a joke, the twist is intended to make the listeners laugh, but with a parable the twist is intended to shake up our view of the world – to challenge the way we think about the world around us and, particularly with Jesus' parables, to challenge the way we think about God.

The problem for us is that these parables have been interpreted and reinterpreted so extensively for so many generations it's hard for us to experience the same kick, the same twist that challenged Jesus' first listeners. For many of us, just hearing the words "The parable of the Prodigal Son" brings forth images of the unconditional love and forgiving grace of the father, and rightfully so; but for the next few minutes let's try to put those images off to the side and see if we can capture some of the original kick of this Parable.

Jesus tells us there was a man who had two sons, and already at this early point in the Parable we will remember that the image of two sons plays a foundational role in the history of the people Israel. Adam and Eve had two sons – Cain and Abel; Abraham had two sons – Ishmael and Isaac; and Isaac had two sons – Esau and Jacob. Keep in mind the common practice in this period was for the older son – the firstborn – to receive the bulk of the inheritance. All of the sons would share in the inheritance when the father died, but the firstborn son was the real winner when it came to the division of estate. Yet when we look back over the history of Israel, we see time and time again that this custom was overturned.

God favours the younger Abel's offering over Cain's; Abraham's firstborn, Ishmael, is not the child of the promise, it is the younger son Isaac; and Isaac's firstborn, Esau, trades his birthright to his younger brother, Jacob, for a bowl of stew. Later on when Jacob, whose name is changed to Israel, had twelve children of his own, it's not Judah – not the oldest son who is the star – it is Joseph, the youngest son, who will become second in command over the entire land of Egypt. Similarly, it is not the older son, Aaron, who will lead the Israelites out of bondage in Egypt, but the younger son, Moses. Even King David was the youngest and smallest of the sons of Jesse. The history of Israel is a history of upstart younger brothers, a history of underdogs.

So when Jesus begins to tell this story about the wayward younger son – about this underdog – the people around him would have assumed the younger son was Israel. And it is a story that begins on a sour note. The younger son asks his father for his share of the inheritance, roughly the equivalent of saying, "Father, I wish you were dead". Keep in mind that an inheritance in the ancient world would not have consisted of much in the way of material goods. The value of the inheritance would have been almost entirely in the land; the land was the primary means of supporting you and your family. So when the younger son sells the land and gathers all he owns, and leaves for another country, he is for all intents and purposes saying he has no intention of ever coming back.

Notice that Jesus doesn't give us the details of where this younger son is going. He only tells us this son traveled to a distant country where he squandered his wealth and was wasting his life. The people of Israel knew there were many different nations and many different peoples, but for the most part they still saw the world as consisting of basically two types of people – there were Jews and there were non-Jews or gentiles. This son has sold his inheritance, sold his share in the Promised Land, and has now set out to live among the gentiles as a gentile.

This, too, is a common theme throughout the Old Testament. Time and time again we see the pattern – the people are faithful, but then they forget the covenant and fall away from a right relationship with God. This is followed by a period where the people fall on hard times and cry out to God who restores them.

And what do we see happening with this younger son? He spends his entire inheritance, then finds himself in need – finds himself in the middle of a famine with no land, no food, no family. He is lost, but he is also stubborn. He will not go back.

He is going to take care of himself;
> he is going to keep a stiff upper lip;
>> he is going to think positive thoughts.

He got himself into this jam and he is going to get himself out. So he hires himself out to a citizen of this foreign country, and to us today this may sound like a good start. The young lad is finally getting his act together – at least he is earning a living. But that is not the way it would have been seen by the people listening to Jesus.

To hire yourself out – to be without land of your own to work – was considered to be a form of slavery. Maybe there are people here today who can relate to this – chained to their job with no sense of vocation. The truly free people were the ones with their own land, their own crops, their own livestock. This son has gone from being free in his own land to being a slave in a foreign land, and, if that wasn't enough, he has left his vocation of being a light to nations and now his job is feeding pigs.

Keep in mind that the pig was and is one of the most prominent symbols of uncleanness for the Jewish people, not because pigs were dirty animals, but because pigs didn't fit the normal order of creation for livestock. A pig has divided hoofs and is cleft-footed, but it does not chew the cud. For a Jew to be feeding the pigs – in some sense to be a servant of pigs – was about as far as you could be from your God-given vocation and right covenant relationship with God. And just when we think that things can't get any worse than this we hear the son is so hungry he would have been happy to eat the pods the pigs eat. It's not just that the son wants to eat food that was set aside for the pigs. These pods are not human food. They are what is left over after the food has been taken from them. It's the equivalent of garbage.

This son has degenerated to the point where he is teetering on the verge of losing his humanity; he has hit rock bottom and it is at this point that he remembers his father's generosity.

Back home the hired hands aren't treated like animals;
> back home human beings eat food that is fit
>> for human beings;
>>> back home there is enough food
>>>> for everyone.

The younger son has made up his mind; he is returning home...but he remembers the way he left; he remembers the humiliation he brought upon his father by asking for his inheritance and the humiliation he brought upon himself by squandering it.

Will his father even take him back?

The son has a plan for that – when he sees his father he will make him a deal that can't be refused; he will apologize and ask the father to take him back not as a son but as a hired hand. Certainly that will be enough to convince his father to take him back. So the younger son sets out for home. But while he is still far off, the father catches sight of him and is filled with compassion. He runs and throws his arms around his son and kisses him. Now in that culture it was considered highly undignified for a senior to be running anywhere; and here not only is the father running, but running to embrace the son who had rejected him. The father is humiliating himself in the eyes of the onlookers.

All the way home the son has been rehearsing for this moment and now he has his opportunity. He blurts out, "I am no longer worthy to be called your son. Treat me like one of your hired hands." But the father will have none of it. He doesn't even seem to hear the request; he is already making plans to restore his son. He says, "Quickly bring out a robe; not simply a clean set of clothes for this son but the best clothes – a new robe, new sandals, and a ring for his finger." The son is not just being welcomed, his status as a son is being given back to him. His identity, his humanity, is being restored.

I am sure there are people here who know exactly what this is like; who have hit rock bottom, have turned to God and experienced the Amazing Grace, the unconditional Love of God.

The Pharisees and scribes would have been no different – they knew full well the Grace and Love of God; he had rescued, restored, and redeemed the people Israel time and again. You can almost imagine them wiping tears from their eyes as they heard Jesus speaking of the father's embrace. Not only had God redeemed them in the past, he had promised to redeem them in the future. They must have been imagining
> a time when God would once again be with them,
>> a time when the Romans would be expelled,
>>> a time when all the nations of the earth

would be flocking to Jerusalem for the big celebration feast that would come at the end of the age.

But this is not the end of the story. Jesus goes on to talk about the older brother – the brother who was out working in the field when all this commotion took place. He hears the music; he hears the dancing; the celebration has started without him. He asks one of the slaves, "What's going on?" only to learn that his brother is back and the father has killed the fatted calf to celebrate. The older son becomes angry and refuses to join in the celebration and, when the father comes out to plead with him to come in, notice how the son begins. "Listen!" the son says to the father.

He is about to lecture his father on how the world works and how the father should behave. And what are his objections? He has been working like a slave for the father. He has never disobeyed the father's command, and yet the father has never given him even a goat to celebrate with his friends.

Now remember why Jesus is telling this Parable in the first place – the Pharisees and scribes are complaining that Jesus is welcoming and eating with tax collectors and sinners. Pharisees were known for their zeal in observing the commandments of God and the Scribes. The Temple authorities were known as the ones who assumed responsibility for arranging the temple celebrations and feasts. If there is going to be a celebration they are the ones who decide where, when, and how the celebration will be given, as well as who will and will not be invited. The celebration was not supposed to begin without them.

This is the moment where Jesus delivers the punch line, the twist of the parable. He says to the Pharisees and the scribes, "Who have you become? You are no longer the underdog. You have lost touch with God's plan and promises for the entire world to be brought into his blessing."

Here Jesus is not saying they no longer have a place in the celebration. The father comes out to plead with the older son; the father wants him to come in and celebrate. So what is keeping the older son away? Why won't he come in and join the celebration? He thinks the family lines have been redrawn; he thinks he is an only son – the one who played by the rules, the one who is deserving of a celebration.

The father says, "Yes, you are deserving, but don't forget about your brother. Yes, he acted foolishly. Yes, he lived shamefully, but what does he deserve? Does he deserve to be teetering on the verge of losing his humanity? Does he deserve to be treated like an animal? Does he deserve to have no hope? Is that the kind of father you think I am? No, when your brother came back it was like flesh was being put back on dry bones; it was a return to life from death. It was a resurrection. We had to celebrate a resurrection. We had to celebrate new life."

In the end we are not told what impact these words had on the older son or how he responded, we are left only with the question of how we will respond. Are we able to share in the celebration the way God has arranged, or will we try to dictate the terms under which we will come in? Will we say, "Sorry, God, the church is filled with hypocrites and self serving people – if you

want me to come in you will have to clean them out." Are we still able to cheer for the underdog –
    for tax collectors and sinners,
        for prostitutes and murderers,
            for drug addicts and for everyone else
who has been made to feel like less than a child of God, like less than a human being? Or are we expecting a party where only our friends are invited?

When the wayward children of God come home smelling like pigs, reeking of an unclean world, who will they find waiting for them? Will they find the older brother guarding the doors to the Church? Or will they find the amazing grace and unconditional love of the Father in Jesus Christ, with his arms stretched wide on the cross to embrace them?

In the end, the question is not so much, "Am I the older son or am I the younger son in this parable?" Rather, the question is, "Do I share the heart of the father; do I rejoice when I see a wayward child of God come home, or do I get bent out of shape because they don't look like me, don't talk like me, don't act like me?"

The first murder recorded in the Bible is the death of Abel at the hands of his brother, Cain. When God came and inquired of Cain what had happened to his brother, Cain responded by saying, "I don't know. Am I my brother's keeper?"

With this parable and with his ministry and death Jesus answers by saying, "Yes, you are your brother's keeper," not because it is a duty assigned by God, but because it is a sharing in the very heart of the Father Almighty, sharing in his heart filled with compassion, and sharing in his heart filled with mercy.

Amen and amen.

A Fragrant Offering

March 28, 2004

John 12:1-11

Last year I came across a story about a woman who lived through the war in the former Yugoslavia. She tells it like this:

I am a Muslim, and I am thirty-five years old. To my second son who was just born I gave the name "Jihad", so he will not forget the testament of his mother – revenge. The first time I put my baby to breast I told him, "May this milk choke you if you forget." So be it. The Serbs taught me to hate. For the last two months there was nothing in me – no pain, no bitterness, only hatred. I taught these children to love. I did. I am a teacher of literature.

I was born in Ilijas and I almost died there. My student, Zoran, the only son of my neighbour, told me, "You are good for nothing, you stinking Muslim woman." My former colleague, a teacher of physics, was yelling like mad and he kept hitting me wherever he could.

I have become insensitive to pain. But my soul? It hurts. I taught them all to love and all the while they were making preparations to destroy every-thing that is not of the Orthodox faith. Jihad – War. This is the only way.

I first read this story last summer, and for the most part had forgotten about it until this past week when I saw on the news that the Israeli army had assassinated the leader of the Islamic Extremist group Hamas. I wonder how many newborn babies in Israel and Palestine will grow up being fed on a steady diet of revenge and hatred; how many will grow up with the names like war and Jihad?

All plans for an end to the violence seem like so much wasted time in a world that thinks the only way to answer violence and death is with more violence and death.

Well, the world wasn't so different in Jesus' day. Israel longed for God to come and redeem them; to save them from their Roman occupiers and reestablish the everlasting throne of David. There was no love lost between the Jewish people and the Romans, and many expected the coming messiah would be a military hero, a king who could muster an army and wipe out the Romans.

So when Jesus arrived on the scene claiming to be the messiah, he most certainly wasn't what most of Israel was expecting; but this alone would not have been enough for Jesus to be considered worthy of attention. There were many false messiahs during this period of time, but in the end they didn't pose a real problem since they could be easily dismissed or defeated by the religious leaders of the day. But Jesus is different from all the others – when he performs signs, people from the various Jewish sects begin to desert and believe in Jesus.

But what is it they are deserting? Deserting Israel? No. All of the religious groups claimed to have the monopoly on what it meant to be the true Israel, what it meant to be the faithful people of God.

When Jesus comes, working signs and wonders, people begin to see that he holds the key to what it means to be the true people of God; they begin to believe in him. But at the same time

Jesus also becomes a threat to the way of life of the religious leaders of the day.

He threatens their power;

he threatens their honour;

he threatens their financial interests that are tied to their positions. Jesus was turning their world upside down.

So what do the religious authorities do? They act exactly the way we expect threatened people to act. They come out fighting. They reach into their arsenal and pull out the worst weapon this world has to offer – death. Jesus must die. It's the only way. Most of us have been around the block enough times to know how this works. First there is a threat; then there is an attack. What comes next? A counter attack, of course. That's just the way the world works. That's just the way it is.

Or is it the only way? How does Jesus respond; how does he answer these death threats? Let's go back and take another look at our Gospel reading for this morning.

John begins by telling us it was six days before the Passover, and here we need to keep in mind that numbers in the bible are rarely used simply for their numeric value. Any time we see a number in scripture we need to ask ourselves what other symbolic values the people would have associated with that number.

When we look back through the Old Testament we see the image of six days is foundational to the pattern of life in Israel – six days for work – one day for Sabbath rest. It is a pattern meant to reflect the activity of God. In six days God created the heavens and the earth and all that is in them, but on the seventh day he rested.

Here in John's Gospel we find Jesus at the beginning of a six day period that will end with Passover; and not just any

Passover. This time Jesus will be handed over and crucified followed by the Sabbath.

But what can Jesus' crucifixion possibly have in common with this pattern of life; in common with the pattern of creation? I mean, aren't they kind of contradictory stories? On the one hand the beginning of God's creative activity, and on the other hand pain, suffering, and death of the Son of God? What could these two stories possibly have in common? Well, remember the final words Jesus says from the cross in John's Gospel: "It is finished." And if we look back to the account of creation we will see the first line in the Book of Genesis after the account of the sixth day reads: "Thus the heavens and the earth were finished."

So John is very purposefully drawing our attention to the fact that Jesus is not simply walking around doing nice things for people. Jesus is engaged in the process of re-creating the world; and more specifically he is re-creating humanity – restoring the image and likeness of God within us.

Notice where this six day period begins -- not at the centre of the Jewish world – not at the temple in Jerusalem. It begins with a meal at a friend's house in a little town outside of Jerusalem. God's re-creation begins, not in the halls of power, but in the ordinary everyday routine of life.

We are told Martha is serving the meal when something very unusual happens. Martha's sister, Mary, comes in carrying a pound of very expensive and very aromatic perfume. She pours it out on Jesus' feet and then wipes his feet with her hair. As unusual as this sounds to us, it would have been even more unusual, even scandalous, to the people who were in the room. Hair was, and in some places is, one of the more sensual parts of the body. Imagine being at a dinner party and watching a woman with a long dress hike it up to the top of her thighs -- well, letting down your hair in this culture was roughly the equivalent. It would have been considered totally inappropriate behaviour.

What was she doing? What was she trying to say to Jesus? What was she trying to say to the other people in the room? Didn't she have any sense of what was appropriate and inappropriate? What could she be thinking?

And as the fragrance from the perfume is filling the room, so, undoubtedly, is the tension. Uncomfortable glances across the room among the disciples – is anyone going to say anything about this? Is Jesus going to say anything about this? And finally it's Judas Iscariot who breaks the tension saying, "Why wasn't this perfume sold for three hundred denarii and the money given to the poor?" Here we get a sense of just how costly this perfume was. Remember the parable about the day laborers? They were paid one denarii for one day's work. Here the perfume's value is set at three hundred denarii – three hundred days of work. When you take into account sabbath and holy days, this is the equivalent of one year's wages.

And how is this expensive perfume used? It's poured out on the feet of Jesus and then wiped off presumably onto the ground. What a waste.

You can bet Judas wasn't the only one thinking this. Right from the beginning we are told his motives were less than pure; that he was a thief who helped himself to the common purse that Jesus and his followers used to fund their activities. But why does John choose to tell us this detail now – is he just looking back with the benefit of hindsight and saying, "Aha, now I know why Judas said that"? Or is there more to it than that?

Well, remember the six days; remember the new creation imagery John is using. What happened six days prior to the finish; what happened on the first day? "God said, 'Let there be light'; and there was light. And God saw that the light was good; and God separated the light from the darkness." *(Genesis 1:3)* In their motives, in their actions and in their responses toward Jesus, Mary and Judas are being separated – light from darkness. But if that is the case, then how can Mary's inappropriate and wasteful actions be seen as light?

When Jesus speaks he says, "Leave her alone, so that she can keep the perfume for the day of my burial." The Greek text here is kind of puzzling. It actually reads something like, "Leave her alone, against the day of my burial she kept this." It's difficult to really get a clear sense of what Jesus is saying, but what is clear is that Jesus did not see the outpoured perfume as a waste. In fact, he seems to be telling them that any remaining perfume should also not be sold, but kept for his burial.

It wouldn't have required any supernatural power on Mary's part to know Jesus' burial was nearly at hand. Jesus himself predicted his own death, and the threats to his life were not hidden, but were everywhere visible. Mary knew that the closer Jesus got to Jerusalem the higher was the risk of losing his life, and Bethany wasn't that far from Jerusalem. Mary knew it wouldn't be much longer and if he were to die the death of a criminal, which seemed very likely, there might not be time for a proper burial.

But what about the inappropriateness of letting down her hair to wipe Jesus' feet? How can this be seen as light? On the night Jesus was betrayed he poured water into a basin and washed his Disciples' feet and then wiped them with a towel. Here Jesus sees Mary's action as a preview of what the disciples will also see as an inappropriate action; having Jesus – their Teacher and their Lord – acting like a slave toward his disciples.

In this action we catch a glimpse of what the re-created humanity will look like. The new creation will be marked by washing each others' feet; serving one another, not out of a sense of compulsion or duty, but out of a deep sense of love for God and for all of those who are created in his image and likeness. But if that is happening – if humanity is in the process of being re-created into the image and likeness of God – what can Jesus mean when he says, "You always have the poor with you, but you do not always have me"? This seems somewhat out of place given Jesus' ongoing concern for the poor throughout the Gospel. So what is he getting at here?

For starters we need to be clear that Jesus is *not* saying, "Some people are rich and some people are poor and that's just the way it's always going to be." We have to remember all that has just happened. Jesus is saying, "Don't get hung up on the idea this perfume was wasted. If you are looking at the bottle of perfume and counting all of the ways it could have been used more appropriately you are going to miss the point."

Remember at the feeding of the five thousand when Jesus tested his disciples by asking where they could buy bread for all the people, and Philip responded that two hundred denarii would not be enough even for a morsel for each person. What about three hundred denarii? Maybe if we had sold this perfume we could have given them all a little something to eat. Just imagine all the great ministries we could offer if we just had enough money. Jesus says if you are thinking along these lines, you are missing the point.

There is going to come a time when Jesus' life will be poured out; when it will seem like his life was wasted; when the crowds will turn their backs on the disciples; when the money given in support of their movement will stop flowing. What will they do then?

When Jesus is crucified will his followers go back to their lives as if nothing had ever happened? Will the world go back to the same old order? And what about the poor? Will they go back to having little or no hope? That is precisely what the religious authorities are counting on; that the way the world has been is the way it will always be –
    those with power,
        those with influence,
             those with military muscle –
they will be the ones calling the shots.

Once they rid themselves of Jesus as well as any trace of his handiwork, namely Lazarus, their way of life will be back on track, back to normal.

I always laugh when I read verse ten. It says, "So the chief priests planned to put Lazarus to death as well." Now stop and think about it for a minute. The religious authorities know this Lazarus fellow is the cause of the decline in their membership. Maybe they call it Temple decline or something like that. Well, that problem seems easy enough to deal with. All they have to do is kill Lazarus – you know, the one Jesus raised from the dead – and the one who had the power to raise him from dead. Yeah, we're going to kill him too.

The religious authorities have become so blind they think they can kill the one who brings life out of death; so blind they seek to kill the one who is working signs and wonders in the name of God. They will not even entertain the idea they may not be bearing faithful witness to the Lord of Heaven and Earth – the same Lord who has promised to bless
> not just a few,
>> not just a handful,
>>> not even just a nation,
>>>> but all the families of the earth.

I know the stories we started with this morning were taken from major events on the global scene in places where many of us have never been. So how can we possibly deal with issues so complex and distant? I chose those stories not because those of us gathered here today have the resources and gifts to deal effectively with them, but because at the heart of each story is dehumanization.

The Muslim woman was treated like something less than a human being. Something less than one who has been created in the image and likeness of God. And the same is true in the struggle between the leaders of Israel and the Palestinian authorities. Both sides treat each other as something less than human; and in some cases they are even treated as if God wanted to get rid of them altogether. We know the consequences of this kind of thinking – the world is filling with the stench of death.

But we don't have look across the ocean, across the country, maybe not even across the street to find people who are being treated like something less than a true human being, something less than a beloved child of God. The world outside our door is filled with people who feel worthless, useless, and empty.

But the good news is that Jesus is re-creating us all – redeeming us all, restoring us all – not through the power brokers of our day, but through his costly and fragrant self-offering that is spreading throughout the world, one human heart at a time.

There is darkness in our world; there is no denying it. But it is people like you and me – children of the light, filled with the Spirit, gifted for service – who bear witness to the fact that in Jesus Christ we have seen what it means to be truly human. In Jesus Christ we have seen what it means to be created in the image and likeness of God. In Jesus Christ the light has come into the darkness of the world and the darkness cannot overcome it.

Thanks be to God.

Amen.

What's Riding on It?

April 4, 2004

Luke 19:28-40

I remember reading a story a short while ago about a church community in South America that was struggling to provide the basic human needs of their people -- homes, food, and clothing.

It was an exciting time for this group. You see, there was going to be an election and one of the candidates in the election was very socially minded – he intended to fight to restore the dignity that the people deserved as human beings.

And as the election approached and people were growing more and more excited, a journalist asked one of them, "What will you do if your candidate doesn't win the election?" And this person's immediate response was, "Well, that would show that God doesn't care; why would we continue to worship a God who doesn't care about us?"

In order to understand this person's response we need to realize that in South America during the 1960's there began a new theological movement that would later be labeled Liberation theology. It came about in the midst of terribly oppressive conditions for the majority of the people. The rich were getting richer and the poor were getting poorer. The primary thrust of the movement was that in Jesus, God had revealed himself as having a preference for the poor, and as such, the action of the church should bear witness to this preference by standing in solidarity with the poor over and against their wealthy oppressors.

When we look at the Gospel of Luke, from which our reading this morning comes, it's not too difficult to imagine how they came up with these ideas. We certainly hear this kind of language in Mary's Song of Praise to God. She sings, "[The Lord] has brought down the powerful from their thrones, and lifted up the lowly; he has filled the hungry with good things, and sent the rich away empty." *(Luke 1:52-53)*

Certainly this announcement would come as good news to those who lived under oppressive rule and severe poverty. But at the same time it doesn't seem to capture the fullness of the good news. It seems to forget the next verse in Mary's Song: "He has helped his servant Israel, in remembrance of his mercy, according to the promise he made to our ancestors, to Abraham and to his descendants forever." *(Luke 1:55)* If God is to remember the covenant with Abraham, we need to keep in mind this promise included the blessing of all the families of the earth, without preference.

It's easy for us to get caught up in the idea that somehow God has a special interest or a preference for a particular group of people, especially when that group of people includes us. It was particularly easy for the people of Israel to fall into this kind of thinking. After all, God had shown a preference for them – they were the chosen people, called by name to be God's people. Surely God would not abandon them; surely God would send them a King – a King like David – one who could slay this Roman Goliath and reclaim the city of David, reclaim Jerusalem.

Remember the general outline of David's rise to being King. For a time, he lived as an outcast leading a motley crew of followers in the Judean wilderness until the death of Saul and Jonathan, when he was anointed as King over Israel. One of his first acts upon becoming king was to go to Jerusalem and take the city as his capital. Well, up to this point in Luke's Gospel Jesus has been leading a motley crew of followers across Galilee until this moment, the moment he reaches Jerusalem. These are exciting times – there is a charge in the air; people are filled with expectations about Jesus' identity – perhaps this is the long awaited King, the Messiah.

We are told that as Jesus approaches Jerusalem, when he is near to Bethany and Bethphage, he sends two of his disciples on an errand. He tells them to go ahead into the village and they will find tied there a colt that has never been ridden. The disciples are instructed to untie the animal and bring it back to Jesus. They are even instructed as to what to tell anyone who asks why they are taking the colt. The question is: why is Luke giving us all this detail? The whole account of Jesus' entry into Jerusalem is twelve verses in length, and five of them are taken up with this business about the colt.

Scholars have had a real battle over whether or not this passage is meant to highlight Jesus' supernatural powers. Some argue this episode is intended to show that Jesus had the ability to foresee the events he described to his disciples, while others insist it shows how much preparation Jesus had done prior to returning to Bethany. In the end, it seems to me the question of foreknowledge is not the real issue here. The two things Luke mentions over and over again in these verses are the colt and its being tied or untied. But what can a tied colt possible have to do with Jesus?

Remember back to when Jacob gave his final blessing to his sons. When he blessed Judah he spoke of a coming ruler from that tribe who would tie a colt to a choice vine. (Genesis 49:10-12) Jacob's blessing was the tribe of Judah would enjoy never-ending rule over Israel and that the fulfillment of this rule would be measured by the immense abundance of the vine.

Keep in mind the Jewish vision of the age to come did not include sprouting wings and floating off on clouds. Their vision of the age to come was about a return to the garden – a return to the time when the vine would be so abundant and strong that you could tie a donkey to it and the donkey would not be able to eat its way through; the vine would grow faster than the donkey could eat. It is this kind of imagery the disciples have in their minds as they go looking for the colt.

When the disciples find the colt and begin to untie it, they are confronted just as Jesus had told them; they are asked what they are doing. There were property laws in Israel. You couldn't just walk up and take a colt without compensating the owner...unless, of course, you were the King. So when the disciples tell the owners that the "The Lord needs it", it is a confirmation of Jesus' status as King. The disciples have just invoked the rights of a king on behalf of Jesus and it worked. So as they rush back to Jesus they must have had visions of Zechariah's prophecy dancing through their minds:

> *"Rejoice greatly, O daughter Zion! Shout aloud, O daughter Jerusalem! Behold, your king comes to you; triumphant and victorious is he, humble and riding on a donkey, on a colt, the foal of a donkey. He will cut off the chariot from Ephraim and the war-horse from Jerusalem; and the battle bow shall be cut off, and he shall command peace to the nations; his dominion shall be from sea to sea, and from the River to the ends of the earth."* (Zechariah 9:9-10)

So when they come back with the colt to the crowd of pilgrims making their way to Jerusalem with Jesus, they throw their cloaks on the donkey and set Jesus on it. Keep in mind Jesus never told the disciples what he planned to do with the colt. It is purely the disciples' initiative; they grab Jesus and put him on the colt.

In a symbolic way they are making the same confession Peter made earlier: "Who do they say that Jesus is?" By putting

Jesus on the colt and spreading their cloaks on the road they proclaim, "You are the Messiah of God". The scene is meant to remind us of the anointing of King Jehu who was called to purge Israel of the idolatry brought by Ahab and Jezebel. Here we begin to get a sense of what kind of king this crowd is expecting. Surely this one, the one who comes to bring the peace of heaven, will begin by getting rid of the idolatrous foreign influences, namely, King Herod and Caesar.

And we see also that the crowds of disciples are not the only ones witnessing this event. Pharisees are in the scene as well. They see the same thing the disciples do – Jesus riding on a donkey toward Jerusalem – but instead of seeing a king coming to bring God's peace, they see a teacher who has lost control of his disciples. They cry out to Jesus, "Teacher, order your disciples to stop." But Jesus replies, "I tell you, if these were silent, the stones would cry out."

When I read this verse I have this vision in my head of the Pharisees looking at Jesus as if he were crazy and saying, "What are you talking about? – the stones would cry out?" Jesus is not simply saying that even a rock could see that he is the King of Israel. He is drawing upon the prophet Habakkuk's words of judgment:

> *"Alas for you who get evil gain for your houses, setting your nest on high to be safe from the reach of harm! You have devised shame for your house by cutting off many peoples; you have forfeited your life. The very stones will cry out from the wall, and the plaster will respond from the woodwork."*
> *(Habakkuk 2:9-11)*

Pay particular attention to the reason why the prophet proclaims judgment – it is because they seek to secure their house by any and every means available and in the process cut off many people. We assume Jesus is rebuking the Pharisees for their failure to recognize him as King – but here we begin to see Jesus has a much broader audience in mind. His response confronts all who would build Jerusalem up into a monumental masterpiece while cutting off access to the gentiles.

Already here we begin to ask what will happen when the crowds of disciples have their expectations challenged. Where will these crowds of disciples be when they learn that Jesus has not come to destroy Rome? Where will they be when Friday rolls around?

One of the things I like about the Lectionary's choice of readings for this Palm Sunday is that along with the triumphal entry of Jesus we also get Isaiah's vision of the servant. What kind of king is Jesus? He is the kind of king who will bear the insult and injury of the world in order to reconcile us with God.

When Jesus comes riding triumphantly into Jerusalem he carries with him the expectations of all the people, and all too often we get caught up in making judgments about the people around Jesus. We think the ones who are waving palm branches, shouting blessings and praises, and laying down their garments are the ones who have it all figured out, while the others who are looking on with disapproval just don't get it. To us it all seems so clear and sounds so good. Yes, this is the way it should be – the crowds praising the Lord Jesus Christ, recognizing that he is the king. We get so excited about the fact he is being called king that we lose sight of what kind of king Jesus sets himself up to be.

It is as if Jesus is a blank screen, and as he rides into Jerusalem the people are projecting onto him all of their hopes, all of their expectations about what the king of Israel should be. They do not see Jesus for what he is; they see Jesus as what he can be for them. And when all of those expectations are not met, when Jesus does not act the way they want, the people turn away. They reject him. The songs of praise quickly turn into the cry, "Crucify."

The question we are left with is: what do we have riding on it? As we see Jesus preparing to enter Jerusalem and we are lined up on the streets singing praises and laying our garments out on the ground, what is it that we are expecting from him; what are we projecting onto him? Do we project the values of our society? Do we project our own individual desires? Do we say to Jesus we are your loyal subjects so long as you live up to our expectations, so long as you live up to our image of what God should be? Or do we see the one who rides into Jerusalem as the one who will bear no image other than the image and likeness of God Almighty?

Palm Sunday is the time of year when we are called to ask ourselves what kind of king we are expecting, to ask ourselves whether we conform to the image of God that is revealed in Jesus Christ. We are called to ask ourselves if the One enthroned on the cross is the one who is shaping us into his image and likeness. That is what is at the heart of proclaiming Jesus is Lord.

Throughout history there have been countless numbers of groups claiming God was on their side. Whether it is nations, races, or political associations, we must guard against the temptation to create a god in our own image. We need to take seriously Joshua's vision at Jericho, when he looked up and saw a man standing before him with a drawn sword in his hand. Joshua went to him and said to him, "Are you one of us, or one of our adversaries?" He replied, "Neither; but as commander of the army of the Lord I have now come." *(Joshua 5:13-14)*

The question is not whether or not God is on our side, but whether or not we are on his side. And if we want to know how to align ourselves with God we need to look no further than God's anointed servant, Jesus, who offered himself in sacrificial love for all of humanity.

    God's salvation,
        God's grace, and
            God's love

are poured out for all people, without preference, through our Lord and King, Jesus Christ.

Thanks be to God.

Amen.

It is Finished

April 9, 2004

John 18:1 - 19:42

    I remember a time when I was about twelve years old, sitting around the kitchen table in my Grandfather's house visiting with some of my relatives. At one point in the conversation my uncle asked, "So Kris, what do you want to be when you grow up?" Well, that was easy. Without hesitation I turned to my uncle and said, "When I grow up I'm going to be a millionaire."

    When my uncle replied, "Yeah, right," I began to realize he was less than convinced so I said, "No, really. I am going to be a millionaire when I grow up." This time my uncle replied, "If you ever become a millionaire, you go out and pick any hat you like and I'll eat it."

    Oh, was I mad. I never forgot what he said. Throughout my teenage years I couldn't walk past a store that sold hats without stopping to pick out the largest one they had and imaging my uncle choking it down. I was going show him; I was going to prove him wrong.

    After a period of time I graduated from high school and set out in the working world to make my millions – I tried almost anything that promised unlimited earning potential. I tried selling cars; I tried selling electronics; I even tried selling vacuum cleaners door to door. I hated it. But what was worse than hating the work was that I just wasn't good at it. But for the most part I thought that

I could live with hating my work so long as I reached my goal, so long as I was a success.

Obviously things didn't turn out the way I had planned. God had other plans, most of which I never would have dreamed possible. But as we come here today remembering what Jesus did on Good Friday, perhaps the one thing that should be clear is that our plans are most often quite different from God's plan, and our ways are quite different from God's ways. It seems that we never fully know what to expect from the God revealed in Jesus Christ.

Our scripture reading for this morning covers the details beginning with Jesus' arrest in the garden of Gethsemane, and continues through his trials, his torture, and finally his crucifixion and death. Those of you who have been here at worship over the past few weeks know how much I enjoy digging into the details the scriptures offer, but given the length of our scripture reading for today I want to do something a little different. I want to take a step back from the details and look at the bigger picture provided for us by John.

At the most basic level we are being shown a legal proceeding in first century Israel, and before we go any further we should begin by looking back into the history of Israel to determine what significance legal proceedings had for the people. It should come as no surprise that legal proceedings, and more specifically the image of a trial, played a central role in the way the Prophets spoke about God.

Remember that Israel was a covenant people; God had chosen them as his instrument – as a means of making himself known in the world – and this relationship was founded upon the covenant received at Mount Sinai. It was a wonderful moment in the life of the Israel, but the covenant was not all sunshine and light. Speaking the word of God; Moses proclaims:

"See, I set before you today life and prosperity, death and destruction. For I command you today to

love the Lord your God, to walk in his ways, and to keep his commands, decrees and laws; then you will live and increase, and the Lord your God will bless you in the land you are entering to possess. But if your heart turns away and you are not obedient, and if you are drawn away to bow down to other gods and worship them, I declare to you this day that you will certainly be destroyed. You will not live long in the land you are crossing the Jordan to enter and possess. This day I call heaven and earth as witnesses against you that I have set before you life and death, blessings and curses. Now choose life, so that you and your children may live and that you may love the Lord your God, listen to his voice, and hold fast to him....." (Deuteronomy 30:15-20)

Can you hear the trial language in those words? "This day I call heaven and earth as witnesses against you." Any breach in the covenant will be tried before the judge – God Almighty. Time and time again throughout the history of Israel we hear the prophets using this language of taking Israel to court for being unfaithful to the covenant.

Here in John's Gospel we have another trial taking place, but who is it that stands accused? Our immediate response is "Jesus", of course; he is
    the one who has been arrested;
        the one who will stand trial before the
        Jewish religious authorities; and also
            the one who will stand trial before Pilate.

It seems pretty clear cut. But remember the words of Moses, "I set before you life and death; blessings and curses." If we are to choose life then we must do what? Listen to the voice of the Lord our God.

Remember how the Gospel of John begins:
"In the beginning was the Word, and the Word was with God, and the Word was God.... The Word became flesh and made his dwelling among us. We have seen his glory, the glory of the One and Only, who came from the Father, full of grace and truth.... From the fullness of his grace we have all received one blessing after another. For the Law was given through Moses; grace and truth came through Jesus Christ. No one has ever seen God, but God, the One and Only, who is at the Father's side, has made him known." (John 1:1, 14, 16-18)

The voice of the Father, the voice of God, comes to us in the flesh of Jesus. And how we respond to that voice is of supreme importance; the stakes are nothing short of life and death. So yes, on the surface the trial is very much about Jesus being judged by the Sanhedrin – judged by Pilate – but at the same time there is another trial taking place, the one where God is the judge. But the question remains, who is being charged at that trial?

Let's begin with the disciples. They have been with Jesus, listening to his voice and claiming to be his followers, but when it comes time for Jesus to be arrested the disciples abandon Jesus out of fear – even Peter who said that he would lay down his life for Jesus, denies him three times.

And what about the religious authorities? Jesus taught and healed in public. They, too, have heard his voice and they have responded by plotting to kill him in order to protect
    their own honour,
        their power, and
           their authority.

Similarly, Pilate can find no cause for the charges brought against Jesus, but instead of hearing Jesus' voice, he gives in to the cries of the mob. Even the crowds of people who had heard Jesus' voice when he taught, and witnessed his healing ministry, turn and demand the release of a known insurrectionist, Barrabas, rather than Jesus.

No one is found to be innocent in this trial. All have failed Jesus; all have failed to recognize who Jesus is; all have failed to recognize whose voice he speaks with. The entire world is on trial – the average person on the street, the followers of Jesus, the religious authorities, and the political authorities are all found guilty. The world is found guilty of failing to listen to the voice of God Almighty. And at this point Moses' words come back to us. "I set before you life and death."

The world stands guilty as charged, filled with iniquity and at odds with the purposes of God. We know the terms of the covenant – we know what should happen – the judgment we should expect is curses and death. Remember the last time God decided to deal with the iniquity that filled the world? He sent a flood that covered the face of the earth. But remember also that after the waters subsided he made a promise:

> *"Never again will I curse the ground because of man, even though every inclination of his heart is evil from childhood. And never again will I destroy all living creatures, as I have done."* (Genesis 8:21)

As John has told us, despite the fact the world has turned against God and his purposes, God so loved the world that he sent his only Son. And so instead of wiping out humanity, God wipes out sin by entering into the world in the flesh of Jesus and taking upon himself the curses and death that should have fallen upon us.

There are sure to be objections at this point. "How can you say that?" some will protest. "Open your eyes and look at the world around you; it's been 2000 years since Jesus died on the cross and the world is still filled with iniquity and sin. How can you say that Jesus wiped out the sin of the world? Aren't we just fooling ourselves? Aren't we just being foolish?"

Well, as Paul said to the church in Corinth, the message of the cross is foolishness to the gentiles when it comes to hunger for wisdom – and our society is no different. The wisdom of our world believes that *where there is a will there is a way*. If we could just come up with the right program or plan and apply the appropriate amount of willpower we could turn this world into a paradise.

As Christians we realize that making plans and implementing them is necessary part of life, but we do not see this process as the solution to the problem of sin.

Instead, we know that in the death of Jesus Christ we have been called into a new covenant relationship with God; a new covenant where we are called to participate in the broken body and the poured out blood of Jesus; a new covenant where we share in the pain and suffering of this world along with Jesus. And in the process we are made into a new creation, a new humanity, a humanity that reflects God's image and likeness.

The problem is that our success-driven society can, and often does, influence what we think it means to be successful Christians and all too often communion with the living God through Jesus Christ is replaced with something like the seven habits of highly effective people. All too often visions of a successful church are based on the wisdom of the world and we lose sight of the fact that when Jesus hung on the cross and said, "It is finished" the wisdom of the world proclaimed he was a complete and total failure.

So what shall we do? Shall we buy into the wisdom of our world? Shall we say Jesus really just brought us some good ideas, some good advice for living a good life? Or will we recognize that on the cross God is finishing what he started so long ago; that on the cross God is re-creating us through the new covenant in the broken body and poured out blood of Jesus Christ?

In that last supper with his disciples, Jesus did not simply ask for a ritual that would memorialize a new philosophy – an action that would remind the world of what a great teacher he was. No, Jesus offers the world the opportunity to share in his unique relationship with the Father – to have the Word alive in our flesh through communion with him.

In the new covenant we are invited to share in the Father's love for a world that has turned its back on God – to share in Jesus' unique relationship with the world by offering ourselves in love to a world that will not love us back.

Will we look like fools? Or worse, will we look like failures? According to the wisdom of the world, chances are the answer will be yes. Why should we expect anything different than Jesus received? But for those who have heard God's voice in Jesus, the cross we bear is the power of Christ and the wisdom of God.

On Good Friday all of humanity sees itself at its worst – convicted of rebellion against God and his intention for creation – but thanks be to God for his compassion and mercy. God will not abandon us in our self-centred sin. Good Friday is not the end for humanity, it is a new beginning – the beginning of the end of sin and the beginning of the end of death. On Good Friday we receive the promise that one day we will see humanity at its best and it will look like our Lord Jesus Christ.

Amen.

No Nonsense

April 11, 2004

Luke 24:1-12; 1 Corinthians 15

I imagine many of you have seen your fair share of these *(holding up a coloured Easter egg)* over the years. Colored eggs and Easter seem to go hand in hand. But I'm sure many of you also know that the practice of colouring eggs is not something originally developed by Christians. Egyptians and Persians were colouring eggs hundreds of years before Christians arrived on the scene; they were part of the festival that marked the arrival of spring, the season of renewal.

The reality is that as Christians spread out from Judea proclaiming the Good News of Jesus Christ, they often encountered Pagan cultural practices, and rather than trying to stamp out these practices, the evangelists simply filled them with Christian content. Practices celebrating the renewal and rebirth of nature were changed to practices celebrating the Resurrection of Jesus.

But things are changing in our society. Churches that once played a central role in the social fabric of Canadian society are on the decline. The mainline church is moving to the sidelines and at the same time there is a surge of interest in new age spirituality and neo-paganism. The other day I was filling my car with gas just down the street, when I noticed a parked car with three bumper stickers. The first one that caught my eye read, "My other car is a…" and there was a picture of a broom. Now my first thought was that maybe this person was a curler and it was a curling broom, but the picture of the broom looked a little too much like the stereotypical witch's broom, which made more sense when I read the other two. The next bumper sticker read, "Goddess worshiper". And finally the last sticker read, "Get ready, now comes the wiccan."

The paganism that Christianity tried to assimilate so long ago is reclaiming its turf, not just in the secular world, but in the church as well. Easter is slowly being emptied of its Christian content and is returning to its function as a spring festival. Far too many pulpits this morning will be filled with the message of spring rather than the message of the resurrection of our Lord Jesus. And it's not too difficult to see why.

If we look at our Gospel lesson this morning we are told about a group of women going to a tomb to properly complete the burial of Jesus, because they didn't have time before the Sabbath. When they arrive at the tomb they find the stone rolled away and the linen burial cloths remaining inside. Two men in clothes that gleam like lightening tell the women Jesus has risen just as he had foretold three times.

So when the women return to tell the other disciples what they saw, what happens? Does everyone jump for joy and sing praises to God? No. They don't believe the women. It all sounds like nonsense. Even Peter, who runs to the tomb to see for himself what happened, is left wondering what it all could mean.

It seems fitting our lectionary reading for this morning should end on this note of disbelief and wonder, because for the most part that is the way our world looks at the story of the empty tomb. It all sounds like so much nonsense.

There has been no shortage of people who have tried to make the Gospel more believable, more reasonable, more acceptable. What happened, they tell us, is the group of disciples that followed Jesus invented the story of the resurrection; after all, their movement had failed, their hero had been executed, and so the disciples fell into a state of cognitive dissonance. That is, they couldn't cope with their dashed hopes and so they created the story of the resurrection as a way of saying Jesus was still alive. Jesus may be dead, but his ideas, his philosophy, lives on. Now that's something our world could believe.

The problem is, we know of at least fifteen other messianic movements – at least fifteen other people – who claimed to be the messiah and had a group of disciples following them both before and after the time of Jesus. All of these would-be messiahs were killed; many of them were crucified. Yet none of the disillusioned disciples from these groups ever claimed their executed leader had risen from the dead. Death was enough to convince them their leader was not the messiah. In fact, death, particularly death on a cross, was considered proof the messianic claims were false.

Yet a short while after the crucifixion of Jesus, his disciples appeared in public in front of their countrymen proclaiming they had seen Jesus and they had spoken with him, that God had raised him from the dead to a new life where death no longer had any power. It was a proclamation that would not win them many friends. They were constantly under threat from religious authorities determined to put an end to the movement Jesus had begun. The writer of our epistle reading this morning was one such person.

Saul was a persecutor of the church, determined to drag every last one of the leaders of this Jesus movement before the religious authorities in Jerusalem, that is, until the day Jesus appeared to him. It was not a great idea – not a good theological argument – but the appearance of the resurrected Christ Jesus who turned Saul, the persecutor of the Church, into Paul, the Apostle to the gentiles. In the letter he wrote to the church in Corinth he states:

> *"Christ has indeed been raised from the dead, the first fruits of those who have fallen asleep. For since death came through a man, the resurrection of the*

dead comes also through a man. For as in Adam all die, so in Christ all will be made alive."
(1 Corinthians 15:20-22)

But Paul isn't simply giving the Corinthian church a theology lesson in the resurrection. While he was away in Ephesus he heard about problems in the church. Now keep in mind in Roman society, status was of supreme importance. The kind of bread you ate, the kind of wine you drank, the color of your clothing, even perfumes and hairstyles, indicated where you fit on the social ladder.

This church that had found so much freedom in the outpouring of God's Holy Spirit began to realize that preaching the resurrection was pretty hard on their status. It was a tough sell for the citizens in the city of Corinth who were saying that the church was a bunch of fools. The social standing of church members in the city was taking a beating, and so they began to think, "Well, maybe the resurrection isn't such a big deal after all." They decide instead the real mark of being a Christian, the real mark that you were a part of this new family of God, was the gift of speaking in tongues. And if speaking in tongues is the real mark then we don't even need to talk about the resurrection – in fact, the church began to proclaim there was no resurrection.

So Paul writes to the church to set the record straight. Listen to what he says:

"If there is no resurrection of the dead, then not even Christ has been raised. And if Christ has not been raised, our preaching is useless and so is your faith.... And if Christ has not been raised, your faith is futile; you are still in your sins."
(1 Corinthians 15:13-17)

That sounds a little harsh. If you don't believe in the resurrection your faith is useless; your faith is futile? Isn't Paul being a little narrow minded here? Well, no. Paul is not simply saying you have to believe in the resurrection to be a Christian as if it were some kind of formula. Paul is saying resurrection is God's plan for salvation. If you deny the resurrection, then you have missed the point of what God did in Jesus Christ and you will also miss the point of what God is doing in the world.

Paul's chief concern is that the church in Corinth is reverting back to the paganism it came out of; that the God revealed in Jesus will simply be added to the pantheon of gods already being worshipped throughout the Roman Empire; that the church will become just another temple dedicated to another god. Paul knew as soon as you get rid of the resurrection you also get rid of the one true God who had acted decisively in history to redeem the world. And once you are rid of the conviction the world changed with the death and resurrection of Jesus, then life can go on pretty much the same as always with no change – no transformation – only the same old death and decay.

But we have grown accustomed to death and decay, so much so that any talk of change, any talk of transformation, any talk of hope for a better world, comes across as so much nonsense … as wishful thinking.

Without the resurrection the disciples go back to being fishermen. Without the resurrection Mary Magdalene goes back to her life as a prostitute. Without the resurrection Jesus was nothing more than a deluded fanatic. But thanks be to God, Jesus *was* resurrected from the dead. So when we look out into our world and see pain, suffering, warfare, bloodshed, violence, and hatred, we know this is not the world as God intends it to be. We know in Jesus Christ, God has something much different planned – a new heaven and a new earth, no more tears and no more weeping.

The Story of Easter is not an annual spring festival for the church, but the ever-present reality of God's transformative power in Jesus Christ. Everything Jesus said and did does not just sit on the pages of the Bible as an account of something that happened a long time ago, but is an account of what God has started and what

God is continuing to do in our lives and in our world through Jesus.

As John Calvin once wrote, *"The gospel is not a doctrine of the tongue but of life. It cannot be grasped by reason and memory only but is fully understood when it possesses the whole soul and penetrates to the inner recesses of the heart . . . .. (o)ur religion will be unprofitable if it does not change our heart, pervade our manners, and transform us into new creatures."* [1]

On this Easter Sunday, let us keep clear in our hearts and minds that with the resurrection of Jesus Christ, humanity received the promise of a future where God's last enemy, "death", will be destroyed. It is an amazing promise, one that challenges our sense of possibility. But just as Paul warned the Corinthians not to trade their hope in the resurrection for the old certainties of Roman society, so he would warn us not to trade our hope in the resurrection for a coloured egg and a spring festival.

God's plan for our future is far more breathtaking than that. In our darkest hour when all seems lost and hope seems like a fantasy, God breaks into our world with Resurrection hope. It is nothing short of a new heaven, a new earth, a new humanity where death has no power and life is eternal.

And that is no nonsense.

Thanks be to God.

Amen.

---

[1] John Calvin, *Golden Book of the True Christian Life (Grand Rapids: Baker Books, 1952), p. 17.*

Beyond the Shadow of Doubt

April 18, 2004

John 20:19-31

Not too long ago I was told a story about a man who was sitting in his hotel room one night somewhere in the U.S.A. when he decided to open up the New Testament he found in the dresser drawer. As he read it he was gripped by the story he found on the pages, so much so, that he decided to attend a Brethren Church in his neighbourhood.

After a few weeks of sitting through the service this man went up to the minister and said, "Hey, this all sounds great. When do we do the stuff?" When the minister asked him what he meant the man replied, "You know, healing the sick and casting out spirits – the stuff."

The minister responded, "Oh no, we don't do that anymore."

I'm sure some of you may recognize the story as that of a man by the name of John Wimber. His conversion experience eventually led him to begin a movement that is known as "the Vineyard" with emphasis being placed on being empowered by the presence of the Holy Spirit to "do the stuff".

As with any religious renewal movement, the Vineyard is not without its critics, but one of the benefits of this renewal for the wider church in North America has been increased emphasis and attention on the Holy Spirit.

In most of our society the church drew back from the Holy Spirit under the influence of the heightened rationalism that came out of the nineteenth century, and instead began focusing upon moral and ethical principles. Determining the will of God was an exercise of the mind, a project that required only logic and reason. And the Holy Spirit fell into the background as a somewhat outdated member of the Trinity.

As we will see from our Gospel reading this morning, the Holy Spirit stands at the centre of the mission the risen Jesus gives to his disciples.

In John's Gospel we find the disciples hiding out together behind locked doors, afraid of the Jewish religious authorities. But why should they be afraid? After all, it was Jesus that the authorities were after, and now that he has been crucified the problem seems to be solved. Besides their grief, what do the disciples have to fear?

Keep in mind Jesus died the death of an insurrectionist – someone who challenged the rule of Rome – but the Romans were pretty smart about these sort of things. They knew killing the leader wasn't always enough to put down a potential uprising. It was always a good idea to crucify the key group of followers – those who were likely to continue where their leader left off.

If someone like the Jewish religious authorities were to identify the disciples as followers of Jesus there was a very good chance they would also be crucified. So they are huddled together trying to find a way to save their own lives. And it's at this moment – the moment they are trying to lock out death – when Jesus, the resurrection and the life, walks into the room

> without knocking,
>> without unlocking the door,
>>> without even walking through the doorway.

Nothing will keep Jesus away from his disciples in their moment of fear.

Jesus says to the disciples, "Peace be with you." This would have been a normal greeting in Jesus' day, but at the same time it has a special significance. It serves to remind the disciples that Jesus is fulfilling the promise he made to them earlier. Jesus said:

> *"All this I have spoken while still with you. But the Counselor, the Holy Spirit, whom the Father will send in my name, will teach you all things and will remind you of everything I have said to you. Peace I leave with you; my peace I give you. I do not give to you as the world gives. Do not let your hearts be troubled and do not be afraid. You heard me say, 'I am going away and I am coming back to you.' If you loved me, you would be glad that I am going to the Father, for the Father is greater than I. I have told you now before it happens, so that when it does happen you will believe."* (John 14:25-29)

After Jesus shows the disciples his hands and side, they are filled with joy, and they should be, but Jesus was not raised from the dead so his disciples could stay holed up in a room sharing their joy with each other. Jesus was not raised just for the disciples; he was raised for the whole world.

Once again Jesus says, "Peace, be with you," but this time he gives the disciples their mission and their purpose. Just as the Father had sent him so now Jesus sends his disciples into the world. But notice what he does first; he breathes on them and says, "Receive the Holy Spirit."

Remember what day of the week this is. John tells us that it is the first day, the day God began his creation. And what is Jesus doing? He's breathing on the disciples. We will remember from the account of Adam and Eve that *"God formed the man from the dust of the ground and breathed into his nostrils the breath of life, and the man became a living being."* *(Genesis 2:7)* In receiving the Holy Spirit the disciples are the beginning of the newly created humanity.

And what is the mission of this newly created humanity – to forgive sins? What can Jesus mean by this? Isn't God the only one who can forgive sins? Yes, but now the Spirit of God dwells with the disciples, and whenever they proclaim the forgiveness of sins, God will forgive them through his Spirit. Maybe to us this doesn't sound like such a big deal. Every Sunday here in worship we proclaim the forgiveness of sins, but for Jews it was a different story. There was only one place where your sins could be forgiven and that was the temple in Jerusalem. Only the priests could perform the ritual and proclaim God's forgiveness.

After all, the temple was the place where the Spirit of God was supposed to dwell – behind the holy of holies – but now where does the Spirit of God dwell? In the lives of the followers of Jesus. In essence, wherever there is a believer in Jesus there, too, is the temple of God Almighty working to re-create humanity in his image and likeness. But we also need to keep in mind that forgiveness of sins did not simply mean being pardoned for individual wrongdoings; certainly, this is part of the meaning, but being forgiven also had a much broader meaning.

Israel was sent into exile because of its idolatry; because of the Israelite's corporate sin as the people of God. To return from exile would mean their sins had been forgiven. But return from exile was much more than simply returning to the land and to Jerusalem; return from exile – forgiveness of sins – meant redemption.

The Prophet Isaiah proclaims:
"Be strong, do not fear; your God will come, he will come with vengeance; with divine retribution he will come to save you." Then will the eyes of the blind be opened and the ears of the deaf unstopped. Then will the lame leap like a deer, and the mute tongue shout for joy. Water will gush forth in the wilderness and streams in the desert." (Isaiah 35:4-6)

Proclaiming forgiveness of sins means much more than the elimination of guilt. It means when the disciples proclaim forgiveness, there God will also work his redemption through the Holy Spirit, in the very midst of the disciples. But if that proclamation is rejected, if the people do not recognize the presence of the living God, then their sins are retained.

And just when it seems like everything is coming together nicely and the disciples will be going out into the world equipped with the Spirit as Jesus has instructed them, we discover not all the disciples were in the room with Jesus.

Thomas is missing. Can you imagine coming back from the outhouse and discovering the risen Jesus had stopped by for a visit and you missed him? We really don't have any idea why Thomas wasn't in the room, but I think almost everyone knows what happens when the disciples tell him they saw the risen Lord. John tells us Thomas was also called Didymus, which means the twin, but the name we most associate with Thomas is "doubter". And that is really unfortunate because when we see Thomas with Jesus prior to his crucifixion he is anything but a doubter. Thomas was a staunch supporter of Jesus and his movement. He was the one ready to go and die with Jesus when they went back to Judea to raise Lazarus from the dead. He was ready to follow Jesus to death until he realized Jesus had no intention of claiming the throne in Jerusalem, until he realized Jesus would be enthroned upon the cross.

When Thomas hears the disciples saying Jesus is risen, and they have seen him, he is not simply saying he doesn't believe in the resurrection of Jesus. You see, resurrection for the Jews was much more than simply a miracle that God could perform. It isn't that Thomas does not believe in miracles – he has seen Jesus perform all kind of miraculous signs including the resurrection of Lazarus. The problem for Thomas is that he believed Jesus was the King of Israel who had come to redeem the people. All the signs Jesus performed pointed to the fact that Jesus was indeed the coming King, but then Jesus had been crucified.

Crucifixion wasn't just an incredibly horrible way to be killed, it was reserved for those who set themselves against the rule of Rome. To be crucified meant you had made a claim upon the throne but you had failed. Crucifixion stated beyond a shadow of a doubt that Jesus was no King. A crucified king was an impossibility. But here the disciples are telling Thomas that, in fact, the same Jesus who had claimed to be the messiah – who claimed to be the king of Jews, and was crucified for it – was now alive. Thomas responds, *"Not unless I see the nail marks and not only that but put my fingers in them as well as my hand in his side will I believe."*

So often we hear these words as if Thomas were dictating the conditions under which he will become a believer – as if he were asking for proof before he will believe that Jesus was raised from the dead – but that is not what Thomas is saying. Remember that resurrection is the ultimate sign of vindication; it is God's ultimate seal of approval.

Here Thomas is saying, "You want me to believe God has vindicated Jesus, that God approves of Jesus and his total failure to deal with the occupiers of Israel, his total failure to redeem Israel? Yeah, right! Show me that God approves of this massive failure."

Thomas is not saying, "I doubt what you're saying is true." What he is saying is roughly the equivalent of when today we say,

"I'll believe that when pigs fly." It is incomprehensible that the king who comes from God should suffer humiliation and death. But even though Thomas doesn't share in the joy of the other disciples, his fate is bound up with the others in the room; he was one of the disciples who followed Jesus and now he, too, is in danger of being crucified for his involvement in the movement. So he remains with the group even if he doesn't share in their joy – that is, until about a week later when again the disciples are together.

Once again Jesus appears saying, "Peace be with you", then turns to Thomas and gives him exactly what he asked for. Thomas sees the wounds in Jesus' hands and touches them with his fingers and puts his hand in the side of Jesus. In the NIV you hear Jesus say, "Stop doubting and believe", but that isn't what it says in Greek. What it says in the Greek is, "Do not be unbelieving, but believe." Now you might say I'm splitting hairs, but every instance in the New Testament where this word is used, it is used to describe pagans -- those who have not heard the gospel or those who have heard the Gospel and have rejected it. Thomas has heard the good news from the other disciples, but has refused to believe it.

It's not a question of Thomas being a good disciple who needs a little extra help in understanding the resurrection. As it stands, Thomas is so bound up in his own vision of what the messiah should look like that when he is confronted with the cross he would rather reject Jesus than change his expectations about how the messiah should accomplish the will of the Father.

Thomas challenges the disciples to show him the impossible, but it is Jesus who responds to the challenge by giving him exactly what he asked for – by confronting him with the reality of his risen and vindicated body that still bears the marks of suffering and humiliation. Only at this point does Thomas finally understand what Jesus had told him before: "I am the way the truth and life." Jesus will not follow Thomas' way. Rather Jesus, in offering himself for the sin of the world, calls Thomas and the rest of the disciples to follow his Way of bearing the image and likeness of God in the world, his way of offering the world God's redemption.

Thomas wasn't the only disciple who wasn't in the room when Jesus appeared. Generation upon generation of disciples have come to this account recognizing that in some ways we are confronted with the same problem as Thomas. How will we – those who have never seen the nail marks and the wounded side of Jesus' body in the flesh – receive the news that Jesus is risen?

Far too often we are left thinking that in this incident with Thomas, Jesus is critical of anyone who is working through questions or doubts, but that isn't what happened to Thomas. He looks out from behind the doors of that room and sees a world where the religious authorities of the day have abandoned the covenant, and at the same time he also sees that the one who looked like the true king of Israel was chewed up and spit out by the powers of the world.

He feels lost and alone. Maybe God will not – maybe God cannot – fulfill his promises. And then comes the unbelievable story of the resurrection of Jesus – about the gift of the Spirit – but the world outside the door still looks pretty much the same as it did before the resurrection. "Show me how the world has changed and I will believe it," he says. "Show me the redeemed world and I will believe."

The same is true in our time. We look out from behind the doors of the church and see a world filled with warfare, crime, cruelty, disease and despair, and it's easy for us to feel like God has forgotten about his church, forgotten his promises. It's easy to feel the world hasn't changed much after the resurrection. It's easy to say, "Show me the redeemed world and I will believe," but we receive the same answer Thomas did: "You, my Spirit-empowered disciples, my new humanity, you are the way I am redeeming this

world. Don't look out into the world; go out into the world and you will see I am there with you,
        healing,
                restoring, and
                      redeeming
through the power of the Spirit. Don't be non-believers; don't stay locked up inside this room. Go out into the world."

We hear the stories that are coming out of Africa. God's Spirit is on the move restoring sight, healing diseases, and bringing life out of death. These parts of the world, filled with disease, famine and warfare, are the same parts of the world where God's Spirit is working wonders in the name of Jesus Christ.

Often the response of the North American church is the same as Thomas' "Yeah, right. I'll believe it when I see it." It is so tempting for us to say, "Those poor Africans. If only they had our education, then they would know God doesn't work that way. If only they had our medical system, then they would realize God only heals people through doctors. If only they had been Christians as long as we have, they would realize God doesn't do the stuff anymore."

We look on, bewildered by the African church that is growing like a wildfire amidst some of the most dehumanizing conditions, and here amidst some of the best living conditions in the world the North American church is too often flickering like a match in the wind, fearful and hiding out.

Jesus' words to Thomas are also directed to us: "Don't be unbelieving. The Holy Spirit is with you, but don't get caught up in the idea that receiving the Holy Spirit is just about having exciting spiritual experiences. There will be times when you will see amazing things, but the Holy Spirit is not given so you can be a member of some kind of holier-than-thou club."

"Look again at nail marks in my hands, and touch them with your fingers," Jesus says to us, "and put your hand in my side." Jesus prepares us for the rejection we will face at the hands of the world precisely because we have received the Holy Spirit. He prepares us for the cross that we will bear, but at the same time he stands as a living proclamation that hatred, rejection, and even death, ultimately have no power.

>The only power that matters in the world is
>>the power of God –
>>>the power of forgiveness,
>>>>the power of redemption

that he offers through Jesus Christ – the same power that is in our very midst, the power of the Holy Spirit. So as the Lord sent the disciples out so long ago, let us also go out from this room without fear as believers in Jesus, our Lord and our God, and let us go out rejoicing in the life that we have in his name.

Amen.

"Follow Me"

April 25, 2004

John 21:1-19

Some people are fortunate in finding their vocation early in life – they grow up or come out of school knowing exactly what is they are called to do and to be, while for others, myself included, finding a vocation is somewhat of a battle.

There was a time when I was willing to try almost anything to make a living and as a result I found I was always moving from one unhappy job to another. When I finally realized I was not going to be happy in any of these jobs I decided to go back to school to do some more training. I didn't have any idea of what it was I wanted to do, but I thought business sounded interesting so I took courses in marketing, management, and accounting. Surely there would be something that would catch my interest.

And sure enough, as I was taking the courses, I discovered that I had a talent for accounting. It was one of those things that just made sense to me; I had a knack for formulas and numbers and so, on most of my tests, I received a perfect score. You can imagine how happy I was. I thought I had finally found it – the one thing I was meant to do with my life. I was a natural accountant. And when I went back out into the work world I did well in every position I had as an accountant. I moved up quickly and before too long I was in senior management. It was at that point in my career that I was expecting to hear, "And he lived happily ever after." But that's not how it worked out. The further ahead I thought I was getting the more I felt like I was going in the wrong direction and the more it seemed that God wanted me to be somewhere else.

It was a strange time. I remember when I finally realized God was calling me to the ministry. I had to quit my job so I could go back to school for my training. I went into my boss's office (he was, and still is, a good friend of mine) and told him I felt God was calling me into the ministry. After a long silence he looked up at me and said, "Yeah, but what if it was just gas?"

I still laugh about that. But I knew where he was coming from – why would God pick an accountant to be a minister? Why pick the guy who is used to sitting in the back room crunching numbers – used to working with formulas and equations where the answer is always certain – to work with people where nothing is for certain? I didn't have the right skills; I didn't have the aptitude for this kind of work. I mean, really, what did I know about ministry? And for the most part I agreed with my friend – I didn't have the skills. But I assured myself that's why I'm going to seminary – to learn the skills to be a good minister. Boy, was I in for a surprise!

More times than I can count I laid awake late into the night at seminary praying to God, "What am I doing here? Why have you sent me here?" God's call that had been so clear and so certain seemed like a distant memory. What if it was just gas?

The situation wasn't so different for the disciples in our Gospel reading this morning. We find Peter, Thomas, Nathaniel, the sons of Zebedee and two other disciples sitting by the shores of the Sea of Tiberius. It appears that after Jesus breathed the Spirit on the disciples and sent them out from Jerusalem they got as far as their home neighbourhood – they got as far as their own backyard before the excitement wore off, before this mission of theirs began to feel a little too big for them.

Peter looks at his friends and says, "Seven of us against the world? Those aren't very good odds. Who are we trying to kid? We can't do this; it's just too big; it's just too hard. Maybe we should go back to fishing and if anyone asks, then we'll tell them about Jesus. I mean we're fishermen, not revolutionaries. We don't have the skills to do what Jesus has sent us to do, and besides, it's been a while since anyone has seen him anyway. Maybe this was all just a big mistake."

Peter says to his friends, "I'm going fishing," and the other disciples go right along with him. The disciples head off into familiar terrain – they set out to employ their skills, go back to doing what they know best ... and after a full night's fishing they catch nothing. They have been hard at work all night long and they have nothing to show for it.

But just as a new day is dawning, just as the light of a new day is beginning to dissolve the darkness of night, the disciples hear a voice calling out to them from the shore. "Friends, haven't you any fish?" The word that the NIV translates as 'friends' actually means something more like 'children'. In the Greek it is a way a respected person who is on terms of fatherly intimacy speaks with those whom is he is addressing. Who could this person be that speaks to the disciples as if he were a father to them?

The disciples respond by saying, "No, we haven't caught anything all night long," and so the stranger on the beach calls out again. "Throw your net on the right side of the boat and you will find some." Now the disciples were experienced fishermen – it's not as if they are sitting in the boat saying to themselves, "Why didn't we think of that?" You can bet that after a night of fruitless fishing they have tried every trick in the book, used every bit of their expertise, and still have come up empty. What the stranger on the beach is calling them to do is something they would have done several times throughout the night. It was believed that putting the net over the right side of the boat was good luck, but the disciples weren't having any luck this night.

But there is something about this man on the beach. He is speaking to them as if they were his children. Could it possibly be the Lord? Could it be Jesus? Well, there was one way to find out – they lower the nets on the right side of the boat, and when they draw them back in the nets are so full they can't even haul them into the boat. Yes, it is the Lord, and when Peter hears these words he immediately jumps into action.

We often miss just how comical this scene is. Normally when someone is about to jump into the water, we expect that they would strip off their excess clothing. But here Peter had already stripped down for his fishing tasks, and now when he realizes this is the Lord, he puts his coat back on before jumping into the water! He is caught between his desire to get to Jesus as soon as possible and his concern to be appropriately dressed when he meets him. And Peter doesn't calmly dive in – in the Greek it says he threw himself into the water. He is so determined to get to Jesus as soon as possible that he comes across looking like a complete buffoon. The other disciples make their way to shore the more conventional way, in the boat, careful not to lose the enormous catch of fish they are dragging in the net behind them.

When they finally reach the shore they find Jesus cooking some fish and bread over a charcoal fire, and here we need to keep a couple of things in mind. The last time John specifically mentioned a charcoal fire was at Jesus' trial before the high priest. Remember that as Jesus was being accused, Peter was warming himself by the charcoal fire in the courtyard, and remember also that when he was confronted about being a follower of Jesus he denied Jesus three times.

Having received the Spirit and being sent away from Jerusalem, away from the chief priests and religious authorities, how will Peter respond? Will he deny Jesus here, too? We also need to keep in mind that this breakfast is not the first meal Jesus has shared with the disciples near the sea of Tiberius. When Jesus fed the five thousand, it was after he crossed the sea; he fed the multitudes with five loaves of bread and two small fish. So this view of Jesus brings with it the reminder of the miraculous feeding, but also the reminder of Peter's denial.

Jesus tells them to bring some of the fish they have caught and, as if Peter was attempting to make amends for all his failures in one gesture, he single-handedly hauls the net filled with one hundred fifty-three fish up onto the shore. There has been a great deal of speculation about what exactly the number "153" means. Why one hundred fifty-three fish? Well, for the most part there is no conclusive answer. Some think it is meant to symbolize the entire church, others suggest it points to the 153,000 proselytes counted in Israel by King Solomon, *(2 Chronicles 2:17 in the LXX)* symbolizing the complete drawing in of the gentiles, while still others argue that it may have simply been the actual number of fish in the net.

Whatever else the number may have symbolized it was seen as nothing short of a miraculous act of the risen Jesus, which leads us to John's strange comment. John tells us none of them dared to ask, "Who are you?" It seems the disciples knew it was Jesus – not because they recognized his physical appearance, but because they recognized the signs that Jesus performed. We need to keep in mind the disciples are not willing to be led along by just anyone who happens to show them a neat trick.

Remember when Jesus was debating with the Jewish religious authorities he said to them,
> *"Do not believe me unless I do what my Father does. But if I do it, even though you do not believe me, believe the miracles, that you may know and understand that the Father is in me, and I in the Father." (John 10:37-38)*

And there is only one who can make the sea obey his commands. As the Psalmist says:
> *"... the Lord is the great God, the great King above all gods. In his hand are the depths of the earth, and*

the mountain peaks belong to him. The sea is his, for he made it, and his hands formed the dry land. Come, let us bow down in worship, let us kneel before the Lord our Maker; for he is our God and we are the people of his pasture, the flock under his care." (Psalm 95:3-7)

Recognizing Jesus means recognizing the Father in him. And having recognized him they do what they had done so many times in the past – the disciples take time to share a meal together with the Lord.

Notice that John very deliberately mentions this was the third time Jesus had revealed himself to his disciples. But what is so special about this appearance – what is it about the fact that this is the third appearance that is so important? Well, remember who has been at the centre of attention throughout this third resurrection appearance – Simon Peter – the same disciple who denied Jesus three times. Up to this point Peter's joy at seeing Jesus must always have been tainted by the memory of his failure – by the guilt that accompanied the knowledge he had denied Jesus – but this time things will be different.

After breakfast Jesus takes Peter aside and asks him, "Simon, son of John…" (Notice that he doesn't call him Peter – Peter means 'rock' and he wasn't acting very rock-like in the courtyard of the chief priest.) Jesus says, "Do you love me more than these?" And here Jesus is not asking Peter to judge between himself and the other disciples, whether or not he loves Jesus more than they do. Jesus is asking Peter if he loves Jesus more than the fish. To us that may sound a little ridiculous. Of course Peter loves Jesus more than fish, and he tells Jesus so: "Yes, Lord…you know that I love you." But then Jesus reminds Peter what that means: "If you love me you will feed my lambs." Jesus isn't asking, 'Which do you like better, me or fish?' he is asking, 'How many sheep have you seen that eat fish?' Clearly none – how will Peter be able to feed the sheep if he is trying to go back to his life as a fisherman?

Three times Jesus asks, "Simon, son of John, do you love me?" and three times Peter's response is, "Yes, Lord, you know I love you." For each of Peter's three denials, Jesus gives him the opportunity to confess his allegiance to Jesus. But more than that, Jesus is telling Peter he is going to leave the fishing business that he knows so much about – he is going to leave it for good – and instead he is going into the sheep business, which at the moment Peter knows absolutely nothing about.

"I want you to look after my sheep; I want you to feed my lambs; I want you to feed my sheep, because I love you and I have redeemed you; I want you to work for me because out there are other people I love, and I want you to tend them. I want you to be my love sitting with them, praying with them, crying with them, celebrating with them. And how can you do it? By coming the way I came. You will have to suffer a lot because you have to share in the pain of the world if the world is to be healed through my life in your life, through me in you. You will have to listen to the pain of the world to hear its silent crying as well as its strident and angry crying, and it will break your heart day by day, just as it broke mine, but I have sheep out there, and they need feeding, Peter, and I want you to do it. All you have to do is follow me."

But Jesus' words weren't meant for Peter alone. Remember how many there were in the boat? Seven disciples – seven, the number of completeness. What Jesus says to Peter is meant to be heard by all disciples.

"Follow me." That's what I heard when I prayed to the Lord during those dark and difficult nights. "I don't want you to go back to being an accountant. I want you to follow me into every dark place you come across in this world so my light in you might bear witness to the dawn of my new creation; my light in you might testify to the fact that darkness no longer has any power."

I want to be clear here. Jesus is not saying we are all called to leave behind our careers; he is calling us to re-evaluate our

vocations. Am I doing what God has called me to do? In my daily life, in my daily work am I tending and feeding his sheep, or am I fishing for those things that will
>feed my ego,
>>feed my lifestyle,
>>>feed my desires?

Is my life's work something I do on weekdays and my discipleship something I do on evenings and weekends, or is my life's work – my vocation, my calling – the way Jesus reaches out to the people I see everyday at the job site, or in the office, or at the school? They, too, are the Lord's sheep and need to be fed. And if they don't get fed by us, we can be sure our society will feed them a steady diet of self-interest, and materialism.

Jesus says to us, "Follow me; and
- tell them I love them;
- tell them I died for them;
- tell them I am alive for them;
- tell them there is a new creation;
- tell them the God who made them yearns to be near them, and
- tell them if they find me they will find him – the one who sent me, the Father almighty.

It's easy to get all pumped up around Easter. People come out to worship in large numbers. The music and services are uplifting. But now, three weeks later, the enthusiasm and emotion is wearing off and we may begin to feel this Jesus project is just too big for the likes of people like us. Can't God find
>someone with better skills,
>>someone with more of an aptitude for this kind of work,
>>>someone for whom this stuff comes naturally?

The real question we need to answer is the one Jesus asked Peter: "Do you love me?" If our answer is, "Yes Lord," then we qualify. If we love Jesus, then we can love his sheep, too. That is all that's required. It will not be always be easy. As Jesus told Peter, there will be times when we will be led places we don't want to go, but through it all we will not be alone, we will be led by Jesus.

We will follow him through suffering into joy;
we will follow him through tears into laughter;
we will follow him through death into life.

Thanks be to God.

Amen.

The Lamb is My Shepherd

May 2, 2004

Psalm 23; Revelation 7:9-17; John 10:22-30

This past week a man walked into the office of his minister and said, "I got caught."

"Got caught doing what?" the minister inquired, not knowing quite what to expect.

The man sat down and said, "I've been lying to my wife. I've been telling her I was drawing extra money out of our account to pay down our mortgage, but really I've been using the money to play in the stock market; I lost it all."

The minister asked, "How much did you lose?"

"Forty thousand dollars. My wife checked our mortgage statement and she found out I was lying. Now she wants a divorce."

The lives of two human beings appear to be crumbling before their eyes – their marriage teeters on the verge of destruction – and for what? A chance at making a big score, a chance to have all the things that our world tells us are so important – big homes, fancy cars, maybe even a chance to be pampered.

The same day I was told the story of this man and his personal crisis, I was driving home from the church when I realized the commercial on the radio was for the lottery. It had the voice of a winner describing the feeling of winning the *649* jackpot: "…isn't it everyone's dream to win the lotto?" she said, and then the commercial ended with a voice singing, "Just imagine."

Hitting the jackpot, winning the lotto, quick and easy riche – is that really everyone's dream come true? I thought to myself, *certainly this can't be what the Christian hopes for*, but then I remembered the man who had just blown forty thousand dollars on so-called 'hot' stock market tips he found on the internet. And it wasn't just a case of a newcomer to the church who wasn't very far along in his Christian faith journey. He was an influential and long time member of that congregation. How had he come to the point where lying to his wife in the hope of making a killing on the stock market was consistent with being a follower of Jesus Christ?

Well, the reality for too many Christians is that there is one day out of seven where they have an opportunity to hear and remember
    what God has done,
        what God is doing, and
            what God will do in our world.
The other six days we are bombarded with a very different view of the world – a world where money, status, and power are treated as if they were gods.

Christians constantly find themselves confronted by a world that does not recognize the One true God, the God who formed the covenant, the God who revealed himself in Jesus Christ.

But this is by no means a new situation. The early churches started by Paul and Peter also lived in a world where the Greek and Roman pantheon of gods were everywhere visible and very much a part of everyday life. If you walked down the street you would be confronted by the statues of the gods hewn out of marble: tall, muscular, holding a sword, or a hammer, or a lightening bolt in their hands. And the temples were not just centres for cultic worship, they were also places where much of the town business was transacted.

Imagine living in these cities as a Christian, being surrounded by the images of a pantheon of pagan gods and trying to proclaim good news about the one true God – the same God who had commanded his people not to make physical images and idols. From the moment the people of Israel were freed from their bondage in Egypt, they were commanded not to make idols, but as we see time and time again throughout scriptures, the people were lured away by these pagan rituals and pagan practices.

But why? What was it that was so enticing about the worship of these pagan gods?

It most certainly was not because they believed all rivers lead to the same ocean, that all religious practices point to the same divine source. Pagan worship was and still is very practical.
- If you have a problem in your daily life,
- if your crops aren't growing,
- if your health is failing,
- if you are having problems getting pregnant, or
- if you can't find work,

we're told it's just because you aren't in proper sync with the gods or the world around you.

Worship of the pagan gods guaranteed success so long as you kept the gods satisfied. If you were doing well and having success, it was proof the gods approved of what you were doing; and if you are having problems, it's because you had failed in some way or another to appropriately honour the gods.

Now take a moment and think how many times you've heard someone say or perhaps have said yourself, "This or that is happening to me because God is angry with me for something I've done." When we say things like that, are we really talking about the God revealed in Jesus Christ, or is it an indication that paganism is creeping into our faith?

This morning's readings are drawn from a variety of different parts of the bible: one from the Psalms – the hymnbook for Israel – another from the Gospel of John, and the last one from John's apocalyptic vision, but all of them use the image of a shepherd to talk about God.

Without a doubt, one of the most well known scriptures is our first reading, Psalm 23. Many memorized it as children, and most others will at least have heard it at funerals where it is a perennial favourite. Those of you who have worked with people suffering from various forms of dementia will know if you pull out a King James Version and read Psalm 23, you will find many who normally have difficulty remembering what day it is, reciting the words without stutter or stumble. It's not long, it's not complicated, and yet this psalm reaches into the depths of our human experience and speaks to us a word of comfort: "The Lord is my shepherd. I shall not be in want."

The image of God watching over us as a shepherd watches over sheep, protecting us, caring for us, rescuing us when we are in trouble, is indeed a comfort, but we also need to remember that throughout the ancient world the image of a shepherd was also used to describe kings. To say the Lord is my shepherd was to say that the Lord is my king, the ruler of my life. And in instances where the demands and commands of the rulers of this world are different than the will of the Lord, saying the Lord is my shepherd may place us in a very difficult situation. Yet at the same time we know with the Lord as our shepherd, with the Lord as our king, we will not be in want. He makes us lie down in green pastures and leads us beside still waters. But here again we need to remember why shepherds take their flocks to green pastures and lead them to still waters.

Too often we get caught up in imagining ourselves relaxing in green pastures besides a pond with a bright blue sky and puffy white clouds reflecting in the still water. Too often it becomes an image of getting away from the daily grind to a retreat of total serenity, but that is not what this psalm is saying. Without green pastures the sheep will die; without a pool of water to drink from, the flock will die. The shepherd restores the souls of the flock. He literally saves their lives.

Even in the midst of the most painful times of our lives, even while we walk through the valley of the shadow of death, we know the shepherd, the one who saves our lives, is with us. There is no evil the shepherd cannot handle, no darkness the Lord cannot overcome. We are comforted by the fact that the Lord is ruler over all and protector of his flock, comforted by his rod and his staff.

Even in the midst of our enemies, even when we face trial or trouble, the Lord knows and abundantly meets our needs. And not only that, but also the goodness and steadfast love of the Lord will pursue us all the days of our lives. His goodness and steadfast love are seeking us out even now so that we may dwell in the house of the Lord forever.

Keep in mind that dwelling in the house of the Lord is not simply a way of talking about heaven. It's a way of talking about God's presence in our very midst,
> first in the tent of the tabernacle,
>> then in the temple,
>>> then in the very flesh of Jesus Christ, and
>>>> now by his presence with us in the power of the Holy Spirit.

Dwelling in the house of the Lord is not simply a promise for our future, it is a promise available to us here and now as well.

Unlike paganism, which proclaims if you want to be healthy, wealthy, and wise then just offer the right sacrifices, follow the right program, say the right prayer, and you will be blessed. The true Lord that David wrote Psalm 23 about is a God who cares for his people, who provides for their needs especially when they are being persecuted by their enemies.

David does not say the Lord prepares a table and wipes out my enemies. He says the Lord prepares a table in the presence of my enemies. In times of persecution, times of trouble, times of anxiety, the lord is there, shepherding and caring for his people. Whenever we begin to associate success as Christians with the absence of pain and suffering we are standing on the threshold of paganism.

It is no coincidence that in our Gospel reading this morning we find Jesus at the temple during the Feast of Dedication, teaching about what it means for sheep to listen to his voice. The Feast of Dedication is the celebration that we know today as Hanukah. It is a celebration that marks the rededication of the temple after it had been desecrated by offering the blood of pigs upon the altar in the temple where Antiochus Epiphanes, the Seleucid king, had dedicated to the Greek god Zeus Olympius.

When the Maccabees reclaimed Jerusalem, they cleansed the temple and re-dedicated it to the Lord. And now in Jesus' day he uses the occasion of the Feast of Dedication to challenge the religious authorities in Jerusalem.

They gather around him and demand a plain answer to the question of whether or not Jesus is the Christ – the messiah. Jesus responds by telling them that he has already given them a plain answer to the question in the works and miracles that he has done in his Father's name – but notice that he then goes on to say, "You do not believe because you are not my sheep. My sheep listen to my voice; I know them, and they follow me."

The Religious authorities are asking Jesus if he is laying a claim on the title and office of the messiah. But Jesus tells them it's not a question of claiming a title or an office, it is a question of recognition. Remember what Jesus taught about being the good shepherd. He said the sheep will only recognize the voice of the shepherd; they will not follow a stranger. In fact, they will run away from him because they do not recognize the stranger's voice. *(John 10:5)* "Do you recognize me?" Jesus asks. Because if you don't, it can only mean one of two things; either I am not the shepherd, or you are not the Lord's sheep.

We have to understand this would not have made a whole lot of sense to the religious authorities. To talk about the Lord's sheep was the same as talking about Israel. If some were going to recognize the shepherd and others were not, it would be the Jews who recognized him and it would be the non-Jews who didn't.

But here Jesus is telling them that recognizing the messiah is not a birthright. Those who recognize the shepherd will recognize him because they know his voice. It will be the same voice that has led them to green pastures and beside still waters; the same voice that has led them down paths of righteousness.

To recognize the voice of the shepherd is to recognize the voice of the Father. Which is precisely what Jesus says: "I and the Father are one."

> Even though they are circumcised,
>> even though they offer sacrifices at the temple,
>>> even though they pray to the God of the covenant,
>>>> even though they were born into one of the twelve tribes of Israel,

they are not one of the sheep. And it's not simply because they have rejected Jesus. If they do not recognize the Father in Jesus it is because they don't know the Father, and how can you claim to be a child of the covenant, one who is meant to bear God's light to the world, when you don't even recognize him?

Why is Jesus saying these things at the Feast of Dedication? Because he knows many have lapsed into a kind of paganism – worshipping at the temple of the one true God, but all the while worshipping a national god whom they expect to promote their national and ethnic interests. That god is no different than Zeus for the Greeks, no different than Jupiter for the Romans, and is certainly not the God of covenant, and not one who is supposed to be worshipped in the temple.

It is in our reading from Revelation this morning that we find John's vision of true worship, but what stands out is not so much what is being said as who is there. John tells us that there is a multitude so large it could not be counted, a multitude of people drawn from every nation and tribe.

Keep in mind that the word 'nations' was commonly used to describe nations other than Israel, and the word 'tribes' was a word used more specifically for Israel. All peoples and all languages, both Jew and gentile, are mixed together before the throne of the Lamb worshipping God.

For most of us it is not all that unusual to hear Jesus described as a lamb. In John's Gospel, Jesus is described by John the Baptist as the Lamb of God who takes away the sin of the world, but here in the Book of Revelation the image of the Lamb has an additional purpose.

Earlier in the book, John describes seeing a book sealed with seven seals which no one in heaven or on earth could break, and he begins to weep because no one is found who is worthy to open the book. But then John is told, "Stop weeping; behold, the

Lion that is from the tribe of Judah, the Root of David, has overcome so as to open the book and its seven seals." And when John turns to see the lion of Judah, the one who is filled with strength enough to open the seven seals, he sees a lamb looking as if it had been slain.

The image is meant to be jarring. It is meant to make us stop and think; since when is a butchered lamb anyone's image of strength? We are challenged to re-examine what we think strength means.

In our reading for this morning the slain Lamb has already broken six of the seals and is being worshipped by the multitudes, but notice the question John is asked by one of the elder's: Who are these people? We have already been told they are from every nation and tribe, from all peoples and languages. What else does the elder want John to see? When John says to the elder that the elder is the one who knows, the elder proceeds to tell John that these are the ones who have come out of the great tribulation, and they have washed their robes and made them white in the blood of the lamb.

Bear in mind that to face tribulation and be seen standing in heaven before God waving victory branches is an impossibility for paganism, but then again so is a God who looks like a slain lamb.

To experience tribulation meant you had failed to measure up – you had failed to keep the gods satisfied – but here tribulation is not only acceptable, it appears to be something of a certainty.

To wash your garments in the blood of the Lamb is to say you have shared in the suffering of the slain lamb; that you too will look like the slain lamb by bearing faithful witness to him in the world.

If the lamb is our shepherd, we will go where he leads us, even if he leads us to a cross. But some are sure to protest here. If the shepherd is a true shepherd, he should protect us from danger; he should protect us from the cross. I mean, isn't that why Jesus went to the cross, so we wouldn't have to? The answer is *no*.

In laying down his life for the sheep, the shepherd shows us that his love is stronger than fear and death. When we walk though the dark valleys in our lives, we are not afraid because we hear the voice of the shepherd calling to us through the darkness: "Don't be afraid; I know my way through this valley. Listen to my voice; I am right here with you." The shepherd doesn't prevent us from bearing our cross; he shows us it is nothing we need to fear, that the cross has no power over us.

Six days a week the world tries to tell us it knows a better way to live – a way to block out the pain and suffering of the world, a more practical way to achieve salvation than through the death and resurrection of Jesus.

But we are those who gather in the midst of the pain and suffering of the world, amidst the tribulation and the dark valleys of this world, confident not in our own ability to overcome them, rather we are confident in the voice of our Lord Jesus who calls us to follow him without fear. For we know he who sits on the throne will spread his tent over us and never again will we hunger, never again will we thirst.

The Lamb at the centre of the throne is our shepherd. He will lead us to springs of living water, and he will wipe away every tear from our eyes.

Thanks be to God.

Amen and amen.

Commanding Love

May 9, 2004

John 13:31-35

I remember a time, just a few years ago, when my first year of theological training was drawing to an end. I had returned home to Calgary for visit with family and friends when we received some bad news.

My mother who had recently finished her chemotherapy treatment was back in the hospital; something wasn't right. I received a call from my sister who had gone with our mom to the hospital. The doctors had checked her condition and results were not good. The cancer was back and this time it was very aggressive. There was nothing more the doctors could do. They suspected she only had a few weeks to live.

I remember driving to the hospital wondering what I was going to say. Nothing in my training had prepared me for this. I still felt more like an accountant than I did like a minister. And to top it off, my family was not what you would call a church-going group. What could I possibly say to my mother – how could I even begin to talk about God at a time like this?

When I arrived at the hospital I walked into her room filled with anxiety. I walked up to her bed and hugged her; but before I could even get a word out of my mouth she said to me, "I'm sorry." Sorry? What could she possibly have to be sorry for at a time like this?

She told me about how she had watched me growing more involved in the church and she felt she had held me back by not taking me to Sunday school when I was little. And for that she was sorry. Lying on her deathbed with, as it would turn out, only a matter of days to live, my mom was worried about *me*. So without thinking I said to her, "You taught me everything I ever needed to know about God; you taught me how to love."

I was reminded of that story when I read our Gospel lesson for this morning, with Jesus preparing his disciples for his death. Judas sets out from the room to betray Jesus who now knows time is in very short supply. The hour he has tried to prepare his Disciples for is rushing towards him. He is running out of time to tell them everything they need to know. His death is only hours away and the reality is that the disciples have
    learnt so little,
        understood so little,
            grasped so little
of what it is their teacher and master has been doing. How will they manage when Jesus is no longer there with them?

Well, the ultimate answer to that question is received in the resurrection appearances and at Pentecost with the arrival of the Holy Spirit. But if the Disciples do not have even the most basic understanding of who Jesus is and what it is he is doing, will there even be a group of disciples to appear to after he is raised from the dead, or will they all scatter, all go back to their former lives and their homes?

It's at this moment, hours from his crucifixion and death, that Jesus gives his disciples the simplest, the clearest, and the most difficult summary of all he has been saying and doing. In this moment when time is of the essence, Jesus gives the disciples the core content of what it means to be his followers. He commands them to love one another.

Sounds easy enough, doesn't it?

After all, our world is filled with messages of love. Try walking through a shopping centre without seeing the word love inscribed on some product or advertisement. Try turning on the radio without hearing a song with the word love in it. Try watching a television program without hearing someone saying the word love. It seems to be everywhere, and yet a recent survey reports that on average one in three marriages in Canada ends in divorce. One out of every three couples who proclaim their undying love for one another, who vow only death will part them, will not have enough love to keep their marriage together.

The kind of love our world has grown so fascinated with comes to us on fuzzy teddy bears and inside greeting cards, or is something that happens behind closed doors with the lights turned out. It most certainly is not the love that comes to us in Jesus.

So what is it then that Jesus means when he says, *"A new command I give you: Love one another. As I have loved you, so you must love one another"*?

Perhaps the place to begin is with the question of what Jesus means when he says this is a 'new command'. It is not as if the disciples would never have heard such a command before; in fact, in the Book of Leviticus we read the following command from the Lord: *"Do not seek revenge or bear a grudge against one of your people, but love your neighbour as yourself."* *(Leviticus 19:18)* So what's so new about this command Jesus is now giving his disciples?

The newness is not so much a matter of never hearing words like this before; the newness relates to the manner of love, the type of love, the depth of love: "As I have loved you, so you must love one another."

At this point it's easy for us to jump to the conclusion that Jesus wants us to copy him. We look back over the Gospel and see him

feeding the hungry,
    healing those with diseases, and
        acting like a servant by washing his disciples' feet.

Instinctively we say, "Ah yes, that is what he means when he says all people will know we are his disciples, if we do the things Jesus did." And certainly there is truth in that, but it's only part of the truth.

What is so often overlooked when we come to this passage is one of the central points in the whole of John's Gospel – who is Jesus? We go back to the beginning of the Gospel and John tells us,

"In the beginning was the Word, and the Word was with God, and the Word was God... The Word became flesh and made his dwelling among us."
(John 1:1 & 14)

When Jesus says, "as I have loved you, so you must love one another" he is not just talking about the last few years he has spent with the disciples. He is talking about love he's had for humanity since the beginning.

It was out of love he created human beings in his image and likeness and breathed life into us; and when we rebelled against him in the Garden he did not wipe us out and start over, but clothed us before sending us out of the Garden.

Even when the wickedness of humanity reached a high point and he sent the flood, it was not to be the end for humanity. Out of love he preserved Noah and his family to make a fresh start. But again humanity turned against him, seeking to make a name for themselves by building the Tower of Babel. And again he did not destroy humanity, but instead formed a covenant with Abram to save humanity.

Out of slavery in Egypt he delivered Abraham's descendants, but time and time again they turned away grumbling against him as he led them through the wilderness, and chasing after the idols and gods of foreign nations once they arrived in the Promised Land.

Through all the grumbling and complaining, through all the idolatry and rebellion, one thing remained constant: God's steadfast love for humanity, and it's this same love that now stands before the disciples in the flesh of Jesus.

Remember how our reading this morning begins, with Judas leaving the room to go and betray Jesus … and what is Jesus' response? Anger? Indignation? Hatred? No. Jesus says, "Now is the Son of Man glorified, and God is glorified in him."

Stop and think about that for a minute. When is Jesus glorified? Now, at the same moment one of his own disciples has left to betray him, to turn him over to his enemies. This is the moment when the glorification of the Son of Man begins.

Think about this in terms of your own witness and ministry. When we begin to encounter hurdles and obstacles in our faith journey, how often do we turn around and say it is an opportunity for glory? I suspect not very often. In moments such as these we are far more likely to feel like God has turned his back on us.

Over the years we have grown so accustomed to associating glory with success that we no longer stop and ask where is the glory here. We assume Jesus is talking about the glory of Easter, the glory of the resurrection, but that is not what he says.

Now that he has been betrayed,
    now that his crucifixion and death are a certainty,
        now is the moment of glorification.

Five times in two verses Jesus uses the word *glory* to describe this moment.

So where is the glory?

Well, as we'll see later on in the Gospel, Jesus prays to the Father, "I have brought you glory on earth by completing the work you gave me to do." *(John 17:4)* Jesus glorifies the Father by being obedient to the commands the Father has given him. He will not conform to what the religious authorities want the messiah to be; he will not conform to what his disciples want the messiah to be. Jesus will only conform to the commands of the Father; he will only be the kind of messiah the Father wants him to be.

In the midst of Israel, a nation eagerly waiting for God to come and wipe out their enemies, to restore their fortunes and make their name great, God sent his Son
    to save them,
        to remind them of their vocation,
            to show them how to bear god's light to
        the world.

What is the glory God wants the world to see? Love; and not just the kind of love you share with
    the people you like,
        the people you are related to,
            the people who share the same interests and opinion as you. The glory God wants the world to see is the kind of love revealed on the cross, sacrificial love, love that cannot be overcome by death.

Where is the glory? The glory is revealed in the fact that nothing – not even the most murderous plans of humanity, not even the worst instruments of torture, not even the worst kind of human betrayal – can stand in the way of the steadfast love of God. The cross is much more than a once and for all act of atonement. It is a glimpse into the very heart of God, a heart filled with compassion and love for a world that does not love in return. In Jesus we see obedience is not simply a question of will power. It is a matter of sharing in the love of God, sharing in the heart of the Father.

Jesus says, *"As the Father has loved me, so have I loved you. Now remain in my love."* The way of obedience, the way to keep the command of Jesus, is
>to remain in his love,
>>to abide in his love,
>>>to share in his love.

When Jesus commands his disciples to love one another as he has loved them, it is much more than a set of rules and regulations to be followed; it is an invitation to share in the very heart of God.

All too often when we talk about what it means to be obedient to the commands of God, our minds automatically click into a legalistic mode; what are the rules and how do I ensure I don't break them? But here we are reminded that obedience to the commands of God is not an exercise in keeping a strict set of rules, or keeping to a code of conduct. Obedience to the new command of Jesus is an exercise in keeping people, a discipline of looking at the world through the eyes of God and loving the world with the heart of God.

In our world that thinks love is a warm feeling we have for certain people, it's often difficult to make sense of what Jesus is asking of us. If love is a feeling, how can we possibly develop warm feelings for those people who don't treat us well? Too often the solution has been to develop a list of tasks that most people agree are loving things to do. If we give people food and clothing when they need it, then we are loving them; no need to worry about developing that warm and fuzzy feeling. But as important as it is to help people who are in need, creating a list of loving deeds falls far short of what Jesus is calling us to do.

Jesus says to us, think of those people. You know the ones – the ones who really make your blood boil...
> like the ones who cut you off in traffic;
>> like the ones who don't seem to care about anyone or anything;
>>> like the ones who are always doing wrong and seem always to get away with it.

Jesus asks, "When you look at them do you see a child of God? Do you see a lost sheep? Do you see a human being created in my image and likeness? Do you see them with my eyes? Do you see that
> I died for them,
>> I rose for them,
>>> I live for them?

Or do you see them as enemies?

In a world where love comes and goes with changing seasons and changing hormones, Jesus' command still comes to us like new –
> a new way to see our world;
>> a new way to see our neighbours;
>>> a new way see our enemies.

Jesus doesn't promise that loving one another as he has loved us will be effortless, but he does promise,
> *"If you obey my commands, you will remain in my love, just as I have obeyed my Father's commands and remain in his love. I have told you this so that my joy may be in you and that your joy may be complete."* (John 15:10-11)

Through his resurrection and in the power of the Holy Spirit, Jesus continues to teach us everything we need to know about God. He continues to teach us how to love.

Thanks be to God.

Amen.

Remember the Future

May 16, 2004

Revelation 21:10, 22:1-5

Growing up, I can remember that any time someone mentioned the word pilgrim, I had a picture in mind of a person wearing one of those round wide brim hats, square toed shoes with a buckle on them, carrying a musket, and chasing a turkey. It wasn't until much later that I realized pilgrims were much more than a group of people who celebrated thanksgiving. Pilgrims, I learned, were defined by the fact that they were on a journey — not a vacation, not aimless wandering, but a sacred journey.

But it's not really a surprise I didn't understand what a pilgrim was. Pilgrimage is just not something our society has much interest in. Yes, there are a number
>who make the journey back to the Holy Land,
>>who go to see the walls of the old city,
>>>who want to walk the via dolorosa — the

supposed path that Jesus walked on his way to be crucified. But for most in our society, a pilgrimage seems like a luxury, some-thing that costs too much time or too much money.

Things were quite different for the people in Jesus' day. Every year huge numbers of Israelites, both those living in the land and those living amongst the gentiles, would make the pilgrimage to Jerusalem for the Passover festival. They came to remember and celebrate the mighty works of God who had led them out of slavery in Egypt and delivered them to the Promised Land.

We often forget Jerusalem is on a mountain and the road up to Jerusalem would have been a long hard walk. Mile after uphill mile, it seems like a long way even today in a car. You wind up through the sandy hills from Jericho, the lowest point on the face of the earth, through the Judean desert, climbing all the way. Halfway up you reach sea level, and you still have to ascend a fair sized mountain.

I imagine Jesus walking up this long road, his disciples following along behind, when they catch the first glimpse of Jerusalem. Looking up, way up, they see the largest structure in the Holy City gleaming in the sunlight; it's the temple.

Now imagine what it must have been like walking closer and closer to the centre of Jewish religious life. I often think it must have been something like an American traveling home across the ocean and first catching sight of the Statue of Liberty off in the distance. Off in the distance the disciples see the centre of their national identity, the centre of their national pride. It is a moment of excitement.

This particular journey must have been especially exciting, walking with Jesus, the one who was claiming to be the messiah. As they followed behind they must have had
    visions of arriving in Jerusalem,
        visions of some climactic moment where
        he would assume the throne,
            a moment when he would reveal his
            true identity,
reveal to the world that Israel was God's favoured people.

But all the excitement of arriving in Jerusalem, all the excitement that surrounded the celebration of the festival of Passover, comes to a grinding halt after the meal Jesus shares with his disciples. Jesus tells them one of them will betray him. And now the mood has taken a decisive swing to the serious. Jesus prepares his disciples for his departure – he prepares them for his death – but notice what he does *not* do.

With so little time left with his disciples he doesn't give them a quiz. He does not say to them, "Repeat back to me everything I have taught you so I can be sure you have learned everything." He doesn't say, "Recite my teachings over and over again so you will remember them." In fact, it is quite clear that at this moment the disciples still do not understand Jesus' teaching.

Jesus tells the disciples, *"Whoever has my commands and obeys them, he is the one who loves me. He who loves me will be loved by my Father, and I too will love him and show myself to him."* A disciple named Judas is puzzled. This is not the same Judas who would betray Jesus, not Judas Iscariot. He asks Jesus, "But, Lord, why do you intend to show yourself to us and not to the world?" He has missed the point. He is still expecting that glorious moment when the world will be confronted by the irrefutable reality that Jesus is the Messiah, but if Jesus is only going to reveal himself to those who love him, how will the rest of the world come to that realization?

This is the point at which our Gospel reading for today begins – with Jesus answering Judas' question. Judas asks, "Why do you intend to show yourself to us and not to the rest of the world?" And Jesus answers the question by saying, *"If anyone loves me, he will obey my teaching. My Father will love him, and we will come to him and make our home with him."*

Far too often we read this saying of Jesus without remembering it is in response to the question Judas asked, and it's not too difficult to see why. The response doesn't seem to be particularly related to the question. Judas asks how Jesus will show himself to the world and Jesus answers by talking about loving him and keeping his words, by talking about his teaching and also about Jesus and the Father coming to make their home with those who love Jesus. What does this have to do with the question of how Jesus is showing himself to the world?

For one thing, it shows us just how far the disciples are from understanding what Jesus is doing. Judas thinks the journey is over, that Israel's pilgrimage is drawing to a close in Jesus. He thinks they have arrived. Now that the messiah has come, surely he will reveal himself. He will claim the throne and begin his reign over the earth, and then all the peoples and all the nations of the earth will come to Jerusalem to worship God in the Temple.

But it is clear Jesus does not share Judas' vision of what it means for him to be the messiah. Yes, he will reveal himself, but only to those who love him. Yes, he will be enthroned, but upon a cross rather than in the palace. And yes, he will begin his reign, but not as the ruler of a nation and not with the sword, but as the one who will absorb the sin of the world, one who will respond with love in the face of hatred, life in the face of death.

Far too often we hear these verses as if Jesus were trying to lay a guilt trip on us. "If you don't do the things I want you to do, then I guess you really don't love me, because if you really loved me then you would do the things I want you to do." But this is not what Jesus is saying. Jesus is trying to tell the disciples, and trying to tell us, the only way we are able to hear his words, the only way are able to keep his teaching, is by loving him.

If you cannot love, then you cannot hear his word, you cannot hear God; and if you cannot hear his word, you most certainly cannot keep his word.

This is not some new concept Jesus has just thought up. It is not something new to the disciples. Listen to the prophet Zechariah:

> *"This is what the Lord Almighty says: 'Administer true justice; show mercy and compassion to one another. Do not oppress the widow or the fatherless,*

the alien or the poor. In your hearts do not think evil of each other.' But they refused to pay attention; stubbornly they turned their backs and stopped up their ears. They made their hearts as hard as flint and would not listen to the Law or to the words that the Lord Almighty had sent by his Spirit through the earlier prophets. So the Lord Almighty was very angry." (Zechariah 7:9-12)

In Jesus, the Word of the Lord has become flesh. To love him is to listen not just to what he has said in the past, but also to what he continues to say to us now and into the future. But we need to remember
    if our hearts are as hard as flint,
        if our hearts are not soft and tender,
            filled with compassion and mercy,
                if we do not love Jesus,
                      we will not hear his word.

This is what Jesus means when he says those who do not love me, will not obey my teaching.

The Greek here actually adds much more emphasis than we find in the English translations. It reads something like, 'Those who do not love me, by no means, or in no way will keep my words.' In other words, keeping his teaching, keeping his words, **cannot** be separated from loving him.

Think about that for a minute. There is no shortage of people who claim Jesus was a great teacher. He had some really good ideas, taught us some fine principles, but here Jesus himself says if we are thinking this way, we haven't understood his teaching. We have missed the point. If we come to the conclusion we can be obedient to Jesus' word apart from entering into a loving relationship with him, then by no means and in no way have we understood him or his teaching.

This, of course, leaves the disciples with a bit of a problem. Jesus has called them to love him, but he has also told them he is about to leave them and not only that, but where he is going they cannot follow. Being separated from Jesus is not just a possibility, it is a certainty. How can they enter into a loving relationship with him, and how will they hear his word, when he is no longer with them?

This is the moment Jesus expands on something he told them earlier. He said, "I will ask the Father and he will give you another counsellor to be with you forever," Now Jesus tells the disciples this Counsellor, the Holy Spirit, whom the Father will send in his name, will teach them all things and will remind them of everything he has said to them.

The first thing we should be aware of is the word the NIV translates as 'Counsellor' does not have a precise English equivalent. The word in Greek is *Paracletos* and is translated in various English Bibles as *'helper'*, *'counsellor'* or *'advocate'*. The word in Greek literally means one who appears on another's behalf. Jesus has promised the disciples they will not be left as orphans. He will come to them through the Paraclete, the one whom the father will send in the name of Jesus, the Holy Spirit who will appear to them on behalf of Jesus.

Yes, Jesus is leaving, but that in no way prevents his disciples from having access to him. Both he and the Father will dwell with those who love through the presence of the Holy Spirit. But unlike Judas, Jesus does not see this as the end of the pilgrimage, the end of the journey.

>His leaving the disciples,
>>his death,
>>>the promise of the Holy Spirit,

are not indications the disciples have arrived, that they have reached the finish line. The gift of the Holy Spirit is intended to be a provision for a new leg in the journey.

Notice the two aspects of the work of the Holy Spirit Jesus singles out here: the Holy Spirit will teach them all things, and remind them of everything Jesus has said. One looks forward, the other looks backward.

This has been the pattern of the faith since the beginning – remembering what God has done and promised, then following along where God leads until the promises are fulfilled – but time and time again we see along the way the people stop listening. They arrive in the Promised Land and think their journey is over. They stop listening to the voice of God that led them through the wilderness. When they arrive in the Promised Land they start to think they can take care of themselves. They forget God has called them to take care of one another.

God sends his word in the mouths of the prophets but the people do not listen to it because their hearts are hardened. "Faith isn't about listening," they tell themselves. "It's about
    keeping the appropriate rites and rituals,
        keeping appropriate attendance,
            keeping appropriate behaviour.

Their hearts are hardened from chasing after the ways of the world around them. They look like the world around them rather than like the children of God Almighty. They can no longer hear the voice of their Father. And now in Jesus, the word of the Lord has come to people in the flesh and they still are not interested in listening, still not interested in what he has to teach them.

Their memory isn't very good either. They remember the part of the promise God made to Abram – "I will make you into a great nation and I will bless you; I will make your name great…" – but they have forgotten the part of the promise where God also said, "…and you will be a blessing."

Those who love Jesus, those who have not hardened their hearts, will hear the word of the Lord even when he is no longer with them. The Paraclete, the Helper, the Counselor, the Advocate, the Holy Spirit who brings to us the word on behalf of Jesus, will
> continue to accompany us on our journey,
>> continue to teach us as we travel,
>>> continue to remind us of everything Jesus

said. This will be important in a world that does not recognize God in Jesus. The disciples will be under constant pressure to conform, under constant pressure to assimilate to the values and practices of the world around them.

Here Jesus assures his disciples when they face those pressures and hold fast to Jesus in love, when they refuse to settle for a second-best, compromised discipleship, they will experience his peace, a peace the likes of which the world can never give.

Here we need to remember that Jesus was not the only one in world promising 'peace.' Peace was also the promise of the Roman Empire. Rome had two kinds of peace to offer the world: the *Pax Romana*, and the *Pax Deorum* – the Roman peace and the peace of the gods.

The Roman peace was offered by the military might of Rome. They would bring peace by the sword and anyone who threatened the peace and security of the empire bore the force of Roman military might. The other peace Rome offered was the peace of the gods: so long as you offered the right sacrifices and kept the right rituals then the gods would ensure success in battle and there would be no natural disasters like earthquakes or floods.

This is not the peace Jesus offers. The peace of Jesus is not like anything the world has to offer. His peace comes to the disciples as the very presence of God dwelling in their midst. Jesus tells his disciples these things to assure them they will not be alone when they face rejection and persecution, when they

continue to listen,
continue to follow,
continue to journey.

Far too often we as Christians get caught up in the idea that the peace Jesus is offering is very much the same thing that Rome was offering – giving us security from all things and all people who might threaten us. We often treat his peace as if it were the same as the peace of the gods, trying to reduce the Gospel to a formula, or a handful of principles to be followed – that once we think the right thoughts and act the right way, then we will have arrived and nothing will ever threaten us and nothing bad will ever happen to us. Once we have arrived, we can kick up our feet and wait for Jesus to come and congratulate us for getting it all right.

What Jesus says next leaves no room for that kind of thinking. He says if you loved me you would rejoice that I am going to the Father, because the Father is greater than I. Jesus is not trying to tell the disciples about the nature of the trinity, he is telling the disciples they still do not love him, they still do not hear his word, because if they did, they would know Jesus has not come to sit on the throne in Jerusalem; they would know he has not come to be everything the disciples wanted him to be.

The Father's plan for Jesus is much greater than simply being a powerful king in Jerusalem. The Father's plan for Jesus is nothing short of the fulfillment of all that has been promised since the beginning. If the disciples loved Jesus, they wouldn't try to
keep him for themselves,
keep him for their nation, but instead
would listen and keep his word.

Our faith as followers of Jesus is not static, and motionless. Our faith is alive and vibrant,

>   constantly on the move,
>   constantly listening
>   constantly journeying
>   constantly growing.

It is a faith that requires relationship, requires us to love Jesus, to open our hearts to his word.

So the question is not so much where are we going, but who are we following on the journey. The Holy Spirit comes along side of us, comes to us on behalf of Jesus to teach and to remind, to challenge us to remember the future God has planned for us.

As we see in John's vision, the New Jerusalem is not a place we can find with the right tools and techniques. It's not a place on a map, but a place that will be delivered to the earth from heaven, not when we arrive at the appointed place, but when we arrive at the appointed time.

As we continue to be confronted by pressures to conform to and be assimilated by the values of our world, and as we continue to open our hearts to Jesus on this pilgrimage to the New Jerusalem, we will receive his peace, and our hearts will not be troubled and neither will they be afraid.

Thanks be to God.

Amen.

Opening an Open Mind

May 23, 2004

Luke 24:44-53; Acts 1:1-11

I remember back a few years ago when I lived on the UBC campus while attending theological school, when I walked between the two main buildings of the school I would often see a car with a bumper sticker. Bumper stickers fascinate me because I think of them as a kind of evangelistic tool for the secular world – an attempt to promote secular values. I remember this bumper sticker read, "Minds are like parachutes – they only work when they are open."

Every time I saw that bumper sticker I shook my head. Sure it sounds clever at first, but an open parachute only works when filled with air. Surely a mind filled with air is not the image they are trying to promote. Surely it's not their intent to promote air-headedness. Obviously the image they were trying to conjure up is of a person safely floating down to earth with an open mind as opposed to a person hurling downwards toward the earth and toward certain death with a closed mind. The message the bumper sticker proclaims is that a closed mind is a dangerous, perhaps even a deadly thing. I think most of us at some point or another will have heard about the supreme value of having an open mind in our world; sayings like, "If only people were more open-minded, then the world would be a better place to live."

We might expect people who claim to have an open mind would be those who are willing to listen to all sides of an argument and weigh them carefully before arriving at any decisions or conclusions, but by and large that hasn't been my experience of dealing with self proclaimed open minded people. I have found the term 'open-minded' doesn't describe how a person reaches a conclusion; rather, it is a title awarded to those people who arrive at the 'right' conclusions. It is a way of congratulating people who have reached the same conclusions as most of the other self-proclaimed open-minded people.

Often it is with this view of an open mind that we hear our Gospel lesson for this morning. We are told that Jesus opened the minds of the disciples to understand the Scriptures. And it is easy for us who equate open-mindedness with knowledge and education to think Jesus is somehow downloading all the right answers into the minds of the disciples, giving them the ammunition they will need to persuade everyone they meet that Jesus is the Christ – the one who fulfills all that is written in the Law and the Prophets and the Psalms. But that is not what Jesus is doing here.

To start with, we need to understand the broad problem that confronts us in all of the Gospels – the problem that Jesus the Christ, the Messiah, came into the world. He came to Israel and no one recognized him. Even his own students, his own disciples, the ones who thought Jesus was the messiah, didn't understand what he was talking about when he said he was going to be killed and then raised from the dead after three days. Yet at the same time most everyone in Israel was anxiously expecting the arrival of the messiah. Most everyone was studying the scriptures so they would be ready, so they would know how to recognize the coming of their new king. Still, when he came none of them saw Jesus for who he is.

The people expected the fulfillment of God's promises would mean an earthly ruler – that their coming king would look a lot like David. But we need to remember at the heart of the faith of Israel is the claim that their true King is none other than God himself. The only reason Israel had a king was because they wanted to be like the nations around them.

Prior to their first king, Saul, the people were not ruled by a monarch at all, but by God himself – raising up leaders, judges to meet the needs of the people as it was necessary. The Jewish hope was indeed that God would reign supreme over the world, but he would do so by keeping his promise to David that there would always be a Davidic descendant on the throne in Jerusalem. No one was expecting this Davidic descendent to be enthroned in heaven.

Too often we get caught up thinking people in Jesus' day just weren't as smart as we are. We wonder why they couldn't see that Jesus was the messiah. We think that surely we would have got it, we would have seen, we would have heard, we would have understood that Jesus was the messiah and what that meant. Why couldn't they see he was the fulfillment of all the promises? Despite the fact everyone in Israel
    expected God to act,
        expected God to send a messiah,
            expected God to finally reign over
                the earth … no one,
    not the regular people on the street,
        not the religious leaders,
            not even the disciples
expected God to come in the flesh of Jesus. No one expected him to be born of the virgin Mary. No one expected him to suffer under Pontius Pilate. No one ever expected him to him to be crucified, to die, and to be buried. Certainly, no one expected him to be raised from the dead and no one ever expected him to ascend into heaven to be enthroned at the right hand of the Father.

In our world, when we encounter people who seem to be unable to comprehend a given issue or topic, we assume the problem is inadequate education, or perhaps there is a problem with the person's intellectual abilities. So it's easy for us to think if the people in Jesus day knew as much as we know or were as smart as we are, then they would have recognized Jesus just like we do now. But we need to remember the scriptures never point to a lack of brain power or a lack of adequate education as the cause for a failure to recognize God's actions or understand his will for the people. Instead, we see the cause singled out by scriptures for this kind of failure is idolatry.

The first eight verses of Psalm 115 are one of the clearest expressions of the relationship between idols and those who worship them:

Not to us, O Lord, not to us but to your name be the glory, because of your love and faithfulness. Why do the nations say, "Where is their God?" Our God is in heaven; he does whatever pleases him. But their idols are silver and gold, made by the hands of men. They have mouths, but cannot speak, eyes, but they cannot see; they have ears, but cannot hear, noses, but they cannot smell; they have hands, but cannot feel, feet, but they cannot walk; nor can they utter a sound with their throats. Those who make them will be like them, and so will all who trust in them.
(Psalm 115:1 – 8)

What happens when people put their trust in idols? They become like idols made of silver and gold.

Their eyes close so they cannot see;
   their ears close so they cannot hear;
      their hearts close so they cannot
     have compassion;
         their minds close so they cannot
        understand.

But notice that in this psalm, all of Israel worships the living God who is in heaven, the living God who does whatever pleases him. The idol worshippers are those from the foreign nations, those who are outsiders, but as we see in the prophets, that is not always the case. Listen to what the Prophet Ezekiel says:

> *Therefore, speak to them and tell them, 'This is what the Sovereign Lord says: When any Israelite sets up idols in his heart and puts a wicked stumbling block before his face and then goes to a prophet, I the Lord will answer him myself in keeping with his great idolatry. I will do this to recapture the hearts of the people of Israel, who have all deserted me for their idols.' "Therefore say to the house of Israel, 'This is what the Sovereign Lord says: Repent! Turn from your idols and renounce all your detestable practices!* (Ezekiel 14:4-6)

Notice it is no longer the foreign nations who are rebuked for worshipping idols, but everyone in Israel – God says, "All have deserted me for their idols," and notice also we are no longer simply talking about idols that are made of silver and gold or wood and stone. The idols Ezekiel is talking about are set up where? In the hearts of the people.

So idolatry is not simply a matter of worshipping an inanimate object. Idolatry is a matter of worshipping an image of God that is contrary to the image that has been revealed through the Law, the Prophets and the Psalms.

Here in our Gospel reading Jesus has been raised from death to life. He has appeared to the disciples on several instances, talked with them, shared meals with them, and now tells them, "This is what I told you while still with you, that everything must be fulfilled that is written about me in the Law, in the Prophets and in the Psalms." Jesus is not pointing out the texts that would have allowed the disciples to have the proper expectations about him. He is not saying if you go back and look at the scriptures you will find references that specifically prove he is the messiah. What he is saying is that the whole of scripture reveals God's identity. The whole of scripture reveals God's image and he is the fulfillment of the scriptures. Jesus is saying he is the true image of God.

And once the disciples recognize Jesus is the image of God, their minds are opened to understand the scriptures. But notice again the summary of the understanding Jesus gives his disciples is not a text that can be lifted from any of the Old Testament texts. "That the Christ will suffer and rise from the dead on the third day" is not a quotation from any scripture in particular, it is the very heart of God that is behind all of the scriptures – that God, the Almighty King, will be revealed in the fact he is willing to suffer and die in order to recapture the heart of his people who are lost in their idolatry. How far will God go to recapture the heart of his people? How far will he go to redeem them? He will go to his death, even death on a cross, and back again to reclaim his children.

> Any other image,
> > any image that does not have room for a God
> > willing to suffer for humanity,
> > > any image that does not look like Jesus,
> > > > is idolatry.

Just as Ezekiel had proclaimed the Sovereign Lord saying, "Repent! Turn from your idols and renounce all your detestable practices," so now Jesus calls the disciples to proclaim repentance for the forgiveness of sins, first in Jerusalem, then to all the peoples of the earth. It is much more than simply saying "Sorry" to God for doing bad things and God saying back to us, "Oh don't worry about it." Repentance means turning away from those things which separate us from God – leaving behind the idols we have set up in our hearts. Forgiveness of sins means the restoration of a right relationship with God, all those things separating us from God have been removed. And all of this is made possible through the revelation of God in Jesus the Christ.

I realize in our pluralistic world saying Jesus is the only true image of God and we are called to proclaim repentance to the all the people of the world is likely to come across as closed-minded, maybe even arrogant. But we need to keep in mind why this story of the ascension is even included in Luke's Gospel.

Luke was not just trying to fill space. Remember how the Gospel ends, with the disciples worshipping Jesus and then returning to the temple to praise God continually. What lies at the heart of the ascension story is much more than a simple recollection of an historical moment.

It is only at this point we understand why it is that this group of Jews, who were thorough monotheists, came to the point where they felt it was appropriate to worship Jesus – a human being. This is the only time in the Gospel of Luke where we are told they worshipped Jesus. At other points we are told people honoured him, but only here, only now in the light of the resurrection and ascension of Jesus, have the disciples been drawn out of their idolatry.

With the ascension, the disciples, and we along with them, are confronted by the fact that Jesus' resurrection was not a temporary fix. He was not raised from the dead so he could assume the throne in Jerusalem. Now the minds of the disciples have been opened to understand. They are no longer blind and deaf like the idols they worshipped. Now they see that Jesus is indeed the long awaited messiah, the King of Israel, but he is much more than the one who came to rule over the land of Israel. Jesus is the Almighty King enthroned in heaven who rules over all of creation, over all of the nations.

The message of the ascension leaves little room for a god who has colleagues, a god who is one among many, and equally leaves little room for a god who is so far away that we cannot know much about him. The ascension confronts us with the God who is fully revealed in Jesus Christ and who is fully sovereign, who does whatever pleases him.

The question ascension poses for us is, "What do we think it means to have an open mind?" Does it mean having big ideas and little gods? Or does it mean being opened by the revelation of Jesus Christ to the God who is large enough to bear the immense pain and suffering of the world so the world may have full communion with him – so the world may fully share in the life he offers?

It is no surprise that in times like these where each new day seems to bring with it new horrors and new atrocities, our world grows ever more defiant against the claim that Jesus reigns supreme over all the nations. It is not just the global crises, but also those crises of our own individual lives when we may feel we are alone, we have been abandoned by God. It is times such as these when people are most likely to object to the sovereignty of Jesus.

The truth is we don't know what awaits us around the corner. We don't know whether tomorrow will bring sorrow or joy. We don't know what to expect, but we do know *who* to expect. We know who is coming. We may not know exactly when he is coming, but we know that just as he ascended into heaven, so he will come back to us from heaven.

We know the last hour belongs to Jesus who was raised from the dead and ascended to the Father. And if the last hour belongs to him then there is nothing for us to fear in every hour, every minute, every second until then. All are within the reach of his outstretched hands and all are under his control.

But until that hour we have work to do. Jesus who reigns in heaven has given us a task. He says to us, "You are my witnesses; wait to be clothed in the power of the Holy Spirit, then go and bear witness in everything you are and in everything you do.

Wherever there is pain, wherever there is suffering, be my witnesses. Tell them I am coming back. Be my witnesses. Tell them that nothing, not even death, will keep me away from my children."

May our minds be opened to understand.

Amen and amen.

Towering Achievements

Pentecost Sunday, May 30, 2004

Genesis 11:1-9; Acts 2:1-21

Shortly after I had discerned my call to the ministry, I returned to University to take some humanities courses in order to round out my mostly technical accounting education. One of the courses I enrolled in was a Greek and Roman History course that was quite interesting, especially given the influence of Roman society on the early church.

As the course was drawing to an end, we came to that time in history where we would briefly look at the impact Christianity had on the Roman Empire, and some of our readings for the class were early Christian writings defending Christianity against those who considered the religion to be a threat. I was really looking forward to that lecture, really expecting to learn something that would be useful in my new vocation, but just before class started some students came in and took their usual seats a couple rows ahead of me.

I realized they were talking about the readings so was interested to hear what they had to say. I remember hearing one of the young women saying, "I don't know why anyone would want to be part of that religion; those people just sound so sheepish." I don't remember much of anything else that was said in that lecture. I was so angry. How could she say that about Christians – how could she belittle the faith of these people without even a second thought?

Normally after classes ended I would find a quiet place to stop and do some reading, but not that day. I remember leaving that lecture and storming around the campus of the University of Calgary,
> arguing with her in my head;
>> challenging her on the statements she had made;
>>> showing her she was mistaken.

Until I was literally stopped in my tracks by a voice that said to me, "and how long ago was it that you used to say those things about Christians?" At that time, I had been a believer for about five years and the truth is I had probably said things that were even worse than that about the Christian faith and those who practiced it.

> Then I remembered my conversion;
>> I remembered how I had been set free by Jesus;
>>> I remembered how I had done nothing to deserve it and asked the Lord to forgive me...and he did.

As it would turn out, the same young woman was in another class with me the following semester, only this time she was alone. She didn't have any friends to sit with, so on the first day when she was looking for a familiar face in the class, she saw mine and sat down beside me. "You were in history with me, right?" she asked.

"Yes," I said. "I remember you." The interesting thing for me was that all of the anger and hostility I had felt was gone. I didn't see her as an adversary or opponent, but simply as a wayward child of God. One question from the Lord had fundamentally changed the way I looked at this person.

While I never did have the opportunity to share the gospel with her, I did take some small delight in watching her facial expression when I told her I was preparing to be a Christian Minister.

I remembered that story as I was preparing for this Pentecost Sunday service – this time in the Christian year that we remember we are not left alone to sort out lives by ourselves; rather, we celebrate the presence of the living God who speaks to us, guides, equips, and transforms us.

Often when it comes to Pentecost we get so caught up looking at all the details we lose sight of the bigger picture, of what place Pentecost has in God's plan for humanity. So I would like to start by going back to the beginning, back to the first eleven chapters of the Book of Genesis where we find the problem that God is sorting out.

Genesis is such a rich book filled with depth of meaning and theology, but the first eleven chapters in particular speak to us about the human condition, about our relationship with God and our relationship with one another. We read about our relationship with God, being created to bear his image and likeness in the world he created. We are intended to be in right relationship with God and with others and with the world around us. But there is a problem. It turns out humanity is not very good at listening.

God gave humanity commands. He set boundaries for how we are to live our lives, but humanity didn't listen. It's not simply that humanity is disobedient to the commands God gave them, but that humanity is willing to listen to almost anyone *except* God. Humanity is more willing to listen to the arguments of a snake – another created being – than to listen to their Creator, the Lord their God.

Cain is more interested in listening to his own selfish pride, so much so that he is willing to commit murder rather than take a second seat to his younger brother, Able. And over time humanity grows so self-interested, so distant from God, that God's heart fills with pain and he is sorry he ever created human beings.

So God comes up with a plan to wash filthy humanity from the earth, but just as he is about to put his plan into action, he remembers Noah, who has done everything the Lord asked him to do. God decides he will start over with this Noah who listens to his voice. Maybe things will be different with him. So after washing away the human wickedness that filled the earth, God starts fresh with Noah and promises never again to wipe humanity from earth with a flood.

But Noah's descendants are not any better listeners than their predecessors. This is where our Old Testament Reading for this morning begins.

We are told humanity shared a common language and they were traveling eastward. This may sound straight forward and matter of fact, but keep in mind the word in Hebrew used to describe their direction is the same Hebrew word used to describe the location of the Garden of Eden. Humanity is searching for the Garden. And remember what God has told humanity: The only thing they are given to do is to be fruitful and to multiply, to fill the earth. But humanity is not particularly interested in what God wants. They are more interested in what they want. They want a city. They want a tower that reaches into the heavens. They want to make a name for themselves. So they listen to each other instead: "Let's make bricks," they say to one another.

What is interesting here is that when God comes to check out humanity's monumental undertaking we are told he had to come down to see it. Humanity's towering achievement, the monument that was so large it was supposed to reach into the heavens, is so small to God – so far from the heavens, God has to get up close to see what humanity has done. Notice God's response. If, in speaking the same language, they are able to do this, then nothing they plan will be impossible; so God sets out to confuse their language and then scatters them all over the earth. In an ironic twist, humanity ends up getting exactly what they were trying to avoid ..., being scattered over the face of the earth.

Now to most of us this will sound somewhat unusual. We are not accustomed to hearing about God setting out to upset our plans, intentionally setting up obstacles to our achievements. Some scholars take the easy way out of this situation and say well, this story really just serves an etiological purpose – that the only reason it is included in the scriptures is because it offered an explanation for why different nations spoke different languages.

At one level that may be true, but keep in mind the point of the story is not simply that God decided to confuse the languages of people, but did so because they were listening to each other rather than listening to him. When Adam and Eve listened to the snake instead of God they were cast out of the Garden, and here humanity has repeated the same offense. They have listened to each other, created beings, rather than listening to God, and as a consequence have been scattered from that place in the east where they intended to build their city and make a name for themselves.

Humanity after the flood is just as unwilling to listen to God as humanity prior to the flood. Those created to bear the image and likeness of God seem to be incapable of listening to what it is God wants them to do and to be.

> They are not in right relationship with God;
> > they are not in right relationship with the world around them;
> > > they are not in right relationship with each other as human beings.

So when God sets out to frustrate the towering achievements of humanity, he is not doing it because he is worried humanity is going to accomplish too much. God is worried about

what they will not accomplish – they will not bear his image and likeness and, as a result,
> creation will suffer;
>> humanity will suffer;
>>> God himself will suffer.

And all so humanity can glorify their own name with their towering achievements.

Since the self-interest of humanity has not been purged by the flood, God acts in new way to draw human beings back into right relationship. He makes a covenant with Abraham who is faithful, who will listen – a covenant through which God will call a people to bear his image and likeness to the world; a people who bear his light to the nations; who will show the rest of humanity what it means to be truly human.

This covenant is based upon listening to the commands of God, but in time they, too, forget their calling. They stop listening, so God sends his words in the mouths of the prophets to call the people to listen.

It is not an accident that all the prophets begin their oracles with the words, "Thus says the Lord". The prophets are not simply social analysts and philosophers calling the people to a better way of living. They are calling the people to stop listening to the voices of the nations around them, to stop listening to the counsel of other human beings and return to listening to the voice of God.

So it is no surprise that when Jesus arrived on the scene people thought he was a prophet. Once again the people were hearing the voice of God, but this time God sent not only his voice, but the model for what it means to listen to God. In Jesus, God shows humanity how to listen. And Jesus does listen and faithfully fulfills all that is asked of him. He is faithful even unto death on a cross. And this moment – this moment of supreme torture and humiliation – this is God's towering achievement.

Death, an especially brutal and slow death, is no human being's idea of an accomplishment. In fact, it would be safe to say this would be the opposite of any human being's definition of accomplishment. If that had been all there was to the story we could quite easily dismiss Jesus as a lunatic or a deluded fanatic, but the resurrection of Jesus – God's ultimate stamp of approval – suggests something quite different.

The resurrection stands as the ultimate check on our human desire to listen to any voice other than God's. If Jesus was resurrected it was because he was faithful to his Father's voice. And if he was faithful to his Father's voice then his death was part of God's plan for the fulfillment of his promises.

But this leaves the disciples in a terribly awkward position. They know Jesus is the model of a faithful servant of God, but he has ascended to the Father. How will they hear the voice of God now that the only one who was able to hear it clearly has left them?

This is why it was so important for Jesus to ensure the disciples waited for the arrival of the Spirit before venturing out on their mission. How long would it be before the disciples were erecting their own monumental masterpieces – before they began trying to make a name for themselves – because it is clear from the gospels they weren't above that kind of thinking. Remember how they argued over which of them would be the greatest in the coming kingdom.

Jesus told the disciples to wait in Jerusalem for the arrival of the Holy Spirit, but the question is why? Why wait? Why not get on with the mission right away? Why not send the Spirit immediately? Because God is waiting for the right time; he waits for the arrival of Pentecost.

Now this may sound strange to those of us who are so used to hearing that Pentecost was the moment when the first disciples received the Holy Spirit. We often forget Pentecost was one of the three Pilgrimage festivals of the Jews. It was the festival that was also known as the feast of weeks, a time when Jews from all parts of the known world would come to Jerusalem. They came to offer the first fruits of their harvest and to give thanks to God for providing for their needs.

The Spirit comes upon the disciples at a time when Jews from all over the world are together celebrating God's ongoing care and provision. This is the time when the Spirit suddenly arrives, but notice what it says about the coming of the Holy Spirit – it's noisy.

Often we remember the gospel accounts of the Spirit descending on Jesus. We imagine a peaceful dove gently descending, but that's not how doves fly. They have small, powerful wings and need to flap them strenuously to get into the air. They make a lot of noise, and you most certainly hear them when they come and go. The arrival of the Spirit will not go unnoticed, especially during the busy festival with so many people gathered in the city of Jerusalem.

But it is not noise alone that accompanies the arrival of the Spirit. The disciples see tongues of fire that separate and rest upon each one of them. Often this is seen as the Spirit setting the hearts of the disciples ablaze with passion, but we need to remember fire was not so much an indication of passion in Scriptures as it was associated with the Lord speaking his commands.

God spoke to Moses through flames of the burning bush and wrote his command on the tablets with fire. The tongues of flame point to the fact God is empowering the disciples for proclamation. They will go out speaking the word of God, telling others the Good News of Jesus Christ, the faithful servant who fulfills God's promises.

Imagine what it must have been like for the disciples waiting for the arrival of the Spirit. Surely they would have remembered the charge Jesus gave them to go out to the ends of the earth proclaiming repentance and the forgiveness of sins; but there must have been some questions, some doubts. They may have known how to speak Hebrew, Aramaic, and some Greek but what about those further regions of the world? Who could speak those languages?

Here the first thing that happens upon being filled with the Spirit is the disciples begin to speak in every different language. The obstacle of different languages that God had set in place to prevent human beings from following after each other's voice is removed in order to ensure the Gospel will be heard. God will not allow any obstacle to stand in the way of the Good News of Jesus Christ.

We are told those who hear the noise of the Spirit, who hear the disciples speaking in different languages, were amazed and perplexed, but keep in mind this was much more than an interesting moment for the Jews gathered in Israel. This is nothing short of a crisis.

Something amazing has just happened. It strikes everyone around as being something only God could be responsible for, but what could it possibly mean? If God is pouring out his Spirit, then he should be pouring it out on all of Israel not just on a handful of people within Israel. The whole people of Israel were God's chosen people, not a small group within Israel. The crowd is confronted by the fact that God is empowering not all of Israel, but only those who will listen to his voice.

So it is no surprise when the response of some is that this is not the work of God at all, but the work of new wine. Confronted by the fact God is not acting the way they expect, their reaction is to mock and to laugh, but remember, if they are mocking and laughing at the disciples they certainly are not listening.

In some ways this is the paradox of Pentecost. The moment God poured out his Spirit upon the disciples in order to remove the obstacles that stood in the way of proclaiming the good news, was the same moment of division within the life of the people Israel.

Even within the church, Pentecost remains a source of much division among those who follow Jesus. Too often in the church, Pentecost is treated as if God were
> fulfilling our need to be recognized,
>> empowering us with the ability to achieve our hearts' desires,
>>> equipping us with the skills and abilities to make a name for ourselves.

But Pentecost is ultimately not about the amazing things we do when we are empowered by the Spirit, but what God is doing for humanity. It is the final stages of the plan God began at Babel: the undoing of human self interest, of turning the ears of humanity from constantly listening to the voice of someone other than God.

Often it is easy for us to be led astray, thinking the grand achievements we have planned are really designed to glorify God's name, but every one of our plans, every one of our achievements, must be measured against the faithfulness that is revealed on the cross of our Lord Jesus.

At Pentecost not only do we receive the assurance that God is with us and speaking to us, but that Jesus, the model of human faithfulness, is also with us, challenging us when we turn our ear away from God's voice, and strengthening us when our faithfulness leads us to places of persecution and rejection.

Along with Peter and the first disciples we are empowered by the Spirit to claim the cross of Jesus as the victory which is at the heart of God's work – the moment when we see what listening to God looks like. Without it we are likely to imagine

>> our own goodness,
>> > our own skill,
>> > > our own intelligence, or
>> > our own power

is the towering achievement through which we could eliminate the evil of the world.

At Pentecost we celebrate the first fruits of the harvest – the turning point in God's plan to reclaim the heart of humanity. We receive much more than a set of skills and abilities. It is nothing short of the voice of Jesus dwelling within us, the realization that God does not dwell in some remote place so far removed from the hustle and bustle of our daily live, but is always with us,
>> directing us,
>> > encouraging us, and
>> > > transforming us.

So we can have the confidence to take on the mission that Jesus has given us. We can have the confidence to take on the world, knowing that the love of God is only a whisper away.

>> Thanks be to God.

>> Amen.

The Unwanted God

Trinity Sunday, June 6, 2004

Romans 5:1-5

One of the challenges I face every week is the task of preaching – finding the appropriate words to talk about God – words that teach,
> words that comfort,
>> words that challenge.

It is by no means an easy task. It is not something for which I ever thought I had a natural talent. I remember back to the very first time I ever preached. It was back in Calgary, preaching to the congregation that first introduced me to Jesus Christ. It was a nerve-racking affair. I stumbled and stammered along, speaking too quickly to keep anyone's attention, and then I finally finished.

What seemed like an eternity to me lasted a measly five minutes, but that wasn't the worst part. When the minister of the church asked me how I thought it went, I told him I was disappointed – when I began preparing for the sermon I had so much passion it seemed like there was so much I could say, but when it came to preach, none of the passion came out. I just couldn't find the right words.

Even now, after my seminary training and the experience I have gained in preaching, I still have difficulty finding the right words. It has become something of an unwelcome ritual at my house: every Saturday night I bring my sermon to my wife Sheryl, and ask her to read it. She says to me, "Let me guess ... you think it stinks."

I take comfort in the knowledge that after more than thirty years' of ministry my mentor, the Reverend Dr. Tony Plomp, still gets butterflies in his stomach before he preaches. Proclaiming the word of God is indeed a privilege, but it is not something that can be taken lightly.

This Sunday is somewhat unusual. Normally in the Christian year we celebrate God's actions. At Christmas we celebrate God coming into our world in Jesus; on Good Friday, his crucifixion; on Easter Sunday, his resurrection; and on Pentecost, the gift of the Holy Spirit. But on this Sunday in particular the church remembers not what God has done but who God is. Trinity Sunday is the day the church takes a step back from the grand sequence of events the Gospel describes and reflects on what the word 'God' actually means.

I remember when I first became a Christian it was interesting to listen to people try to explain what *trinity* meant. Explanations ranged from the very abstract with talk of essences to arguments over whether or not the second person of the trinity was created or eternally begotten. Then there were the object lessons that made the trinity so small it could easily be grasped by the human mind.

Ultimately neither of these approaches was adequate because in both cases, talk of the trinity becomes something other people do, either an exercise in philosophical speculation or a trivialization with no real point of contact with our daily lives.

So what I would like to do this morning is take a look at our reading from Paul's letter to the Romans as a way of reflecting on why our view of God matters. More specifically, why seeing God as trinity matters.

Perhaps the place to begin is to say when Paul wrote his letter to the church in Rome, he was not writing so they would have a good theological understanding of the trinity. As with all of Paul's letters, he was writing to address a pastoral issue. There was an issue, or more likely several issues, Paul was seeking to address in his letter and our passage this morning is part of Paul's response to them.

It's important for us to remember that during the reign of Emperor Claudius, rioting broke out among the Jewish population in Rome. The cause of those riots seems to have been the earliest Christian preaching among the significant number of Jews who made their home in the capital city of the Roman Empire.

Peace and security were among the chief concerns of Roman citizens and as such the emperor sought to solve the problem by issuing a decree that expelled all Jews from Rome. For most Romans the decree would have come as welcome news.

You see, generally there was no love lost between gentiles and Jews. We have ample written evidence of the distaste expressed toward their Jewish neighbours, but the distaste flowed both ways. Jews also tended to be equally offended by gentiles. It was a custom among Jews who traveled outside of the holy land to stop before re-entering and shake the gentile filth off of their sandals. They didn't want to track the gentile filth into the Promised Land.

But in the midst of all this bad blood between Jews and gentiles came the Gospel of Jesus Christ that Paul and the other apostles were proclaiming: "There is no gentile or Jew," but a new humanity in Jesus Christ. For more than a decade this simply wasn't a problem for the church in Rome since the Jews had long since been expelled. With no Jews in the city it was quite easy for the church in Rome to imagine a Gospel was really God's plan for the gentiles alone and that God had simply expelled them from the covenant the same way the emperor had expelled them from Rome.

But all of that changed when Claudius died and Nero became the Emperor. When an emperor died, so did his decrees, and as such the Jews were no longer banned from Rome. They began to return to their homes, to their businesses and more importantly they began to return to their synagogues. The small gentile church in Rome was now facing a crisis: wherever they preached about the messiah there were Jews who contradicted their proclamation, and not only that, but they seemed to have history and tradition on their side. How would the church respond when faced with this kind of rejection?

Well, Paul knows when people are faced with a crisis they are tempted to revert back to the security of their old way of life, which in the case of the gentiles in Rome, was paganism. Suffering for your faith was just as unpopular in Paul's day as it is in our time.

To pagans, suffering was not only unpopular, it was a sign of failure. Suffering was sure proof the Gospel wasn't true. After all, if you were doing what your god wanted you to do, then surely your god would grant you success. If your god wouldn't grant you success, it was because your god didn't have the ability to grant you success and, therefore, wasn't worth worshipping. So knowing the fragile gentile church in Rome is under pressure to return to the paganism of their past, Paul draws upon something else that would have been familiar to the gentiles in Rome, he draws upon the Greek philosophy of stoicism.

The stoics were the authors of the "stiff upper lip" approach to life, and their philosophy is still very much alive and well today. Anytime you hear the words "that's just the way the world works" or "that's just the way life is", you are hearing stoic philosophy. The main idea is that the world never changes so we simply need to find a way of coping with the challenges life hands us.

It's not so much that Paul is wanting the church to adopt stoic philosophy. He knows stoicism is part of the fabric of gentile society and that the church is familiar with it, so he uses it as a springboard back to the Gospel.

Stoics taught that suffering produces perseverance and perseverance produces character, but it ended there. Character was considered to be a virtue by Romans. It was an end in itself, something worth striving toward. But this is the point at which Paul springs to the Gospel: suffering produces not only character, but hope. Suffering is not simply an opportunity to build character, it is the beginning of hope.

Makes perfect sense, right? No? In fact, it's kind of counter-intuitive. Isn't it when things take a turn for the better in our lives that we tell ourselves we have some reason to hope? But what Paul is doing here is driving home what's at the centre of this whole issue: remember who is it you are worshipping, he says to the church in Rome. You are worshipping Jesus the Messiah who was raised from the dead. Don't forget he was raised only after he suffered and died. You are worshipping a God who reveals himself in the suffering and death of Jesus.

This is most certainly not the god Rome wanted. Rome wanted a god they could appease and manipulate. They wanted a god who would grant them victory in battle when they offered the right sacrifice. They wanted a god who would guarantee them safety and security. Nobody in Rome wanted a crucified god.

The hope of the church in Paul's day and the hope of the church today is not that everything will work out the way we want it to. Our hope is for redemption. Jesus is the pattern for all of humanity. Just as he suffered and died and was resurrected, so will all those who bind themselves to him in faith. Our hope is for a return to the order God originally intended, with all of God's creation in right relationship with their Creator, not just for a period of time but for all time.

The problem was these Jews who had returned to Rome were tying to poke holes in the church's proclamation, rejecting the claim that Jesus was the messiah. Did suffering really lead to hope, or were the gentiles simply being led astray by a few mistaken Jews? Maybe there was good reason not to believe in a suffering and crucified God.

Paul addresses this concern in the opening sentence of our passage. He says, "Therefore, we have been justified through faith; we have peace with God through our Lord Jesus Christ." When Paul talks about justification he is not just throwing around theological jargon. As a good Jew, Paul knew what justification meant – human beings were justified through being faithful to the covenant. Those who were faithful to the covenant were justified by God; they were marked as members of God's covenant people.

But for the Jews, justification had taken on ethnic and nationalistic overtones. The covenant was seen as a kind of possession of the nation of Israel and being ethnically Jewish was seen as the marker that you were a member of God's chosen people. Faithfulness to the covenant was still important but it was no longer the defining mark of the covenant people.

But the death and resurrection of Jesus the messiah was the ultimate challenge to that kind of thinking. Israel was not to follow a military messiah. They were to follow a suffering servant. And justification – the mark of being a member of God's chosen people – was faith in Jesus the Christ, trusting the suffering servant. In Jesus, God showed humankind what covenant faithfulness looked like. Those who believed Jesus was the messiah and followed his way were justified, were marked as members of God's covenant people, regardless of whether they were a Jew or gentile.

Paul is not simply saying faith in Jesus is the way for gentiles to be brought into the covenant, he is saying that faith in Jesus is the only criteria for membership in the people of God.

Clearly, there were many Jews who disagreed with Paul. Jesus is not the god many of the Jews wanted.
> They wanted a god who was going to be faithful to their nationalistic dreams.
>> They wanted a god who would show the world the Jewish people were God's favoured people.
>>> They wanted a god who would wipe out everyone who stood in their way.

None of the Jews in Rome, Jerusalem, or anywhere else wanted a crucified God.

Paul wants the church in Rome to remember the God revealed in Jesus Christ cannot be confined or limited by their desires, by their expectations, by what they want god to be. The God who is revealed in Jesus Christ offers real hope because he will not fit any mold, any program, any religious system, devised by desires of humanity. When Moses encountered the burning bush, God revealed his name saying, "I am who I am" *not* "I am who you want me to be."

But the truly amazing part is when God reveals who he is through his actions in the world, what we see time and time again is grace, compassion and mercy.

When we go back to the story of Cain and Able we see Cain murder his brother. What response do we expect from God? What would we do if we sat as judge, jury and executioner over Cain? Would our judgment be an eye for eye? Not only does God refrain from killing Cain to pay him back for what he has done to Able, but he also places a mark on him so no one else will kill him either. God responds to Cain's murderous self-interest with mercy and compassion.

When Joseph's brothers sell him into slavery to make a couple of quick bucks off their brat of a younger brother, God raises Joseph up to a place of prominence in the Egyptian palace government, a position from which he will provide food for his brothers when a severe drought threatens their lives. God responds to the brothers' ruthless actions by making Joseph the means of survival not only for this family but for all the people in and around Egypt.

Later, when the people of Israel turned away from God, killed the prophets who spoke God's word, and were carried off into exile, God did not respond by abandoning them, but instead promised to redeem them by leading them back into the Promised Land.

And when God sent his word in the flesh of Jesus and he was brutally murdered, God used the innocent blood of Jesus on the hands of murderous humanity as the means by which all of humanity would have access to peace with God, the way in which humanity would be reconciled to God. The startling truth is that while humanity is chasing after the gods they want, the unwanted God – the God who created the world and everything in it – is chasing after us. He wants us.

He wants us to be near to him;
> he wants us to share in his love;
>> he wants us to be what we were created to
> be: his children;

and God will stop at nothing, not even death, to ensure it.

So it is safe to say God's ways are most certainly not our ways and any talk of God that does not take into account the fact we can never fully grasp, contain, or otherwise pin God down, will in some form or another result in us chasing after the gods we want.

As one theologian said, "All idols started out as the god that someone wanted."[2] The end result of that idolatry is we set ourselves up as a god, and this god we have fashioned in our image

---

[2] Wright, N.T. For All God's Worth, Wm. B. Eerdmans Publishing (1997)

and likeness becomes little more than our puppet doing whatever we ask in the hope of getting what we want. But nobody trembles at the word of a home-made god. Nobody goes out with fire in their belly to heal the sick, clothe the naked, or feed the hungry because of the god they wanted. They are more likely to stay at home with their feet up.

Trinity is much more than a dogma. It is an attempt to find the right words to talk about the God who is so much greater than anything we can say about him. Trinity is a signpost pointing into a light that gets brighter and brighter until we are dazzled and blinded, but which says, "Come and I will make you children of light."

But Trinity Sunday also stands as a reminder that when we stop trying to speak about the God revealed in Jesus Christ, other gods, the gods we want, come clamouring for attention, drawing us away from the God who proclaims that suffering is the beginning of real hope. Not because suffering is good, not because that is just the way the world is, but because God knows of a better world, a redeemed world –

- a world where *"The wolf will live with the lamb, the leopard will lie down with the goat, the calf and the lion and the yearling together; and a little child will lead them."* (Isaiah 11:6)

- a world where *"(God) will wipe every tear from their eyes. (and) there will be no more death or mourning or crying or pain..."* (Revelation 21:4)

God knows of the world that awaits us on the other side of the cross.

Why does the Trinity matter? Because at a most basic level, God longs to recapture our hearts, so much so that he poured out his love for us into the flesh of his Son Jesus and said to us, "This is who I am" and then again poured out his love, but this time into our hearts through the power of the Holy Spirit.

He isn't the god the world wants, but the God the world needs – the only one who take us from suffering through to hope and from death through to life.

Thanks be to God: Father, Son, and Holy Spirit.

Amen.

Sharing a Meal with Sinners

Communion Sunday, June 13, 2004

Galatians 2:15-21; Luke 7:36 - 8:3

I remember being in a bible study a few years ago and the topic for the day was human sin. Normally the group would watch a video presentation and then engage in some discussion. On this particular occasion one of the members of the group was clearly uncomfortable with the topic; she sat restlessly through the video and was first to speak when it came time for the discussion.

"I don't think I'm a sinner," she said. "I've never done anything to hurt anyone else and I do just as many good things as anyone else I know." And then she finished by saying, "I'm not a sinner; I'm a good person." It's safe to say she's not alone in her convictions. I think if we were to go out and ask people if they thought they were good people, most would have a similar response. They would say, "I'm a pretty good person."

My guess is we would have to search pretty hard to find someone who would come out and admit, "You know, I'm really quite a bad person." In fact, when we do encounter people with that sort of self-image, we usually think they should be shipped off for counselling to improve their self-esteem. For many people just like the woman I met in the bible study, there is a kind of unease or discomfort when it comes to talking about human sinfulness. Most people would be willing to concede they are not perfect, but surely they are not sinners, surely they are not sinful.

Part of the problem for us is that the word *sin* has a variety of meanings. In biblical Hebrew there are more than fifty words that mean sin, which in and of itself should tell us something about just how important this issue was and is for those who take their relationship with God seriously.

Of those fifty different words, three are used most frequently. One of the words means to fall short of the goal, to miss the mark. This is the kind of sin that can be incurred without ever knowing about it. It is most frequently associated with the holiness codes found in the Book of Leviticus. The second of the three most common words means to revolt against God. This one is an intentional sin, often translated in our bibles as *transgression*. It means to knowingly defy the commands of God. The last of the most common words for sin means *iniquity*, to bear moral guilt before God.

So it's interesting that for so many in our world the word *sin* has come to be almost entirely associated with the last kind of sin – the guilt we bear before God for our moral wrongdoing.

All sense of Levitical holiness and most of the sense of human desire to usurp God's rule over the earth tend not to be in our minds when we read the scriptures. But we need to remember these other forms of sin were very much in the minds of the first people to have listened to Jesus and who listened to the apostles when they set out on their mission.

One of the consequences of our western emphasis upon the moral aspects of sin is that our image of God has tended to be distorted. We tend to see God sitting on his throne in heaven putting an 'X' beside our names when we do something morally wrong, and the people with the most 'Xs' get fire and brimstone, while the people with fewer 'Xs' get zapped into heaven and receive eternal life and peace. But we need to be clear this is not a biblical understanding of how God responds to sin.

Sin has one consequence and that is separation and alienation from God. Sin creates a relational problem. It results in our being unable to relate to God, unable to communicate with God. When our relationship with God is out of alignment all our other relationships suffer as well; our relationship with our environment suffers and our relationship with other human beings suffers.

The other thing we need to keep in mind is when we find ourselves in the midst of this relational problem, unable to properly relate to God, to our neighbours, and to the world around us, we are not simply left alone to find our way back to God, or left alone to pull ourselves up by our own bootstraps. Despite the fact it is always humanity that turns away from God, God is always the one who is initiating reconciliation, always the one
> seeking us out when we have wandered,
>> reaching out to us,
>>> calling us back, and
>>>> welcoming us home.

Reconciliation, a restored relationship, is never something we do. It is always something God does for us. We are brought back into proper relationship with God purely by grace.

Paul knew firsthand what it meant to be restored to a right relationship with God. Remember he was one of the most fervent and zealous persecutors of the church, going out with documents in hand to arrest the leaders of this new Jesus movement and bring them back to face a trial before the Sanhedrin. He was determined to clean up, once and for all, the mess Jesus and his followers had created … until he was confronted by the risen Jesus himself. He came to see what he was persecuting was nothing short of the means by which the whole world would receive the grace of God – the means by which the world would be brought into right relationship with God.

In a twist of irony, our scripture reading from the letter to the Galatians finds Paul in the position of having to defend his mission and ministry to the gentiles in the face of stiff opposition from other members of the community of Christian believers.

An argument has arisen in the church over the claim that Jews cannot eat with gentile sinners – and here we should be aware that the kind of sin they are talking about is the breaking of the Levitical purity laws. The food laws the Jews observed were intended to mark off God's holy people, not so they could boast about being God's people, but so that as a people they would stand out as a beacon – a light pointing to God. Many Jews who came to believe Jesus was the long awaited messiah and received the Holy Sprit did not see the kosher food laws being inconsistent with faith in Jesus the Christ. They still saw the Jews as God's light to the nations, and still saw their vocation in terms of their call to be a holy people. If Paul wanted to preach to the gentiles, that was fine, but should the gentiles come to faith in Jesus, then they needed at a very minimum to obey the food laws or, more preferably, convert fully to being a Jew.

Now it's important for us to keep in mind when Paul says, "we know that a man is not justified by observing the Law, but by faith in Jesus Christ…" the Jewish Christians he is arguing with would have agreed with him. Paul is not trying to convince them they can be justified by faith and can not be justified by works of the Law. That was common knowledge among believers. What they are wanting Paul and the gentile believers to accept, is the *proof* of them being reconciled to God through faith in Jesus Christ was to keep the kosher food laws that marked God's people from the rest. If you have faith in Jesus, the consequence will be a new life of holiness as it was prescribed by God in the Law.

Paul says, "Well, that sounds fine in theory, but look at how it works out in practice. You say eating with gentiles makes me unclean, makes me a sinner. If that's the case, then I am not reconciled with God. I'm not justified, and the reason I am considered to be a sinner is that my faith in Christ is measured in terms of keeping the Law. So, in fact, the grace of God, the reconciliation offered through Jesus Christ, is only considered to have been effective so long as I observe the Law. And if that is the case, then it is no different from saying we are justified through the works of the Law. And if our relationship with God could be restored through keeping the Law, then Christ died for nothing."

That's a strong statement. Paul meant it to be a strong statement. The argument may sound complex but at a most basic level Paul is trying to say anytime we set something alongside faith in Jesus Christ as the mark of being reconciled with God, we set up obstacles to entering into the grace of God.

Those who confronted Paul said God is gracious to gentiles if they have faith in Jesus *and* prove their faith by observing the kosher dietary laws. That may sound a bit bizarre to us, but what if we say God is gracious to those who have faith in Jesus *and* prove their faith by not drinking, not smoking, not dancing, or any other number of 'sins' that Christians have found detestable over the years. Now that's not to say Paul had anything against the food laws, nor do I want to suggest he is simply proclaiming that now anything goes. Paul's point is that the definitive proof of God's Grace *is* faith in Jesus Christ. Anything in addition creates obstacles to entering into a renewed covenantal relationship with God.

In our Gospel lesson this morning we see Paul wasn't the first one to confront this kind of problem. Each of the various sects within Israel had their own particular set of beliefs about how to be faithful to the covenant. The sect of the Pharisees believed the mark of covenant faithfulness was rigorous observance of the Law. Now we hear Simon the Pharisee has invited Jesus to a meal at his home and something very unusual happens. A woman who had heard Jesus was nearby – a woman with a bad reputation, quite likely a prostitute – comes into the house where Jesus was sharing the meal. She is crying and her tears fall on his feet. Then she wipes his feet with her hair and kisses them and pours perfume on them.

We may be used to hearing this story about how Jesus sees this woman, we may be used to seeing her actions as actions of love and devotion, but that's not how it looks to Simon the Pharisee. What does he see? He sees a woman with a bad reputation, a woman who was likely a prostitute, come into his house and do all kinds of erotic things to Jesus' feet. He must have thought she was trying to entice Jesus into becoming one of her clients.

Simon sees a sinful woman and a false prophet. If Jesus didn't even have enough common sense to know what this woman was and what she was doing, then he most certainly was not a prophet. After all, what kind of a prophet would allow himself to be defiled in a manner such as this?

Jesus interrupts all of these thoughts that are flying through the mind of Simon with a question. When a debt is cancelled, who loves the money lender more – the one with the large debt or the one with the small debt? A no brainer for someone as bright and knowledgeable as Simon. It is the one with larger debt.

Jesus congratulates Simon for his correct answer then turns to the woman at his feet: "Do you see this woman?" Simon must have been thinking, "Finally this man who people are calling a prophet is going to put this sinner in her place. He is going to impress upon her the necessity of holiness before God." But Simon has missed the point of Jesus' question. Instead of pointing out the woman's shortcomings, Jesus points out Simon's shortcomings –

> "I came into your house. You did not give me any water for my feet, but she wet my feet with her tears and wiped them with her hair. [45] You did not give me a kiss, but this woman, from the time I entered, has not stopped kissing my feet. [46] You did not put oil on my head, but she has poured perfume on my feet." (Luke 7:44-46.)

Simon has failed in his capacity to be a good host, which to us may not seem like a big deal, but in that culture, a failure in hospitality carried with it serious social consequences. You could be sued if you failed to appropriately honour your guests, not to mention the damage that would be done to Simon's honour and reputation.

Then to top it all off, Jesus turns around and pronounces the woman's sins have been forgiven, that her faith has made her well, her faith has saved her. Do you see this woman, Simon?
This woman you think is a sinner,
    this woman you think should be severely
    dealt with,
        this woman who offends all of your
        beliefs about what covenantal faithfulness
        means,
her sins are forgiven. She is restored to right relationship with God. Her exile is over. She who was once held captive by sin has been released. Why? Because she proved her faith by bearing the marks of holiness set out in the Law? No, because she brought her broken heart to Jesus and poured out everything she had, tears, perfume, and love at his feet in the hope he could make her well again.

She may have thought it was a long shot, but she had heard Jesus was a prophet, and that he was also the friend of sinners. It was the only chance she had for redemption. What joy she must have felt at hearing those words, "Your sins are forgiven."

But for Simon little had changed. Jesus had simply confirmed what he had suspected from the beginning – Jesus was a false prophet. Not only was he willing to associate with sinners, but now he was even assuming the authority that rightly belonged in the temple. That was the place where God forgave sins. That was the only place on earth where God's *Shekina* presence, God's Holy Spirit, dwelt. But then again, the presence of God had not returned to the temple when it was rebuilt. How long would God withhold his presence? When would their long exile be over?

The sinful woman knew. The Spirit of God that tore his way out of the heavens and descended upon Jesus was in the room. God was present in Jesus, and that could only mean
>restoration,
>>redemption,
>>>forgiveness.

Is that what we think of when we talk about being forgiven? So long as we see sin simply as the bad things we do, we can quite easily say along with most of our world, that I am a pretty good person. I'm not a sinner. I don't need to be forgiven.

But what if sin is not so much bad things we do? What if sin is that emptiness, that darkness within us that fills the place where God belongs, that place we try to fill with ritual, with holiness, or like most in our society, with material possessions?

What if forgiveness is not so much about saying 'sorry' for doing bad things, as it is about opening our hearts to allow God himself to fill that emptiness with his light – allowing God to restore his image and likeness within us?

Isn't that what we celebrate here at this table today – the presence of God in the broken body and poured out blood of Jesus, filling our bodies with broken bread and poured out wine through the power of the Holy Spirit? Isn't that what we celebrate here at this table – God present with us, sharing a meal with sinners and proclaiming forgiveness to all who come trusting that Jesus can set us free and make us well?

May it be so for us today.

Amen and amen.

What Are You Doing Here?

June 20, 2004

1 Kings 19:1-15a; Luke 8:26-39

Earlier this week when I was putting together the order of service for today, I was trying to decide on a title for the sermon and so I asked Morag for her opinion. I said, "Do you think anyone will be upset if I use the title "What are you doing here?"

Morag said, "No, I think that would be fine." In fact, she went on to tell me a story about a time when she was a Sunday school teacher in Scotland; how one day in class she asked a similar question of her students. She asked them if they could tell her what they were doing every week at Sunday school. One boy spoke up and said, "Well, we read stories, we sing songs, and then we give our money to Mr. Cunningham."

I had to laugh when I heard that story, but I also thought the young man's response wasn't so different than Elijah's response in our scripture reading for this morning. Twice God asks Elijah, "What are you doing here?" If we are to understand Elijah's response we need to take a closer look at the events that led up to his arrival at the mountain of God in Horeb.

Our passage begins where another story ends. Most of us will be familiar with the infamous King Ahab and his equally infamous wife Jezebel. Ahab is remembered by the Book of Kings as a particularly deficient ruler of Israel, most especially because of his total disregard for the covenant. Not only did he marry a foreigner, but he bowed down and worshipped her god Baal, and proceeded to set up Temples and *ashera* poles throughout the land – all while his wife Jezebel was killing the prophets of the Lord.

During this slaughter of the prophets of the Lord, Elijah seeks out the king and challenges the prophets of Baal and ashera to a kind of propheting duel. Two bulls are prepared to be presented as burnt offerings, one for the prophets of Baal and the other for Elijah. The five hundred and fifty prophets of Baal will call upon their god to send fire upon the offering and Elijah will call upon the Lord to do the same, and the true God will prove himself by answering with fire.

The prophets of Baal get the first chance, calling upon their god and working themselves into a frenzy, but there is no response. No one answers, no one pays any attention to them.

Then comes Elijah's turn. He calls the people to him, and sets twelve stones around the offering to remind the people they are the twelve tribes that descended from Jacob whom the Lord had given the name Israel. Then he has the people thoroughly drench the offering with four large jugs of water poured out three times – a total of twelve large jugs of water poured out on the offering. Elijah prays to the Lord, and he doesn't simply pray for the Lord to send fire. He prays for the Lord to send fire so the people will know the Lord is turning their hearts back to God.

The fire of the Lord falls on Elijah's offering and consumes it all, even the water that had been poured out. The people fall on their faces and cry out, "The Lord, He is God!" Then the people seize the prophets of Baal and put them to death.

The story *seems* to end in triumph. Elijah has proven the Lord is God in a very dramatic fashion, but not everyone is impressed with his display of power. When King Ahab informs his wife Jezebel what has just happened, she is enraged and she sends a death threat to Elijah: "May the gods deal with me, be it ever so severely, if by this time tomorrow I do not make your life like that of one of them." It's not an idle threat; Jezebel's words take the form of a vow made with her gods as witnesses. She is essentially promising Elijah she will have him executed within a day.

What does this hero of faith do? What does this prophet who has just called down the fire of the Lord do? He runs for his life. He hikes up his robe between his legs so that he can run faster and then he flees not just out of town, but out of the Promised Land as well.

From the border of the Promised Land at Beersheba, Elijah travels into the desert, but he only gets about a day's journey when, weak and weary, he lies down under a tree and prays to God saying, "I have had enough, Lord, … Take my life; I am no better than my ancestors." It is easy enough to understand why Elijah would be weary and tired, and we may even be able to understand why he might ask the Lord to take his life – better the Lord take it than for Jezebel and her idolatrous followers. But what are we to make of this talk about Elijah being no better than his ancestors? What does this have to do with anything?

Well, if we think back, we will remember a time when Elijah's ancestors were also in the desert, a time when they also were on a journey to the mountain of the Lord at Horeb. In the Book of Deuteronomy Moses reminds the people of what happened when they arrived there – how he had stayed on the mountain forty days and forty nights. He had eaten no bread and drunk no water, and the Lord had given him two stone tablets on which were inscribed all the commandments the Lord had proclaimed on the mountain out of the fire. But even before Moses returned down the mountain, the people had turned away from what God had commanded them and had made an idol for themselves in the shape of a calf. So Moses took the two tablets and broke them into pieces – just as the people had broken the covenant. But then once again Moses fell prostrate before the Lord for forty days and forty nights without bread or water in order to intercede on behalf of the people. *(Deuteronomy 9:9-18)*

Here in our passage Elijah is awakened by the angel of the Lord who instructs him to "Get up and eat" and he finds bread and a pitcher of water by his head. A second time the Angel of the Lord comes to him and again instructs Elijah to "Get up and eat, for the journey is too much for you."

Two separate times Moses went forty days and forty nights without bread or water, once to bring the covenant to people and once, after they had so quickly broken it, in order to renew the covenant. And now Elijah will go another forty days and nights with no bread and water on his own journey to the mountain of the Lord.

When he finally arrives at the mountain, what does Elijah do? Does he ascend and fall prostrate before the Lord to intercede for the people? No, he climbs into a cave. Now remember that caves were not a place where people normally lived. Caves were hideouts. When David was on the run from Saul he lived in caves to hide from him, and the prophets who were hiding from Jezebel were being hidden in caves by Obadiah.

So here we find Elijah climbing into a cave to spend the night. He is attempting to hide from Jezebel, but the word of the Lord finds him, asking, "What are you doing here, Elijah?" Elijah responds by saying, "I have been very zealous for the Lord God Almighty, but the Israelites have rejected God's covenant, they have broken down God's altars, and they have killed the prophets of God". Elijah complains that he is the only prophet left, and they are trying to kill him, too.

Why is Elijah here? Because the only things that await him in the Promised Land are death and idolatry. So he has chosen instead to exile himself on the mountain of the Lord.

But God has other plans. He tells Elijah to go out on the mountain because the presence of the Lord is about to pass by. Then all kinds of extraordinary things begin to happen.

A mighty wind comes ... one that is so strong it breaks the mountains apart, but the Lord is not in it. An earthquake and a fire also come, but the lord is not in either of those. Then comes the sound that the NIV translates as a gentle whisper. In Hebrew it literally reads a calm soft noise.

The Lord is in this calm soft noise and, knowing that standing face to face with the presence of God would mean certain death, Elijah covers his face and stands at the mouth of the cave where he hears the voice ask him a second time, "What are you doing here, Elijah?" Word for word, Elijah gives the same response as he gave the first time: "I have been very zealous for the Lord God Almighty. The Israelites have rejected your covenant, broken down your altars, and put your prophets to death with the sword. I am the only one left, and now they are trying to kill me, too."

Not much has changed for Elijah. He still feels like a failure. He performed all kinds of mighty deeds in the name of the Lord to prove to the people the Lord was God and all the others were simply idols, but it wasn't enough. Jezebel was not convinced; in fact, she was determined to end Elijah's life. And not only that, but she was still at the King's side, still ruling beside the King over Israel, still leading the people astray. All of Elijah's work had been in vain. What more could he do? So far as Elijah was concerned, the covenant was finished. Once Jezebel had her way and he was dead, who would be left to speak God's Word?

But one thing has changed since the first time Elijah was asked the question; he is no longer in the cave; he is no longer hiding. Elijah has been called out, into the very Presence of the Lord. And in asking the question of Elijah twice, God is saying:

> *"Don't you remember Moses; don't you remember that he once stood in the very place that you are standing? Don't you remember that before he came up here for the first time to receive the covenant*

that there was thunder and lightning, and a thick cloud over the mountain, and a very loud trumpet blast that caused everyone in the camp to tremble?

"Don't you remember how Moses led the people out of the camp to meet with their God, and how they stood at the foot of this mountain and how I, their Lord, descended on it in fire; how the smoke billowed up from it like smoke from a furnace and how the whole mountain trembled violently, and how Moses spoke and I answered him with my voice?" (Exodus 19:16-19)

And do you remember also that a mere forty days and nights later the people had fashioned an idol for themselves – a golden calf?

But just as the Lord did not abandon the covenant then, just as he didn't abandon his people then, neither will he abandon his people and his covenant now; but Elijah has abandoned God's people. Elijah is now painfully aware that where Moses had interceded for the people when they sinned, he had turned tail and abandoned both the people and his vocation, his calling to be a Prophet of the Lord.

Here God challenges Elijah: did you really think the fire you called down from heaven was going to convince the people? Did you really think that's all it would take to turn their hearts back to the Lord? Did you think these divine special effects would succeed for you while they had failed for Moses? Of course not. So God restores Elijah's vocation, and at the same time he reaffirms his commitment and faithfulness to his people and the covenant he made with them.

"Go back the way you came, take my word back to the people, fulfill your calling and remind them that I am present not only in the amazing and

miraculous events, but also in the soft and calm noises, the whispers that are so easily passed over and never heard."

Later on when the word of God comes to the people in the flesh of Jesus, things haven't changed all that much. God's people are still looking for God to act in a decisive and amazing way, a way that would unite Israel together and strike fear into the hearts of the Romans. That was the proof people were looking for – the one who could do what Elijah did – the one who could draw upon the power of God to rally an army and put to the sword all the idolatrous foreigners who occupied the Holy Land. The one who could do that would not only be a prophet, but the long awaited messiah.

So it's interesting that in our Gospel lesson for today we find Jesus, the one who had come claiming to be the Messiah, confronted by a man possessed by demons. The man didn't wear any clothes and lived among the tombs instead of in a house. By all standards he is a man who is teetering on the borderline between being a human being and being an animal. When Jesus asks the demon its name, the response he gets is "Legion".

Now remember that a Roman Legion was a military unit that consisted of approximately 5,600 troops. So it is no wonder the man is bordering on losing his humanity; he is possessed by an army of demons. So the Legion begs Jesus not to cast them into the abyss, and it just so happens there is a nearby herd of pigs on the hillside.

Luke is not a foolish man. He knows pigs are not herd animals. They are kept in pens and do not graze on the hillside in herds like sheep or goats. Yet Luke still uses the word 'herd' to describe them.

Not only does he use the word *herd* to describe the pigs, he uses the word *swineherd* to describe the people who are looking after the pigs. For the most part it is easy enough for us to dismiss these details. We know Luke is just trying to tell us there is a bunch a pigs around and there are also people who look after them nearby. That is, until we realize in the Greek-speaking world the word *swineherd* was commonly used to describe the commander of Roman troops, and the Roman troops themselves were commonly referred to as a *herd of swine*.

So why is Luke using all this military language here in this story of Jesus casting the demons out of a possessed man? Well, remember much of the Jewish world was expecting the messiah to come and defeat their Roman occupiers.

Take a moment and imagine what kind of biblical images might be running through their minds when they thought about this. Can you think of any biblical stories that feature an army of Israel's enemies being wiped out? How about when Moses parted the Red Sea and the people passed through safely on dry ground, and the enemy army that pursued them was swallowed up and drowned in the waters that closed in after the people had safely passed through.

Here in our passage we have the image of an army of swine rushing into the water, rushing to their death, only this time the one who has been safely delivered is a demon possessed man – a man who used to live among the tombs, who is now clothed and in his right mind and sitting at the feet of Jesus. The same man who had been teetering on the verge of becoming an animal has been restored. His humanity has been restored, and now he can once again bear the image and likeness of God.

The Messiah had not come to wipe out the armies that occupied Israel, but had come to cast out all those things that stand in the way of bearing the image and likeness of God, to remove all the obstacles that stood in the way of being truly human.

But now comes the really strange part – the man begs to be allowed to go along with Jesus. He has experienced first hand the amazing and miraculous power of Jesus and now he wants to follow. He wants to be a disciple, but Jesus refuses – he sends the man away saying, "Return home and tell how much God has done for you."

Since when does Jesus turn people away who want to follow him? After all the time we spend talking about following Jesus, it sounds somewhat strange to hear Jesus himself turn away a willing follower, but we need to be clear that, while Jesus does prevent the man from following along with the other disciples, he still gives him a vocation. Jesus calls him to go home and to tell how much God has done for him. And it is no trivial thing. Think of this man's friends and family. The last time they saw him he was a raving madman, but now he is restored not only to his right mind, but also to the possibility of normal family relationships back at home.

Imagine if this man had gone with Jesus. Would his family, his friends, his neighbours ever know what had happened to him, or would they just assume that he continued to be demonized? Perhaps they would hear rumors of a healing, but that could easily be dismissed as wishful thinking. It's more likely his friends and family would think he had finally killed himself. No one really expected he would return home after seeing him in that condition – but that's what Jesus wants people to see.

Someone whom everyone had written off, someone who no one thought had a chance at living a truly human life, will return home, and will tell the great things Jesus had done for him. When the gospel spreads out from Jerusalem and the people hear the Good News about the God who so loves the world that he will not abandon them to sin and death, when they hear about the God who had promised all families of the earth would be blessed, they will remember the demonized man who returned home clothed and in his right mind who gave testimony about how Jesus had set him free. The man may not be with Jesus, but he is paving the way for spreading the Gospel.

Elijah is told to go back the way he came – back to the Promised Land and the covenant people – while the man who was freed from an army of demons and who begs to go with Jesus is sent back home. When we come here, when we come Sunday after Sunday seeking the presence of God here in our sanctuary, do we hear God asking us, "What are you doing here?" We might answer, "We are here
> to meet God,
>> to worship,
>>> to stand in his presence,
>>>> to receive his comfort and
>>>>> forgiveness,"

and there is nothing wrong with that. But God challenges us to remember the ones we have left behind, the ones who are not here with us, the ones who are outside the doors of our sanctuary. What does what we do here have to do with them?

The Lord says to Elijah, "How can I speak my word through you when you are hiding in a cave and not even in the same land as my people?" And to the man who has had the legion cast out Jesus says, "What kind of witness are you bearing when those who know you best will not see what the Lord has done for you?"

We are left with the startling realization that sometimes our desire to be near God keeps us from those places where God wants us to be. There comes a point at which our worship can serve as a hiding place from the world, rather than a way to fully engage in our vocation, our calling as Christians to take out into the world what we have received here.

And not only looking for and finding God in his dazzling displays of power – not only in the wind, earthquakes and fire – but also listening for the voice of God in soft and calm noises in our world; listening for the voice of God in the painful weeping of God's children; listening to our neighbours; listening for God's voice in the sounds that our world is too busy and noisy to hear.

What are we doing here? We come here to draw near to the Lord, to remember God's promises to his children, and to remember also that we have been given a task to go out from the safety and security of this sanctuary to the places where God's word needs to be heard, and to tell of everything the lord has done for us.

We are called to go out into the world as a living reminder that even though it seems the world has forgotten God, God has not forgotten the world. He is faithful to his promises and will never abandon us. Not an army of demons – in truth, not even death – will itself will keep our Lord from renewing the covenant and drawing us back into his arms.

Thanks be to God.

Amen.

A Double Portion

June 27, 2004

2 Kings 2:1-14; Luke 9:51-62

As I stand here to preach this morning I cannot help but think of what is happening a short distance away in Richmond Church. Today is the day Tony Plomp will preach his last sermon as the minister of Word and Sacrament for that congregation prior to his retirement. After more than thirty years as the minister there, the idea of retirement is not all that easy for Tony to come to terms with. You see, as I am sure you are aware following the retirement of Bob Garvin, retirement from the ministry is somewhat different than retiring from any other kind of work.

In most other careers there is no requirement that you be separated from the friends and the community you have been a part of for the past number of years. It will not be an easy adjustment for Tony, as I am sure that Bob Garvin can attest. In many ways it will be a much deserved break, but at the same time it will be a challenge not only to be apart from the people you have grown to love, but also to learn a new way of following Jesus, a new way of serving after so many years of serving in a particular way.

So I found it interesting that our passage from the second Book of Kings for this morning in some ways is a story of a retirement. While being whisked off by chariots of fire and carried up into heaven in a whirlwind represents something of a more final retirement than most people experience, at the same time we need to recognize this is the not just a spectacular finish to the life of Elijah. It is also the end of his ministry, the end of his vocation.

As we look at the details of this story we find even for this hero of the faith there are mixed feelings about reaching the conclusion of his ministry. Notice the first thing we find in our reading is a description of how the story is going to end. That's somewhat unusual. Normally we don't expect a story to begin by hearing how it is going to end, but that's what happens here. We're told the Lord is about to take Elijah up into heaven in a whirlwind.

So the question is, why do we need to know this at the beginning of the story? Why has the author not simply let this detail come out in the telling of the story? Well, as we get a bit further into the reading we begin to see most everyone in story also seems to know Elijah is about to be taken away from Elisha, and if we are to understand the story, we too need to have this fact in the front of our minds as we proceed.

We are told Elijah and Elisha are journeying to Gilgal when Elijah makes the first of three attempts to separate himself from Elisha. He says to Elisha, "Stay here, please," but in each of the three instances Elisha responds by saying, "As surely as the Lord lives, and as you yourself live I will not leave you." Often this exchange between Elijah and Elisha has been seen in terms of a test; Elijah wanting to test Elisha to see if he will indeed endure, to see how willing he is to follow. But there is no indication in the story that this is the case. Elijah never congratulates Elisha for having stayed with him, for having passed any kind of test. So the question remains, why is Elijah trying to separate himself from Elisha?

I think the key to understanding what is going on here is to remember something of Elijah's history. He was a powerful prophet, working many amazing and wondrous deeds in the name of the Lord, but we need to remember, also, there were times when he failed to fulfill his vocation. Think back to last week's reading where we found Elijah hiding out in a cave on the mountain of the Lord. Why was he hiding? Because Jezebel had threatened to kill him. When God questions him, asking what he is doing hiding out, both times Elijah answers by saying he is hiding from those who want to take his life. As powerful a prophet as he is, Elijah is not a shining example of courage in the face of death – he is quite concerned about preserving his own life.

Now here in today's reading we know the time has come for Elijah to be taken up to heaven and it seems most everyone else knows it, too. We see groups who are in some way connected with the prophets saying to Elisha, "Do you know that the Lord is going to take your master from you today?" If even these followers of the prophets know what God is about to do, then we can be sure Elijah and Elisha also know. Elisha, who spends all of his time serving Elijah, knows his master well. He knows the last time Elijah's life was threatened he left his servant in Beersheba and took off into the wilderness to hide on the mountain of the Lord.

We need to remember that dismissing your servant was something you did when you were leaving your ministry. Here, knowing his Elijah is about to be taken away, it sounds somewhat reasonable that he is seeking to separate himself from Elisha. Why should Elisha continue to follow when he knows this ministry is ending? But the problem is, Elisha knows Elijah's ministry is *not* finished. He knows when God sent Elijah back from the mountain he also told him to complete several tasks. Elijah was commanded
> to anoint Hazael as king over Aram,
>> to anoint Jehu as king over Israel, and
>>> to anoint Elisha to succeed him as
>>> prophet. *(1 Kings 19:15-16)*

The time has come for Elijah to be taken away and Elisha knows none of those things have happened; how can it be that Elijah intends to retire without completing the mission he has been given by God?

So long as the Lord lives and so long as Elijah lives the mission of the Lord must be fulfilled. Elisha will not allow his master to dismiss him because he knows ultimately it is not Elijah that is his Master, but the Lord. When the company of prophets comes saying don't you know the Lord is going to take your master away, Elisha may know they are right, but he doesn't want to hear about it. It doesn't make any sense. How will the mission Elijah has been charged with be fulfilled if God takes him away?

So, after traveling from Gilgal to Bethel, and then to Jericho, they come to the Jordan where Elijah takes his cloak, rolls it up, and strikes the water with it, and the water parts, allowing the two to cross over on dry ground.

When the pair arrives on the other side, Elijah asks what he can do for Elisha before he is taken away; and Elisha asks to inherit a double portion of Elijah's spirit. Too often at this point we look at what Elisha asks for in terms of quantity. It sounds to us as if he is asking for twice as much spirit as Elijah had, but that is not what Elisha is asking. The language of double portion refers specifically to an inheritance.

He is not asking for twice as much, he is asking for the share a first born son could expect to receive when his father's estate was divided up. But what is interesting here is if it were land we were talking about, Elijah would have some control over how it was distributed. He would be in a position to give Elisha what he was asking for, but here Elisha has asked for a double portion of the same spirit. He is asking that Elijah's title as prophet pass to him as if it were an inheritance.

So when Elijah's responds by saying, "You have asked a difficult thing," it seems Elijah is simply recognizing that it is God who chooses prophets, not human beings. It appears to us Elijah is simply recognizing he is not in a position to grant Elisha's request, but that's not the case. Remember God commanded Elijah to anoint Elisha as prophet over Israel, but Elijah only took him on as a servant, as a disciple. Elisha is only asking Elijah to do what the Lord has commanded, but for whatever reason the commands of the Lord have become "a difficult thing" for Elijah.

Here we begin to see some similarities between this story and the story of Moses. Moses was the one who first led the people out of bondage in Egypt, but who did not keep the command of the Lord at Meribah. That action resulted in his being unable to cross over into the Promised Land, as well as resulting in the succession of Joshua as leader over the people.

Now here we find Elijah being unable to keep the commands the Lord has given him as well as travelling to the same location where Joshua succeeded Moses – the same location where Elisha will succeed Elijah. The point of the story is not that Elijah, or for that matter Moses, has fallen out of favour with God. As we see in the Gospels, both Elijah and Moses are held in very high esteem.

What we need to keep in mind is that God is on the move. He is constantly working toward drawing the world back to him, so when the leaders of his people can no longer function in their capacity to carry out his commands, he chooses new leaders, those who will pick up where the last leader left off.

Under the leadership of Joshua, the waters of the Jordan were parted and the people passed through on dry ground on their way to begin the conquest of the Promised Land. Here we see Elijah is separated from Elisha by chariots and horses of fire and taken up to heaven in a whirlwind. Chariots and horses are first and foremost instruments of war. That the chariots and horses of fire are still on the earth indicates the conquest is not over. Elijah began the war on idolatry within Israel, and Elisha will continue fighting that battle.

When Elisha sees Elijah being taken from him he tears his garments, a gesture of severe anguish at the loss of his master, but at the same time it also marks the completion of his succession. The clothes he wore as a servant of a prophet are destroyed and left behind, replaced with the cloak of Elijah. And just as the waters had parted when the ark, the symbol of God's presence, had touched the water, here Elijah's cloak serves also as the symbol of God's presence, which parts the waters for Elisha the same way it had parted the waters for Elijah. God's battle for hearts of humanity marches on with Elisha.

But the battle didn't end with Elisha. It is the same battle we see Jesus fighting in our Gospels. It seems everywhere Jesus turns he meets resistance, not only from the foreigners in the land, but also from his own people, particularly the religious authorities.

The more Jesus travels around the land proclaiming the Kingdom of God, the more determined the opposition becomes, so much so that as Jesus heads toward Jerusalem he knows he is heading to his death.

At a moment like this, we might expect Jesus would welcome any kind of support he could find – that he would go out and beat the bushes to gather support and momentum for his movement – but in fact what we see is something quite different. As Jesus encounters people who want to become one of his disciples, they are not greeted with a big smile and a hearty handshake. Instead it seems Jesus makes radical demands of them.

Apparently Jesus hasn't been to the latest church growth seminars. Potential disciples are supposed to feel invited, welcomed, comfortable, but here it seems Jesus isn't as interested in building up his support base – not as concerned with building up his numbers – as he is with transformation, turning the hearts of the people back to God. And potential disciples need to know what they are getting themselves into.

But what's interesting about our Gospel lesson for this morning is that in the midst of the demands Jesus is making of these would-be disciples, there are a number of unmistakable references to the history of Elijah and Elisha. Luke begins this passage by telling us the time was approaching for Jesus to be taken up to heaven. Luke could just as easily have chosen to say the time was approaching for Jesus to be crucified, but instead he chooses to highlight the fact that Jesus will be taken up into heaven, not by chariots and horses of fire after failing to fulfill his ministry, but by dying on the cross as fulfillment of his ministry.

When Jesus and his disciples are not received by a Samaritan village, James and John ask if they should call down fire from heaven to destroy them. We will remember Elijah is the only other one we know of who has called down fire from heaven. Is the faithfulness of Elijah what Jesus wants his disciples to imitate? The kind of faithfulness that is strong when things are going well, but runs and hides in the mountains when their lives are threatened? Clearly not. Jesus calls his disciples not to imitate that, but to imitate him in bearing their cross.

Then there is the would-be disciple who wants to follow Jesus but first wants to say goodbye to his family at home. Jesus responses by saying anyone who puts his hand to the plow and then looks back is not fit for the kingdom of God. We will remember when Elijah called Elisha to be his disciple by throwing his cloak over him, Elisha was in the field plowing, but asked if he could go back home so he could kiss his father and mother goodbye and then follow Elijah.

Often commentators have claimed Jesus is calling his disciples to be more responsive; more committed than Elisha, but to say this is to forget Elisha only returned home to sacrifice his work animals and burn his plow and farming instruments. In truth, the only reason Elijah returned home was to ensure there was no way he could come back later – he burnt his bridges and gave up the inheritance in the land that he was entitled to receive from his father. Is Jesus really calling his disciples to be more committed than this?

So often when we come to this passage we are asking the question, how much? How much does the Lord require of me? How much is enough? When we hear Jesus' words it's easy to feel like Jesus is being too demanding, asking too much. We think maybe there are some really spiritual people out there who have the will power to give what Jesus is asking for, but for most of the rest of us, it just feels like too much. Is Jesus using this opportunity to say that we are not doing enough?

If we look closely we will see the issue is not quantity –
not how much Jesus demands of his disciples,
not what they are willing to give up, but
who they are willing to be.

When one person claims he will follow Jesus wherever he may go, Jesus responds by talking about not having a home ... but notice when he talks about not having a home he does not use the human homes as an example. Instead he talks about the home of the fox and the birds. He chooses to talk about natural habitats. What is the natural habitat of the Jew? The Promised Land. Every Jew had a birthright to a home in the Promised Land, but is this Jew willing to follow Jesus, a Jew who does not consider the Promised Land his home? Following Jesus means that home is wherever God leads you.

When another person says he will follow Jesus after he buries his father, Jesus comes off sounding quite cold and heartless when he says to let the dead bury the dead, but don't forget when Jesus' mother and brothers came to see him, he said his mother and brothers were those who hear God's word and put it into practice. Following Jesus means our family has been extended, no longer based on blood lines and ethnicity but on listening to God's commands and following them.

When another person says he will follow but first he wants to go back and say good-bye to his family, Jesus responds by saying no one who puts his hand to the plow and looks back is fit for the kingdom of God. Now, the key thing to notice here is not the reason why this person wants to go back, but his posture. He cannot follow Jesus if he is constantly looking over his shoulder at what he left behind.

Jesus' words continue to confront us today because to some extent we still see these words of Jesus in terms of what he is asking us to do, rather than who he is asking us to be.

We think Jesus is asking us to be prepared to leave our homes, to be prepared to leave Maple Ridge or Pitt Meadows, maybe even to leave Canada, but what Jesus is asking is whether we are prepared to follow him. Are we those who know our home is wherever there is pain and suffering, wherever there is someone in need? We think Jesus is asking us to be prepared to leave our family behind, but Jesus asks whether we are prepared to follow him. Are we those who know that every human being is a potential family member?

We think Jesus is calling us to be prepared to fully commit without ever wavering in our commitment, but what Jesus is asking is whether we are prepared to follow him. Are we those who know we are heading toward the good new days or are we constantly looking back, remembering the good old days –
the days when crime was low,
    when the air and water were clean,
        when the churches were full.
Do we say if only we could go back to the good old days?

It's not that Jesus is saying there is anything wrong with the good memories we have of the past, but there is something wrong with setting up those memories as the standard by which all other times will be measured. So long as we are focused on the good old days behind us, we are certain to miss the good new days that lay in front of us.

In some ways we find ourselves in the same position as Elisha. We ask to receive a double portion of the Spirit of Jesus. Our master has been taken up into heaven, but we have not been left empty-handed. We have been left with the garment of the Holy Spirit, but to put it on will mean first shredding our own garments, leaving behind all our half-hearted attempts to follow and, instead, clothing ourselves in the Holy Spirit.

Then, clothed in the Spirit, we may follow *wherever* Jesus leads us, to *whomever* Jesus leads us, keeping our eyes fixed firmly forward on him who leads us into his glorious future. While there, we can expect there will be turbulent and chaotic times. We know God does not lead us around the rough waters, he leads us through them on dry ground –
    through sorrow to joy,
        through illness to health,
            through pain and suffering to peace, and
              through death to life
                  we are delivered safely.

Thanks be to God.

Amen.

Sent Out as Lambs

July 4, 2004

Luke 10:1-20

I remember back a few years ago when I was in seminary, one of the courses I was required to take was a class on religious pluralism. I was taught different religions were simply different ways of talking about God, which, of course, led to the conclusion that we cannot say Christianity is the only true path to God any more than we can say the English language is the only true language. Not only that, but if we press the language analogy further, we could begin to see there are multilingual people of faith. People who speak the faith of Christianity and Buddhism, Hinduism, or any other faith.

So when it came to write the paper for the course, I posed the question to my instructor, who happened to be the Anglican Bishop Michael Ingham. I asked how his position of multilingual faith is consistent with the witness of the Christian martyrs. I asked, "How do you honour those who have died for their faith?" And Bishop Ingham answered my question in his comments on my paper by saying he honours the martyrs by ensuring that it never happens again. Never again should anyone have to die for their faith.

At first, hearing that may sound alright, perhaps it may even strike some in society as being self-evident. After all, the *Canadian Charter of Rights and Freedoms* says as Canadian citizens we have a right to our religious convictions. Not only that, but we have a right to life, as Article 7 of the *Charter of Rights and*

Freedoms states, "Everyone has the right to life, liberty and security of the person and the right not to be deprived thereof except in accordance with the principles of fundamental justice."

As Canadian citizens, our government tells us we have a right to security, a right to life, a right to hold our religious convictions, and, as it turns out, that is exactly what the doctrine of religious pluralism hopes to achieve. It hopes to convince us that of these three rights, the two most important are security and life. If maintaining our security and preserving our life requires a modification of our religious convictions, then so be it.

But what seems to be beyond the grasp of the proponents of religious pluralism is it is our religious convictions that define life and security. When faced with the decision of whether to renounce Jesus as their Lord and claim Caesar as Lord instead, a substantially large number of Christians chose Jesus and consequently were put to death. Let there be no mistake about it ... all they had to do was offer a sacrifice to the emperor and they could have saved their lives and enjoyed the benefits of the *Pax Romana*, the Roman Peace which promised security to all loyal citizens of the empire. But they didn't choose the life that was being offered by Caesar, nor did they choose the peace that was being offered by Caesar. They followed Jesus literally to the cross.

In our world there is a special word set aside for people who put their religious convictions before their own security and even before their own life – they are branded *fundamentalists*. Surely those *fundamentalist* Christian martyrs misunderstood Jesus' message of light and love. Surely they missed Jesus' point that being a Christian is really about being a nice person.

Did they really misunderstand Jesus? Did they really miss his point? Well, let's take a closer look at our Gospel lesson for this morning and see what we can see.

Before we look at the beginning of our passage we need to remind ourselves of what Jesus said just prior to this. *"No one who puts his hand to the plow and looks back is fit for service in the kingdom of God."* We will remember from last week that within this statement is an allusion to the Prophet Elisha, the model of faithful discipleship who removed all possibilities of abandoning his calling by burning his plow and farming equipment and cooking his work animals.

It is with this image fresh in their minds that Jesus appoints seventy-two of his followers to go two-by-two to every town and place where he was about to go. But why appoint seventy-two?

Well, remember after leaving Mount Sinai there came a time when Moses was burdened by the demands of the people and cried out to God for help, and God responded by telling Moses to bring to the tent of the meeting seventy men who were known elders and leaders among the people. There God would take the Spirit that is on Moses and put it on the seventy elders so they could share the burden of leading the people.

But as it turns out, there were actually seventy-two elders – seventy gathered at the tent of the Meeting with Moses and two who remained in camp – and when God put the Spirit upon the elders they began to prophesy, not only the seventy with Moses but also the two in the camp with rest of the people.

This was of great concern to Joshua who had heard about the elders who were not with Moses and so he called on Moses to make the elders stop, but Moses told him not to get worked up about these extra elders who had received the Spirit. In fact, Moses goes on to say that if it were up to him he would have all of God's people share in the Spirit.

Now here in our passage we find Jesus gathering together another seventy-two people who will assist him in his ministry, but notice Jesus is not looking for people who will help him bear the burden of an obstinate group of people. The issue now is that it is harvest time. And any of you who have a grain farming background will know harvest does not wait around until the farmer is ready. If you are not ready, or you do not have sufficient people to harvest the crop, eventually the seeds will fall to the ground and you will lose some or all of your crop. There may be nothing left to harvest. It's a very time sensitive moment. For the owner of the land it is a make it or break it moment. Failure at harvest time will have very serious consequences, not the least of which will be whether or not his family will have food for the next year.

But clearly Jesus is not talking about bringing in a harvest of grain. He is talking about the Kingdom of God and the role he plays in its arrival. Remember Jesus is on his way to Jerusalem. He knows the time for his crucifixion is coming quickly and if the people do not recognize him as Israel's long awaited Messiah, the consequences will be severe, no less severe than if they were to fail to recognize harvest time. The stakes are high. The consequences are nothing short of life and death.

It's not until the next verse that we really begin to understand why the stakes are so high. Jesus sends the seventy-two out telling them, *"Go; I am sending you out as lambs among the wolves."* Stop and think about that for minute.

In claiming to be the Messiah, Jesus was claiming to be the King of Israel, and keep in mind one of the chief metaphors for describing a king was the image of a shepherd. What do we see this shepherd doing? Is he protecting the sheep by guarding them against the wolves? No, he sends lambs out into the midst of the wolves –
    not the sheep,
        not the largest and fastest,
            not the ones most able to fend for
        themselves;

Jesus sends the lambs, the youngest and the most vulnerable, into the midst of their enemies.

Does that sound like a good shepherd to you? What can Jesus possibly be thinking when he sends out these seventy-two followers? It's obvious he is not recruiting the religious leaders of Israel, those who should be in the best position to know how to recognize the Messiah and be in the best position to convince others Jesus is the Messiah.

The religious authorities are too busy planning Jesus' death, so the task falls not on the leaders of Israel, but upon ordinary and vulnerable people just like you and me. But that still leaves the question of why? Why send out the vulnerable lambs into the midst of the wolves who by nature seek to devour them? Two times in the prophecies of Isaiah we hear about lambs dwelling with the wolves. The first is the description of the coming of the true king of Israel:

> *A shoot will come up from the stump of Jesse; from his roots a Branch will bear fruit. The Spirit of the Lord will rest on him-- the Spirit of wisdom and of understanding, the Spirit of counsel and of power, the Spirit of knowledge and of the fear of the Lord – and he will delight in the fear of the Lord He will not judge by what he sees with his eyes, or decide by what he hears with his ears; but with righteousness he will judge the needy, with justice he will give decisions for the poor of the earth. He will strike the earth with the rod of his mouth; with the breath of his lips he will slay the wicked. Righteousness will be his belt and faithfulness the sash around his waist. The wolf will live with the lamb, the leopard will lie down with the goat, the calf and the lion and the yearling together; and a little child will lead them. (Isaiah 11:1-6)*

The second mention of lambs and wolves is the description of the new heaven and the new earth:

"Behold, I will create new heavens and a new earth. The former things will not be remembered, nor will they come to mind... I will rejoice over Jerusalem and take delight in my people; the sound of weeping and of crying will be heard in it no more... The wolf and the lamb will feed together...." (Isaiah 65:17-25)

Here in our passage Jesus sends out the seventy-two not as lambs to the slaughter, but as a sign
>of the breaking in of the Kingdom of God,
>>of the beginning of Jesus' reign over the earth,
>>>of the dawning of the glorious new creation.

They are sent out not so much to convince people Jesus is the messiah as to press the people of Israel into making a decision.

Jesus prevents the seventy from taking with them even the essentials for the journey – no money, no shoes – and interestingly, they are not even to stop and greet someone on the road.

So when the followers arrive in the towns they are sent to, they will be in need of hospitality – they will not have money to buy their own food and their feet will most certainly need washing. If they were to greet someone on the road, the person who greets them might provide for their needs and that is not what Jesus wants. He wants the followers to arrive in theses towns in need. How the people of the town respond to their need, how hospitable the people are toward the followers of Jesus, will be the criteria by which the town will receive either blessings or curses.

If the followers are welcomed, peace will remain with them and the followers are instructed to remain there and perform healings, whereas if the followers are not well received, they are to wipe the dust from their feet. Remember the followers were required to wear no sandals so their feet would be dirty and the hospitable thing to do would be to offer to wash their feet, but if that does not happen then they are wipe their own feet as a testimony against the lack of hospitality they received. This is much more than a symbolic gesture. Wiping the filth off of their feet was essentially saying the town was unclean – the holy land is being redefined. Its boundaries are no longer determined geographically but by the response to Jesus and his followers.

This is why we hear it will be more tolerable for Sodom on that day than for that place. Despite the fact we often associate Sodom with sexual misconduct, Jews have always seen the primary transgression of the inhabitants of Sodom as a failure to treat the guests hospitably. The failure to be hospitable to the followers of Jesus is seen as being worse than the failure in hospitality of the inhabitants of Sodom.

The question is why?

Why is the response of these towns so important? Why is it they face a fate worse than Sodom, that is, total destruction, for their failure to be hospitable? Doesn't that seem a bit extreme?

Keep in mind what the seventy-two say to Jesus when they return from their mission: "Even the demons submit to us in your name," and Jesus responds by saying, "I saw Satan fall from heaven like lightening." Jesus is describing the defeat of Satan and all the powers in the world that are opposed to the rule of God. Think back to Jesus' temptation in the wilderness, the beginning of the Battle with Satan. Now the followers of Jesus have been drawn into the battle and participate by proclaiming the Kingdom of God is near.

If you were a Jew living in one of these towns visited by the followers of Jesus, you would have thought they were crazy. The Kingdom of God is near? How can that be? God's people are being ruled by a pagan emperor! No, they knew the dawning of the Kingdom would begin with a battle alright, but it would be a battle with the Romans. That's why they needed a military messiah –

someone who could begin the second conquest. What they needed was another Joshua.

Now along comes a group of people following a man who claims to be the messiah – whose name in Hebrew is literally Joshua – but he is not calling together an army of military warriors. He is calling together a motley band of followers whose only weapon is peace. And not the peace that Rome had to offer, not the peace that was purchased and maintained by military might, but with the Sabbath peace, the peace of dwelling in the presence of God.

God's chosen people have been led astray by the tempter into believing the Kingdom of God will look exactly like the kingdom of Rome except with a Jewish king on the throne – believing the way the kingdom will be brought in is through their mighty military Messiah, through warfare and bloodshed. They were expecting the great reversal that would see God's chosen people being exalted and vindicated.

But Jesus confronts the people with the fact they have been deceived. They have been deceived into believing the best way to deal with the wolves is by becoming bigger wolves with bigger teeth, the better with which to devour their enemy. They fail to recognize as chosen people they were called to be a light to the wolves, a people who would show the wolves what it means to be created in the image and likeness of God, to be truly human.

Jesus reminds them indeed there will be a great reversal, indeed the powerful will be brought low and the lowly will be lifted up, but if they chose to behave like Rome, God's chosen people will suffer the same consequence. Woe to you, Chorazin; woe to you, Bethsaida; Capernaum will not be exalted. Why? Because they weren't nice to Jesus' followers? No, because instead of choosing the kingdom of God under the reign of a messiah like Jesus, they wanted the kingdom that was like Rome under the reign of a messiah who looks like Caesar.

Why did the martyrs choose death before offering a sacrifice to the emperor? Because they knew the kingdom of God was nothing like the kingdom of Rome. They knew the Lord was nothing like Caesar. They knew the real battle was not with Rome but with every power opposed to the reign of God. But they also knew what victory looked like. They knew on the cross Jesus exposed once and for all the great deception: that the Kingdom of God was not about power, wealth, fame and privilege. Also, on the cross Jesus revealed once and for all that the way to bear the image and likeness of God was through sacrificial love.

The question is, do *we* know it?

The reality is that religious pluralism in society has been quite effective. Most people believe under no circumstances should our religious convictions cause us pain, never mind death. In fact, it is more common to find people who believe the opposite: that religion is the aspirin for the headaches of the world. They see religion as a vehicle for self-improvement and self-fulfillment, a means of fulfilling our spiritual needs, and since they think different religions are like different languages, it really doesn't matter which religious convictions we choose as long as they meet our needs and do not cause any one else any discomfort.

In a world of formless, undemanding deity and vague spirituality, we are sometimes tempted to weasel out of our encounters with Jesus, to cast away the particular God of Abraham, Isaac, and Jacob – the God revealed in Jesus Christ – in favour of a more generic one of our own making.

We may be tempted to make the faith as broad, as universal in its appeal as possible. So we talk about "love" without giving "love" the cruciform shape that makes Christian love so demanding. Or we talk about self-fulfillment, or whatever vague virtues our society may be in the market for at the moment.

But Jesus often provokes conflict with our most cherished values and widely held beliefs. Jesus sometimes speaks to us in ways that are hard to understand. Sometimes Jesus makes demands of us that seem far out of range of our abilities.

Faced with the choice of offering a sacrifice to the Emperor or death, Christian martyrs chose to follow Jesus literally to the cross, chose to bear the image and likeness of God.

Our challenge, as people who have been called to follow Jesus, is not simply to believe that God was in Jesus, but that God was in Jesus, *reconciling the world to himself.* We cannot make this faith mean anything we want. Certainly there is mystery, room for wonder, questions, disagreement, but there are also these nasty particularities that make the gospel unavoidably abrasive, harsh and so very interesting.

If we will dare to come forth and follow, if we will dare to believe that when he said, "Follow me," he was talking to us, he promises
> *not* that we might have the right to life,
>> nor the right to security,
>>> nor the right to practice our religion
>>> in safety.

He promises
> we will share in his victory,
>> the enemy will have no power over us, and
>>> our names will be written in heaven.

We will share in the fullness of the new creation, the new heavens and the new earth, where there will be no more weeping and no more crying, only the peace and the joy of full communion with God.

Thanks be to God.
Amen.

What Must I Do?

July 11, 2004

Luke 10:25-37

I remember some time ago seeing a commercial on television that showed a man being beaten and robbed and left in a back alley of some major city. It was raining and dark and the streets were full of puddles. The man lying in the alley was calling out to people who were passing by on the street, but no one stopped, until a well dressed man with a compassionate look in his eyes saw the victim and came to his aid.

Then the announcer came on and said, "It's about caring," and as the one man reached out his hand to help the victim, the words "The Church of the Jesus Christ Latter Day Saints" appeared on the screen.

Clearly, the ad was attempting to do a modern day recreation of our Gospel lesson for this morning: the parable of the Good Samaritan. It's one of those stories that has passed into folklore and has succeeded, confusingly, in changing the meaning of the word *Samaritan* in the English language.

If you look up the word *Samaritan* in the Oxford English dictionary, the first definition you will find reads: "a charitable or helpful person," and only secondly do we find the definition reading: "a member of a people inhabiting Samaria during biblical times." When we hear the word *Samaritan*, so often we do not remember the parable Jesus told so much as we remember what many consider to be the moral lesson of the parable – "When you see someone in the ditch, go and help them."

This was the point the commercial I just mentioned was trying to make. But we need to remember Jesus was not simply wandering around Palestine teaching his disciples hard and fast, timeless moral truths. If we are to have any chance of understanding what Jesus himself meant and what is at stake in the wider conversation with the expert in the Law, we need to take a closer look.

As Jesus and his followers are walking to Jerusalem, Jesus is confronted by an expert in the Law who we are told is intent on testing Jesus. Remember Jesus has just finished sending out seventy-two of his followers to test the hospitality of Israel. We also will remember the stakes were high. Those towns which were not hospitable to the seventy-two faced a fate worse than Sodom – nothing less than total destruction. Now we find someone who has heard enough about what Jesus and his followers are saying and doing, and he is intent on putting a stop to it.

This expert in the Law, this expert in the application and argumentation of the Law, is going to challenge Jesus publicly. He is going trap him in his own words. He is going to publicly humiliate Jesus and put an end to this foolish movement before it gets out hand, before they get to Jerusalem and create a serious problem.

"Teacher," he asks, "what must I do to inherit eternal life?" The question sounds innocent enough. How could it possibly be used to trap Jesus?

We have to keep in mind that the question was intended to appear harmless, but notice the lawyer does not simply ask what he must do to receive the kingdom of God. He uses the language of inheritance.

Inheritance was the reward promised to those who belonged, to those who were members of God's covenant people. God had promised to make Abraham into a great nation, promised them a land and promised also to bless them, but that inheritance had been continually pushed into the future, until at this point those blessings were associated almost entirely with "the age to come" – the age when all God's promises would be fulfilled and the people would live in the Kingdom of God.

Jesus has just finished making some pretty lofty claims – "He who rejects me, rejects the one who sent me," and "No one knows who the Father is except the Son and those to whom the Son chooses to reveal him." To the lawyer this would have sounded like heresy. The Jews were God's chosen people. They were the ones who knew the Father, but here is this Jesus fellow talking as if he were the one who would do the choosing – as if the membership in the covenant depended on him. The lawyer intended to trap Jesus in one such saying and discredit Jesus by revealling his heresy.

But Jesus shrewdly turns the question back upon the expert in the Law. Jesus asks him to answer his own question. Now it is the lawyer's honour that is on the line, his reputation as an expert in the Law is at stake, so he draws upon Leviticus 19:18 to answer his own question. He responds to Jesus saying, "Love the Lord your God with all your heart and with all your soul and with all your strength and with all your mind, and love your neighbour as yourself."

So Jesus evades the trap the lawyer has set for him by declaring that yes, this expert in the Law has indeed answered the question correctly, but he also throws in something of a challenge. The lawyer began with the question of "what must I do…" and here Jesus concludes by emphasizing the importance of not simply knowing the answer, but putting it into practice by saying "*Do* this and you will live."

During this period the importance of the *study* of the Law had reached its peak with many Pharisees claiming the study of the Law was of higher rank than practicing it. Not only has this expert in the Law failed to trap Jesus in saying something heretical, but his own words have been thrown back in his face, with Jesus saying the equivalent of "go practice what you preach."

But the lawyer is not prepared to give up quite yet. He will not be content until he has justified himself. Keep in mind that the word 'justify' is legal terminology. When two people have a dispute they go before a judge and argue their case. When the judge rules, the person who receives the favourable judgment is justified. Now if we look at what just happened, Jesus has pronounced the lawyer's answer as being correct. Jesus has justified the lawyer, but that was the last thing the lawyer wanted. The lawyer was not interested in receiving a ruling from Jesus on the correctness of his understanding of the Law; he was interested in using his knowledge of the Law to accuse and condemn Jesus.

The lawyer will not be satisfied until he has drawn Jesus into a debate where he can prove himself to be the winner and at the same time prove Jesus to be the loser. So this time the lawyer takes a different angle. He asks, "And who is my neighbour?" knowing this question could not be answered with a simple exposition of the Law. It required interpretation. It would require Jesus to lay his cards on the table about who he believed the covenant people truly were, and then the lawyer would be in a position to hammer Jesus with the Law.

Debate over the definition of a neighbour was not simply an academic exercise. When God created the world he brought forth order out of chaos. He separated the light from the darkness, separated the water and dry ground. God's creation was based on order, and those things that fit within the normal order of creation were considered holy and clean, while those things that did not fit within the established order were considered polluted or unclean.

The same was true for people. Humanity had fallen away from God – had fallen away from what they were intended to be. Humanity had become unholy, unclean. But in his mercy, God separated the Jews from the rest of the peoples of the world to be a holy people, to be a clean people through the covenant, and this holy people would be the light to all the other unclean gentiles. The chosen people were the ones who were supposed to show the world what God intended humanity to be.

The lawyer knows that as Jews they had an obligation to be a light to the nations, but in order to meet that obligation they must remain holy; they must keep the covenant. So with the question of who is my neighbour, the lawyer is trying to press Jesus into extending the boundaries too far – to press Jesus into saying even the gentiles were neighbours. Then the lawyer would have Jesus right where he wants him. Then the lawyer can argue that 'If we are to love our neighbours as ourselves, and if our neighbours are unclean gentiles, then instead of being a light to the gentiles we will have become unclean, and instead of drawing the gentiles to God, the gentiles will have drawn us away from the covenant and away from God.'

But once again Jesus will not fall into the trap the lawyer has set for him. Instead of offering a hard and fast definition of a neighbour, Jesus responds with a story. It should come as no surprise to us that the first two characters in this story are people who by definition must be extremely cautious about their purity. Both the priest and the Levite were temple officials who would not be able to perform their duties in the temple if they came into contact with a corpse. They would need to endure a long ritual cleansing before being able to return to the temple. Both the priest and the Levite see the man, but they cannot tell if he is alive or dead, so they decide it is better to maintain their purity than to risk the consequences of touching a dead body and defiling themselves.

It was a common practice in telling stories to have three characters, the third of which would break the pattern that was established by the actions of the first two, so at this point in the story the lawyer and the rest of Jesus' followers would have been expecting the next person to do what the first two had not done. But who would they have expected this third character to be? Not the high ranking temple authorities. Not even the low ranking temple authorities. That left only one kind of person: the average Israelite on the road.

So just as expected, the third man breaks the pattern established by the first two men, but what was totally unexpected was this third person, the one who had pity on the man in the ditch and helped him, was not your average Israelite, but a Samaritan. The relationship between Jews and Samaritans was not simply one of dislike; they hated each other. Both claimed to be the true inheritors of the promises made to Abraham and Moses, and both considered themselves to be the rightful possessors of the land. To the Jews, the Samaritans were not simply gentiles, they were also a people who practiced an heretical corruption of the faith of Israel.

This is the kind of person who stands out as the hero of Jesus' parable. Not only does the Samaritan stop, but he goes far beyond the social standards for helping someone in need,
> bandaging the mans wounds,
>> pouring out his own oil and wine,
>>> giving the man his donkey to ride and
>>>> ensuring that the victim has a roof
>>>> over his head and provisions for
>>>> the next few days.

Everything was given without expectation of reward or repayment by someone that everyone considered to be an enemy and most certainly not a person anyone would consider to be a candidate for inclusion as a neighbour to a Jew. Then, as with the first exchange with the lawyer, Jesus turns the question back on him asking, "Which of these three was a neighbour to the man who fell into the hands of robbers?"

The expert in the Law cannot even bring himself to say the word Samaritan; all he can muster is "the one who had mercy on him." In the Greek it literally says "the one who did mercy". So the lawyer who began by asking what must I do and who is my neighbour now answers his own questions by saying the one who does mercy proves himself to be a neighbour.

And notice Jesus does not ask the lawyer if he thinks the Samaritan is his neighbour; he asks who turned out to be a neighbour to the half dead Jew lying in gutter. Underneath the straight-forward moral lesson of "go and do likewise" we find a much more demanding challenge. Can you recognize the hated Samaritan as your neighbour? Because if you can't, you might be left for dead in the gutter.

What lies at the heart of the confrontation with this expert in the Law is a clash between two very different visions of what it means to be Israel, what it means to be God's People. For the lawyer, God is the God of Israel, and neighbours are Jewish neighbours. For Jesus, Israel's God is the God of grace for the whole world, and a neighbour is anyone in need.

The lawyer's question about the neighbour is designed to smoke out Jesus' supposedly heretical views on God's wider plans for the whole world, and at the same time to show the lawyer was correct in challenging Jesus. And it does indeed produce from Jesus an answer about the wide-reaching grace of God. But the parable that Jesus tells makes it clear these views are not heretical. Rather, they are the fulfillment of the commandment the lawyer himself has just claimed is foundational to being God's covenant people.

What is at stake then and now is the question of whether we will use the God-given revelation of love and grace as a way of boosting our own sense of isolated security and purity, or whether we will see it as a call and challenge to extend that love and grace to the whole world. As the church, and as Christians we cannot be content with easy answers which allow us to watch most of the world lying half dead in the road while we walk by on the other side of the street.

The question posed by the parable of the Good Samaritan is not simply are we charitable people, or even are we caring people. The question is what do we think it means to be God's people. Do we think it means barricading ourselves behind the doors of the church, protecting ourselves from the filth of our world, or does it mean rolling up our sleeves and getting our hands dirty – reaching out to those who the rest of the world has left for dead?

Just like the lawyer, we need to be challenged as to how far we think God's love and grace extends. We need to be shaken into seeing that the Grace of God cannot be contained or limited by any categories –
    not by clean and unclean,
        not by Jew and gentile,
            not by neighbour and enemy.
God's love revealed in Jesus Christ shatters all those categories and leaves us with the startling realization that God's love knows no boundaries. God's love is limitless and those of us who claim to be God's people, who claim to be created in his image and likeness, are called to go and do likewise.

But all too often we can find just about any excuse not to love our neighbour, whether it be class, race, denomination, gender, disease, mental infirmity, a checkered past, a checkered present, or simply that we think we don't have the time.

In the end, all our excuses are challenged by the love of the God who shattered the boundary between humanity and God,
    by coming in the flesh of Jesus,
        by reaching out not to the self righteous,
        but to the sinners and the outcasts,
        the humble and weak,
            by shattering the limits death had
            established over life.

The parable of the good Samaritan reminds us that being God's people means reflecting the love God has for us in how we love others, and if we will remember – if we will go and do likewise – we will find
    not only are we charitable or caring,
        not only are we a good neighbour,
            but we are children of God and heirs
        of a love that will not die.
We will find we are inheritors of eternal life.

Thanks be to God.

Amen.

Better Hospitality

July 18, 2004

Luke 10:38-42

I remember back to a time when I was a teenager in Calgary. During one summer vacation I set out to go for a bike ride around Glenmore reservoir. At the end of my block I stopped to make sure I had everything I would need for the journey: a bottle of water, cassette tapes, and batteries for my Walkman. Then, just I was adjusting my headphones and preparing to ride off, I looked up and saw the clear blue Alberta sky stretching all the way to the Rocky Mountains on the western horizon; not a cloud in the sky. As I took in the beauty of the day I happened to catch a glimpse of the church at the end of the block.

It was Sunday. I watched as people arrived and entered the church and I sat on my bike shaking my head. How foolish. I mean, just look at this day, sunny, bright and beautiful, and here were all these people dressed up to sit in a stuffy church and listen to some stuffy minister deliver some stuffy sermon. They didn't know what they were missing. Besides, I thought to myself, if I really wanted to worship God I could do it outside in the fresh air and sunshine. Not that I ever did.

And now as I stand here more than fifteen years later on another hot summer day, I find I'm the stuffy minister delivering the stuffy sermon while much of the world drives by thinking we are crazy for wasting such a lovely morning cooped up in the church. How I got from there is a long story, but the challenge of our Gospel lesson for this morning has a great deal to do with it.

We're told Jesus and his disciples were traveling together when they arrived in the village of Bethany where Martha and Mary lived, and Martha opened her home to Jesus. Now the word in Greek that is translated as *opened* is somewhat of a technical term that relates to extending hospitality. Martha has made a formal invitation of hospitality to Jesus.

We remember from the earlier story of the sending out of the seventy-two, hospitality was the measure by which towns would be judged. Those who received the followers of Jesus with hospitality would be blessed with teaching and healings, and those that did not respond hospitably were no longer members of God's covenant people.

So it would seem Martha and the village of Bethany are off to a good start. Martha has officially welcomed Jesus into her home as her guest. However, we soon realize there is somewhat of a problem. Martha's sister, Mary, is also in the house, but instead of helping Martha with all the work that needs to be done in caring for their guest, Mary is sitting at Jesus' feet listening to what he is saying.

The real problem between Martha and Mary wasn't the workload Martha had in the kitchen. That, no doubt, was real enough, but it wasn't the chief thing upsetting Martha. Neither was it, as some commentators have claimed, that both sisters were romantically attracted to Jesus and Martha was jealous of Mary's adoring posture, sitting at the Jesus' feet. If there were any such feelings, the scriptures do not even hint at it.

No, the real problem was that Mary was behaving as if she were a man. In that culture in many parts of the world to this day, houses were divided into male space and female space, and not only was the space sharply divided, but so were the roles of men and women.

Mary had crossed an invisible, but very important boundary within the house and another equally important boundary within the social world. The public room was where the men would meet; the kitchen and other quarters unseen by outsiders belonged to the women. Only outside, where little children would play and in the married bedroom would male and female mix. For a woman to settle down comfortably among the men was bordering on scandalous. Who did she think she was? Everyone would have thought only a shameless woman would behave in such a way. They would have thought she should go back into the women's quarters where she belonged.

As backward and sexist as that may sound to us, the issue was not primarily a matter of superiority and inferiority, although we can be sure there were people then who thought that way just as there are today. But what was at stake was not so much the question of whether men were superior to women, but what the appropriate division was between the two halves of humanity?

You'll remember last week I talked a bit about the difference between clean and unclean – how God had ordered creation in a certain way and if God's people were going to reflect God's image and likeness, then they needed to ensure God's order of male and female was not simply cast aside.

And just as the public room was male space, to sit at the feet of a teacher was also decidedly a male role. Too often we associate sitting at someone's feet to be a devoted, dog-like, adoring posture, as if the teacher were some kind of rock star or sports idol. When Saul of Tarsus "sat at the feet of Gamaliel" *(Acts 22:3)* he wasn't gazing up adoringly and thinking how wonderful the great rabbi was. He was listening and learning, focusing on the teaching of his master and putting it together in his mind.

To sit at someone's feet meant, quite simply, to be their student. and to sit at the feet of a rabbi was what you did if you wanted to become a rabbi yourself. In this period in Israel's history there is no sense of learning simply for the sake of learning – no sense of listening to Jesus simply to learn something new. Education was not an end in itself. Mary has quietly taken her place as a would-be teacher and preacher of the kingdom of God. She is acting as if she were one of Jesus' disciples.

Since it seems Jesus is the only one Mary will listen to, Martha goes to him with her protest. Notice the difference between the postures of the sisters – while Mary is sitting at Jesus' feet listening to him, Martha comes near to Jesus to make him listen to her. The sisters take entirely opposite approaches to dealing with their guest, and now Jesus has essentially been asked to judge which one is acting appropriately.

It's not too difficult for us to imagine what everyone would have expected Jesus to say. They would have been expecting Jesus to
>remind Mary of her place,
>>remind her she is not a man,
>>>remind her that while she has an
>>>important place in society
>>>>it is not in teaching and preaching.

And even for us today it's not all that hard for us to be sympathetic to Martha. Most of us have been in a situation where we have at some time or another been left in jam with too few hands and too much work. If only we had another set of hands, then the work would be finished that much quicker.

Here Martha has an important guest staying in her home and she is trying to make sure she appropriately honours him. This is the moment her sister, who usually helps out, who Martha was counting on to help with the preparations, has decided to act like a social misfit. It's easy to sympathize with Martha when she comes to Jesus demanding he tell Mary to help her.

Martha would certainly not have been prepared for the response she received from Jesus, nor would anyone else in the room. "Martha, Martha," Jesus answers, *"You are worried and upset about many things, but only one thing is needed. Mary has chosen what is better, and it will not be taken away from her."* With a few words Jesus upsets some of the most deep-seated social practices of the day and quite likely left everyone in the room scratching their heads. For many people today it still has a similar effect.

We are so accustomed to hearing Jesus calling his followers, calling us out of our complacency and into action, but here it almost seems as if Jesus is rewarding Mary's life of study over Martha's life of active service. Indeed, there is no shortage of the commentators who see Martha and Mary as models for active and contemplative styles of spirituality which, of course, leads to the belief that Jesus favours the contemplative spirituality of Mary over the active spirituality of Martha. In reality, we know both are important. Without activity we wouldn't eat and without contemplation we wouldn't worship.

Clearly this passage is not intended to be a comment on the preferred form of Christian lifestyle. It is first and foremost about the way in which our encounter with Jesus turns the world as we know it upside down. As Jesus goes up to Jerusalem, he leaves behind him towns, villages, households and individuals who have glimpsed a new vision of the kingdom, and for whom life will never be the same again.

Martha thought she had it figured out. She knew Jesus was someone of importance – maybe a prophet, perhaps even the messiah like some people were saying – and so she does what most hostesses would do when they think they are hosting someone who could be royalty, possibly the next King of Israel. She worries about every little detail. She frets about whether her hospitality will be good enough for him.

She tries to give him everything she can think of. Yet in the midst of all this anxiety and worry she never imagines this might not be doing what Jesus wants.

Jesus says to her, *You are worried and upset by so many things when only one thing is needed.* What could Jesus be talking about? Well, remember back in the wilderness when Jesus was tempted by Satan for forty days and forty nights, he was offered everything a king could ever want, but Jesus' response was to quote Deuteronomy 8:3 *"... man does not live on bread alone but by every word that comes from the mouth of God."*

Then later, when he was teaching in the synagogue, Jesus proclaims the scripture he had just read was fulfilled "in their hearing." *(4:21)* Still later on the journey, Jesus explains the parable of the sower by saying the seed is the word of God and the seed that falls among thorns represents those who hear, but as they go on their way they are choked by life's worries, and they do not mature. *(8:14)*

Martha has become like the seed that fell among the thorns. She has become so wrapped up in fulfilling what she thinks is expected of her as a good host she hasn't *heard* a word Jesus has said. Her anxieties and worries have choked the word of God, and if she doesn't soon recognize it, if she doesn't remedy the situation, she will not bear the good fruit of the kingdom of God.

The one thing she needed to do to be a good host was to remember the dinner party was not the important thing – we do not live by bread alone. To be hospitable to Jesus means sitting at Jesus' feet and listening. It means acting like Mary, who risked harsh social repercussions simply to listen to him.

For doing so, Jesus says it will not be taken from her. Mary's choice to act like a disciple rather than a waitress will not be taken away, not at anyone's request – not because he doesn't want to help Martha, not because Jesus likes Mary better – but because Mary has chosen better. She has chosen to be good fertile soil for the word of God. She has chosen to listen to Jesus, which is the one thing that is needed.

In our world society where women and men are far less constricted by social barriers, it is easy to lose sight of the fact this passage would have been offensive, just as offensive, or perhaps even more offensive, than learning that even a hated Samaritan could be considered a neighbour. And if this passage is to retain any of that original offense in our world, it is most likely to centre upon the idea that listening to Jesus is the one thing we need.

On that morning as I sat on my bike shaking my head at the people who were gathering for worship, I did so as the product of a society which has a variety of different values, each competing to be the most important: power, prestige, wealth, career, health, fitness, perhaps some combination of all of these things. Faith in Jesus was certainly not among the front runners.

Faith was more of an option ... something to give you
a boost when you were down,
hope in times of despair,
comfort in times of sorrow;
helpful at times, but certainly not the centre of your existence, certainly not the only thing you needed.

The question is, do those of us who gather here to worship think any differently? We've come to church this morning to meet God, to be with Jesus. Most of the time, that's the way we think of the Christian life. We come to church, we come to Jesus in prayer, we beat on God's door saying, "Open up!" or maybe even, "Is there anybody home? Jesus, will you receive us?"

The Bible usually tells the story the other way around. The door that needs opening is not that of Jesus. It is the door into our lives, the door of our hearts that we have locked shut. On Sunday, in worship, we are not knocking on God's door; God is knocking on our door. Will we receive Jesus? Will our worship be hospitable to him? Will he feel welcome here? Will he find people who are willing to sit at his feet and listen, or will he find people wracked with worry about many things and forgetful of the one thing that is necessary?

In the end we are never told how Martha responded to Jesus, and perhaps that's the way Luke intended it – that the challenge addressed to Martha would also be addressed to us. Mary, the one who broke the rules, the one who acted like a social misfit, chose better – not because she refused to help, but because she refused to stop listening to Jesus without worrying about the cost.

May God grant us the wisdom to go and do likewise.

Amen.

Don't Worry; Be Ready

August 8, 2004

Genesis 22:1-14; Luke 12:32-40

I never really expected I would need to get used to a change in climate moving from Richmond to Maple Ridge, but we have discovered over the last month that summers in Maple Ridge are much warmer than we are used to. There were a few nights where I considered taking a pillow down into our crawl space to get away from the heat. A couple of those nights I longed for the evenings in Calgary where after a hot day you could expect the temperature to drop sharply, but then I remembered the winters in Calgary and the heat didn't seem quite so bad.

But when I was thinking of the winters in Calgary I remembered an interesting phenomenon that seemed to happen every year. There would be a very cold spell where the temperature would drop below minus thirty degrees Celsius, and during those days there would be a wave of car thefts. People would go out to their car, start it up, then go back inside their house. Or they would go to the store and leave their car running while they ran in to shop. During these times, either by opportunity or design, thieves took advantage of the situation. Every year there would be a warning from the police: "Don't leave your car running unattended," as well as warnings from the insurance companies: "Leaving your car unattended with your keys in the ignition voids your theft coverage."

You can just imagine how the people who had fallen prey to such a thief must have felt – not only would they have their car stolen, but they would also have no theft insurance, all because they were trying to keep warm. Even if they had been very diligent in securing their car at others times, one momentary transgression – a few minutes of letting their guard down – could result in a substantial loss.

As prudent and sensible as the warnings are, the consequences still seem to be somewhat extreme for a momentary lapse in judgment.

Many people are left feeling somewhat uneasy when they come across this morning's gospel reading. It appears to have a similar message with regard to the consequences of letting our spiritual guard down, of not being ready to welcome Jesus when he returns.

Jesus begins with words of comfort and assurance – do not be afraid little flock; do not let worldly concerns cause you worry or anxiety – but almost immediately he goes on to say several things that cause unease, worry, and anxiety for many people. Sell your possessions; be ready and vigilant; watch and wait for the coming of the son of Man and don't let your guard down, not even for a moment, because the Son of Man will come when no one is expecting him.

As uneasy as it is for some to hear these words today, it would have been equally uncomfortable for the people who first heard them albeit for quite different reasons. When we hear Jesus say, "sell your possessions" we might think of our houses, cars, home electronics – our personal possessions – but for the Jews who first heard these words, the first thing that would have jumped into their minds was the land.

Every male Jew was entitled by tribal inheritance to a portion of the Promised Land, the land that had been divided according to the instructions of Moses. Certainly there would have been those who no longer owned their share of the land – perhaps

they had to sell it to pay off their debts, or the parcel was too small to support a family, or any number of other reasons – but that did not mean they had lost their claim on the land. Every fiftieth year according the festival of Jubilee, the Law required the land automatically revert back to its original owner. So those who had sold their land to their fellow Jews could
> regain their liberty,
> > regain their share,
> > > regain their inheritance in the Promised Land.

Not that it always worked out that way, particularly not at this point in history where the land was occupied by Roman overlords. But the people expected the coming messiah would change all that. When the messiah came he would
> reestablish Jewish rule over the Promised Land,
> > redistribute the land,
> > > rescue his Jewish brothers from the bondage of the Romans.

In the midst of all these expectations Jesus comes along claiming to be the messiah, only we discover instead of promising to restore their share of the Land, Jesus is calling his followers to sell their possessions, to give up their share in the Promised Land. Not only that, but chief among the possessions that a Jew might have, other than his share in the land, were the tools of his trade. To sell those would mean giving up your living, giving up your source of income, the means of feeding your family.

Why does Jesus ask this of them? So they might store up for themselves treasures in heaven, treasures that cannot be stolen, treasures that will never decay.

So you can imagine how popular this teaching would have been among those who first heard it – about as popular as it is today. I found it interesting reading the lengths to which commentators will go to take the edge off Jesus' words here. Obviously, they say, Jesus cannot be telling his followers to sell everything. No, the point of this saying, they tell us, is that we need to be more interested in heavenly or spiritual things than we are in accumulating material possessions. And that's a fair enough point, but it doesn't really get to the heart of what Jesus is saying.

It's at this point our Old Testament reading, the story of the binding of Isaac, is instructive. Remember God's plan for the salvation of humanity began with one man: Abraham. Remember how God called him out of his home in Ur of the Chaldeans, away from his family to a land the Lord would show him.

God promised Abraham he would make his descendants as numerous as the stars and they would possess the land, but by the time Abraham was old and nearing the end of life, all he had to show for the promises God had made to him was a single son born of his wife Sarah. Now comes the troubling part. We are told God has decided to test Abraham. God tells him, *"Take your son, your only son, Isaac, whom you love, and offer him as a burnt sacrifice on the mountain that I will show you."*

It is a horrific moment. If anyone today claimed to hear such a command they would quickly be taken for psychiatric evaluation and the child would certainly be placed in protective custody, but in the world in which Abraham lived, the sacrifice of a first born child, tragically, was not all that uncommon.

The problem is, we expect more from Abraham. We expect him to be more critical, more compassionate toward his son. He has
    every reason to question,
        every reason to doubt,
            every reason not to go along with what
        God has told him to do.

We know Abraham loves his son, not only because we are told so at the beginning of the story, but also by the way he acts with Isaac. He does not let the boy carry the knife or the fire, the things that could cause the child harm. Not only that, but Isaac is the child of the promises, and if Isaac dies, all of God's promises die with him. If Abraham has no heir, then no one will inherit the Promised Land, and if he has no child his descendants will certainly not be as numerous as the stars. He will certainly not be the father of a great nation, and all the families of the earth will certainly not be blessed through him.

So from Abraham's perspective, it would appear as if God was taking back his promises, that God was failing to honour the covenant he made with Abraham. Yet Abraham never even hints he is going to do anything other than follow through on God's instruction. He does not delay, but sets out early the following morning to carry out God's plan.

In the midst of this situation which so far appears to conclusively show God cannot be trusted, Abraham always responds as someone confident God will safely deliver his son. He tells the men who accompanied him he and Isaac will return after they worship, and even when Isaac asks where the sacrificial lamb is, Abraham answers by saying God will provide it.

God tests Abraham not simply to see if he will do what he is told – if he will be obedient even if it means an end to the covenant. God essentially says to Abraham, *"Where is your treasure? Has Isaac become your treasure? Does your heart belong to Isaac or does your heart belong to the Lord?"*

When Jesus says to his followers "sell your possessions", it is not so much a command as it is a test. Not a test of whether or not they will do what they are told, but whether or not the Promised Land has become their treasure. Do their hearts belong to their Jewish national identity or do their hearts belong to the Lord who has promised salvation to all the families of the earth?

Even if the followers of Jesus were prepared to say their hearts were fixed on God, and they were seeking treasure in heaven, Jesus knew there was a risk they might start to relax, to assume that simply because they were Jesus' followers, all would be well for them, and they would find themselves unprepared when the moment arrived.

So Jesus begins to instruct them about being ready for service. In the Greek it literally reads to *gird your loins* which means to take the bottom of your robe and tuck it into your belt in order to make it easier to travel quickly. This, along with the call to "keep your lamps burning", points particularly to the first keeping of the Passover where the Israelites were to eat the meal already dressed for the journey so they could be up and off at a moment's notice whether it was day or night. Here Jesus is calling for the same kind of preparedness, the same kind of urgency among his followers in watching for the coming of the Son of Man.

But Jesus knows full well the sense of urgency the people displayed while they were eating the Passover meal gradually eroded as their journey in the wilderness grew longer. When Moses did not return from the mountain, the people were quick to command Aaron to create an idol for them to worship.

Not only that, but as time passed in the wilderness, the people began to grow angry with Moses, saying it would have been better if they had stayed in the bondage and idolatry of Egypt where at least they were certain where their next meal would come from.

Out in the wilderness they found it nearly impossible to trust God to provide for their needs. And so it is no surprise that Jesus shifts the imagery of the next verse, no longer talking about preparing for a journey, but instead picturing his followers as servants waiting diligently for their master to come home from a particularly long dinner party.

In his absence Jesus knew his followers would be tempted, particularly when faced with difficult circumstances, to abandon their calling to be servants of the gospel and instead, revert back to their former nationalistic vision of the kingdom of God. So Jesus reassures his followers that while the timing of the age to come may be uncertain, what is certain is he will come, and when he comes Jesus himself will care for their needs.

Clearly, the issue for us is not our stake in the Promised Land, but in a society as fascinated with material possessions as ours, the call to sell our possessions can't help but strike a sensitive nerve. Many may be willing to listen to a call to place more emphasis on heavenly treasure than on material possessions, but ultimately that avoids the challenge Jesus would have us hear.

The test for us is not how much we are willing to give, not how many of our possessions we are willing to sell, but whether or not we trust Jesus to have full control.

We often hear sayings something like *you can tell where a person's treasure is by looking at their checkbook*, but I don't think that really gets to the heart of what Jesus is saying here. The real issue is, are we willing to give our checkbooks to Jesus and let him spend it as he sees fit? Are we willing to entrust everything we have to God's disposal?

In a world that would have us believe everything we have is the product of our own ingenuity and hard work, Jesus reminds us everything we have – our life, our food, our material possessions – are all gifts flowing from God, our gracious Father, who is pleased to give us not only those gifts, but the kingdom as well. And as such we need not be fearful, worried, or anxious, but ready and willing to respond by offering ourselves in service,
    not once in while,
        not once a week,
            but at all times and places.

When we come to this table to partake of the life Jesus has poured out for us, we do so as those who desire to be faithful servants, as those who wait diligently for their master's knock at the door. We come to this table inviting Jesus to be Lord of our lives.

Amen and amen.

Kindling the Fire

August 15, 2004

Isaiah 5:1-7; Luke 12:49-56

Last month my wife Sheryl and I celebrated our tenth wedding anniversary, but it seems much longer than that. Not because we are beginning to get on each others nerves, but because we actually were dating for about seven years before we were married. We realized this year we have now been together more than half our lives. As we looked back over the time we've been together, we realized we were always kind of looking at the horizon – looking forward to getting to that time when all the major worries and concerns would be behind us and we could get on with living the 'good life'.

At first it was looking forward to graduating from school and beginning our careers. After that we thought everything would be great. Then it was
> after we got married, then
>> after we bought a house, then
>>> after we had a child….

There came a time after we moved to Airdrie and built our house when it seemed as if we had finally arrived. Finally, we would get to enjoy the 'good life'. Then we realized I was being called to the Ministry, and it started all over again:
> after I finish school,
>> after I am called to a congregation,
>>> then everything will be great.

Once again the 'good life' seemed to be just beyond our reach.

Well, along the way we realized the 'good life' was something of a fantasy we were chasing after – a daydream where we envisioned our lives were like a jigsaw puzzle. All we needed were a couple missing pieces and we would be complete.

We weren't alone in this kind of thinking. Not only as individuals, but as a society there is no shortage of people promising the world would be a better place once we followed along with their plan. Whether it be in the arena of politics, economics, spirituality or some other part of life, ideas, plans, and programs for a better life and a better world are all around us.

Life in Jesus' day wasn't so different. The Jewish people had their own vision of the 'good life' forged in the dark times when they were forced from the land, when they were forced into exile. There they heard the prophecies of restoration, the promise of a time when their sin would be forgiven and they would once again dwell in the land with a Davidic king to rule over them. Over and over they recited and remembered the promise Isaiah had proclaimed:

> *They will build houses and dwell in them; they will plant vineyards and eat their fruit. No longer will they build houses and others live in them, or plant and others eat. For as the days of a tree, so will be the days of my people; my chosen ones will long enjoy the works of their hands. They will not toil in vain or bear children doomed to misfortune; for they will be a people blessed by the Lord, they and their descendants with them.* (Isaiah 65:21-23)

They were getting closer to realizing their dreams. They were back in the land, the temple had been rebuilt, but the picture wasn't quite complete. There were still a few pieces of the puzzle missing. There was no descendant of David on the throne, not even a Jew on the throne. They thought they were so close. If only they could find a way to put the last couple pieces in place, then everything would be great. And just like today, there was no shortage of different ideas, plans and programs for how those final pieces of the puzzle could be put in place.

Pharisees, Sadducees, Essenes, Zealots all had their own plan and they all thought if everyone just followed their plan, then they would realize their dream; the picture would finally be complete, they would have arrived at the point where God's promises were finally fulfilled. But along the way the people became so focused on the blessings they had been promised that they forgot the other prophetic words Isaiah had proclaimed.

In our Old Testament lesson for today we hear Isaiah telling a story not about the vineyard people wanted, but a story about the vineyard God wanted. God took vines – choice vines – vines that had descended from his faithful servant Abraham. God plucked them out of Egypt where they were wilting and dying, and planted them in a vineyard on the hill – planted the people in the Promised Land on mount Zion.

This was no haphazard transplant. It was done with great care. God prepared the soil and cleared away the stones. He drove out the idolatrous inhabitants that occupied the land before he planted his people there. He also set up a watchtower. God watched over his people; he dwelt in their midst, protecting them from those who sought to take the vines for themselves. Then God made a wine press, because he was expecting that vineyard would yield a harvest of good grapes, grapes suitable for pressing, suitable for making wine.

Remember that every household would have needed wine. Without it, the impurities in the water would lead to illness and often death. So wine was not a lifestyle option, it was a necessity. God's vineyard was intended to be a source of sustenance. It was intended to provide for the needs of humanity, just as he had promised Abraham –through him God would bless all the families of the earth. But when the time came to gather the harvest, instead of good grapes, God found only bad grapes.

It's hard to miss the point. The people were not bearing good fruit. They were not living up to their calling to be God's people. The question is, if that's all Isaiah was trying to say, why use all the imagery of the vineyard? Why not simply come right out and say, "You are not behaving like the People of God"? Well, vineyards were common in the agriculture world of first century Israel. Unlike in our world, most people had some agricultural experience. Everyone knew basically how a vineyard operated, because most had some firsthand knowledge. So in comparing Israel to a vineyard, Isaiah invites the people to take a step back and look at the world through God's eyes.

He says to them, "Imagine you were the owner of this vineyard, that you had worked long and hard preparing it,
> tilling the ground,
>> clearing away the rocks,
>>> selecting the best vines you could find,
>>>> fertilizing and watering them,
>>>>> protecting them from animals and insects,

and then finally when the time comes for harvest you find only bad grapes."

The word translated as *'bad grapes'* doesn't simply mean rotten or spoiled grapes. The Hebrew word actually means the berries you would find growing on a wild vine. Just imagine, Isaiah says, after all the work, after all the care, the vineyard yields exactly the same fruit you could find growing out in the wilderness. Not only that, but the berries are small and sour, hardly edible and definitely not suitable for making wine.

So the question Isaiah leaves dangling in the minds of his listeners is, "What would you do if it was your vineyard?"

No one can argue with the Lord for saying he will make his vineyard a wasteland, neither pruned nor cultivated, with briers and thorns growing there, because that is essentially a description of the vines that grow in the wilderness. If the vines in the vineyard do not yield different fruit than the vines in the wilderness, then there is no sense in maintaining a hedge and a wall around it. If the fruit yielded by God's people is no different than the fruit of the idolatrous nations around them, then there is no need to keep them separate, no need to keep them safe behind the walls of Jerusalem.

As we know, Isaiah's warning fell on deaf ears, and Babylon poured through the walls of Jerusalem, trampled the city and carried the people off into exile.

But that was not to be the end of the story, not the end of God's people. There would be a restoration. God would be faithful to the covenant he had made, but this will be much more than offering the people a second chance. God will be faithful to his promises – the people will return – but the restoration will not be a simple relocation from Babylon back into the Promised Land. This restoration – this new exodus – will be nothing short of a new act of creation. The Lord says,

> *"Behold, I will create new heavens and a new earth. The former things will not be remembered, nor will they come to mind." (Isaiah 65:17)*

When Jesus arrives on the scene claiming to be the Messiah, everyone is trying to figure out whose camp he is in, whose plan Jesus is going to champion. Was he going to be a Pharisee and demand strict observance of the Torah? Would he be a Zealot and lead a war against Rome? Would he be an Essene and call the people to live an ascetic life of ritual purity and withdrawal from a polluted world? But as we see in our Gospel Reading for this morning, Jesus does not fit within any camp, and he will champion no plan except the plan of his Father. And what does that plan call for? Fire.

Jesus says, *"I have come to cast fire upon the earth and how I wish it were already kindled."* For most people this is not the image that jumps to mind when we think of Jesus. We tend to think of the shepherd going out looking for the lost sheep and carrying them back home on his shoulders, the friend of outcasts, sinners, and tax collectors. We are used to hearing about Jesus our Saviour, our redeemer, but here there is no question that Jesus is casting himself in the role of judge – the one who brings fire. You were expecting peace? "Sorry," Jesus says, "I have come to bring division." Again this doesn't sit too well with us. What happened to Jesus, the prince of peace? What can Jesus possible mean by saying these things?

For starters, Jesus is shattering the idea that the world is in pretty good shape and just needs a few minor adjustments. He is saying if you think I have come to be the icing on the cake of your dreams for the good life, think again. God's plan does not involve making a few minor changes to the old creation, it means the old creation will pass through fire and be transformed into the new creation.

For us, that may sound quite dismal. We tend to associate fire with its destructive capacity, a force capable of destroying hectares of our forests as well as homes, animals, and people – whatever happens to get caught in its path. But remember that fire is chiefly used in the scriptures as a way to describe God's holy presence. God revealed himself to Moses through the burning bush, and descended upon Mount Sinai as a consuming fire.

When Jesus talks about casting fire upon the earth, he is not simply talking about burning the earth with fire, he is talking about subjecting all of creation to the refining presence and holiness of God.

Remember that being exposed to the presence of God had serious consequences. Aaron's sons, Nadab and Abihu, were consumed by the fire that came from the presence of the Lord, for the unauthorized offering they made in God's presence. The presence of God is a dangerous thing and so it remained behind the curtain in the holy of holies in the temple as a protective measure for the people.

But the presence of God that was absent from the Temple ever since it was rebuilt after the exile, has now returned. It is standing in the very midst of the people in the flesh of Jesus who is calling them to follow him into the new creation purged of idolatry, purged of injustice and unrighteousness. And in the process, Jesus is also calling into question some of the core values of their society.

As much as we today think family is important, it was of supreme importance in the first century. The family was the basic building block of society. Loyalty belonged first and foremost to your family. If someone challenged the honour of your family, as a family member it was your responsibility to defend your family's honour. Not only that, but you were also expected to be very careful not to behave in a way that could bring shame upon your family. Here Jesus tells the people that following him will create divisions within families. In the new creation family is not based on blood lines and ethnicity, but upon recognizing that your loyalty belonged first and foremost to your heavenly Father. As a result, everyone who called him Father was a member of your family – your brother or sister.

The message would have been offensive to most who heard it, but with his next illustration Jesus drives his point home. When you see a cloud rising in the west you know it's going to rain, and when you feel the south wind blowing you know it's going to be hot. So how can you fail to correctly interpret the present time?

Jesus challenges the people saying, "Don't pretend that in this present time we have almost grasped the fulfillment of God's promises. Look around you. In this age when the widows are penniless and the orphans have no homes, how can you pretend we are anywhere near the fulfillment of God's promises? How can you pretend that having a Jewish king to outwit and outmuscle Rome is the answer the world needs? "No," Jesus says, "the answer is fire."

In our world filled with promises of quick and painless ways to have the good life, Jesus' words come across as startling. Perhaps to some his words may even sound frightening, but the alternative is far worse. The alternative is to say God has turned a blind eye, a deaf ear and a hard heart
> to all of the warfare and bloodshed,
>> to all of the illness and disease,
>>> to all of the poverty and hunger in the world.

Jesus says no, that is not the case. It is not that God has turned away from the world; it is the world that has turned away from him. Humanity has forgotten they are created in God's image and likeness, that they are intended to be God's reflection in the world. It is the world that needs to be redeemed; it is humanity that needs to be reformed into God's image bearers. And the way that will happen is by following Jesus.

The same way the people followed God's presence in a pillar of fire, now they are called to follow the same fiery presence that has come in the flesh of Jesus, all the way to the cross where all their unrighteousness and idolatry will be consumed by the passion of our Lord on the cross.

So the question for us is, will we follow the burning glory of God Almighty, revealed in Jesus? Will we follow Jesus to the cross?

Will we kindle the fire that burns away all our idolatry, that burns away our wooden eyes – burns away eyes that see only what we want to possess – so we might receive truly human eyes, eyes that will see what Jesus sees, eyes that see the needs of others?

Will we kindle the fire that burns away our wooden ears – ears that hear only our own voice – so we might receive truly human ears, ears that hear what Jesus hears, ears that hear the cries of others in need?

Will we kindle the fire that burns away our wooden hearts – hearts that love ourselves first – so we might receive truly human hearts, hearts that love the way Jesus loves?

May God grant us the wisdom and courage to say 'yes'.

Amen and amen.

The Real Thing

August 22, 2004

Luke 13:10-22

I remember several years ago I approached the session of the congregation I belonged to in Calgary about the possibility that I was being called to the Ministry. They set up a committee who would meet with me over the course of a year to test my call. And I remember in one of our meetings I was asked: what one thing frightened me most as I considered serving as a minister of Word and Sacrament.

I told them two things were equally frightening – the first was being mediocre, of getting to a point where my calling would become little more than a set of tasks to be completed ... a kind of going through the motions. The second thing was funerals. You see, when Sheryl's Grandmother passed away, the minister at the service proclaimed that the family and friends who had gathered for the funeral were never going to see her again unless they accepted Jesus Christ as their Lord and Saviour.

I'm not saying we should not challenge people to thoughtfully reflect on where their loyalties lie, but I am saying that using fear as an evangelistic tool at a time when people are already suffering a great deal of pain is fundamentally contrary to the Gospel.

The words this minister spoke fell on one of Sheryl's uncles like boulders, pummeling him into a suicidal state of mind.

At a funeral ministers have the opportunity to do a great deal of good, but there is also the potential to do a great deal of harm.

It wasn't until later on that I realized the two things I considered to be the most frightening aspects of entering the ministry were much more closely related than I had originally thought. When faith becomes an exercise in going through the motions, then the opportunities for healing, opportunities to do good, quickly turn into harmful situations.

This is very much what we see unfolding in our Gospel reading for today. We find Jesus teaching in one of the synagogues on the Sabbath. We need to keep in mind when we hear the words *Sabbath* and *Synagogue* we are being told much more than simply the place and the day of the week this event took place. The synagogue and the Sabbath were central symbols of Jewish identity.

When the people of the southern kingdom of Judah were carried off into exile it was much more than a devastating defeat. It seemed to most like God had abandoned his people. After all, as the psalmist says, "How can we sing the songs of the Lord in a foreign land?" *(Psalm 137:4)* As a people, their identity had been based upon the Promised Land as well as upon the centre of their religious life, the temple in Jerusalem. But after the temple had been destroyed, after they had been forced to leave the land they had been promised by God, how could the people possibly remain distinct from the world filled with foreign gods?

The answer was that people would remain distinct by gathering at the synagogue for prayer and to study the Torah, the Law. Additionally, the people of Israel would remain visibly distinct by observing the Sabbath. While everyone around them worked every day of the week, Israel would stand out as distinct and unusual because they did not work, but rested on the seventh day of the week.

After the people returned from exile, even though the temple had been rebuilt and was recognized as the cultic centre of Jewish people, the synagogue and the Sabbath continued to play a central role for their understanding of what it meant to be a Jew day by day and week by week. So when Jesus arrives in this synagogue on the Sabbath, everything he says and does has implications for the identity of Israel – what it means to be God's people. And as you can well imagine, there would have been a fair degree of tension in the room before Jesus even began to teach.

Any one who has been in a congregation where there has been a divisive issue will know what it can be like to come to worship; while it may look like everyone is sitting together in the sanctuary, there are two distinct camps, each with their own leaders, each listening to hear whether the teaching will promote their side of the issue or not.

Jesus has been travelling on his way to Jerusalem preaching and teaching a very different vision of the Kingdom of God than most people are hearing from the leaders in the synagogue. Those who are opposed to him would have been waiting for Jesus to say something they could use against him. So as Jesus sits down at the front of the synagogue to teach, you likely could have heard a pin drop as the crowd waited for him to begin speaking; everyone's eyes would have been firmly fixed on Jesus. But where is Jesus looking? Is he looking around the room to make sure enough of his supporters are there? Is he looking at those who oppose him, measuring how serious the threat against him might be? No, Jesus is looking at a woman, a woman who had been crippled by a spirit for eighteen years.

Keep in mind men and women had separate rooms in the synagogue. Women were not allowed in the place where Jesus would be teaching. They would have been in a separate room from Jesus, only able to see and hear through the doorway and window holes in the wall. Through the crowd of men and into this other room Jesus sees this woman.

It's interesting that we are told she has suffered with this illness for eighteen years. It's a long time by any measure, but often numbers in the scriptures have a significant symbolic value in addition to their numeric value. The number eighteen is not one of those numbers that can be immediately associated with anything in particular.

However, just prior to this passage in Luke's Gospel, Jesus had been questioned by some followers about the fate of a group of Galileans who had gone up to Jerusalem to offer sacrifices. While they were in the temple making their offering, Pilate's soldiers had killed them. Apparently when they heard Jesus talking about the need for repentance, some of Jesus' followers wanted to believe the coming judgment that Jesus had announced was reserved for others – for the really wicked people, like the ones Pilate had killed – obviously they deserved judgment, but surely the rest of the people would be spared.

But Jesus challenged them saying, "Do you think that these Galileans were worse sinners than all the other Galileans because they suffered this way?" Then he went on to say, "Or those eighteen who died when the tower of Siloam fell on them – do you think they were more guilty than all the others living in Jerusalem?" It seems there had been a tragic accident in Jerusalem where a tower near the pool of Siloam had fallen over, killing eighteen people and Jesus challenges these followers, asking them what these eighteen had done to deserve such fate.

It was quite common in Jesus' day for people to associate misfortune with divine punishment. If you experience pain and suffering you must have committed a sin in the eyes of God. But Jesus rejects all such ideas saying,
    all have fallen short,
        all have sinned, and
            all need to repent
to reorder their lives in line with God's purposes and will.

So when Jesus sees this woman with an illness that has crippled her for eighteen years, the number eighteen serves not only to tell us the woman had been ill a long time, but also to remind us this illness is not the consequence of divine disfavour.

It was easy enough for people in Jesus' day to dismiss such a person, simply because she was a woman, but a woman with a long term illness would have been an outcast in the community, someone with whom no one with any sense of honour would have wanted to associate. But notice when Jesus sees this outcast woman, this woman that everyone had written off, he does not go to her, he calls the woman forward. He calls her from shadows, from the fringe of her community. He calls her from the place where no one can see her to the place where he is, where everyone will see her and where everyone will see what he is about to do for her.

Jesus says, "Woman you are set free of your infirmity" and with a touch of his hand this woman who could not stand up straight, who was bent over, straightens up and begins to praise God.

Eighteen years of suffering, humiliation, and ostracism have come to an abrupt end, and what is the response? Praise from the healed woman and indignant anger from the leader of the synagogue. All the others may have been entranced by this Jesus, but not the leader of the synagogue. He remembers what's at stake – this day is the Sabbath, one of the primary marks of Jewish identity, one of the things that sets Israel apart from the idolatrous gentiles around them. The Sabbath must be kept holy.

So the leader turns not to Jesus, but to the people gathered in the synagogue, to remind them of the Law. "There are six days for work," he says, drawing upon the Ten Commandments in Exodus 20:19. "So come and be healed on those days, not on the Sabbath."

At this point the leader of the synagogue comes across sounding somewhat cold hearted, but what he was saying was actually a commonly understood practice among interpreters of the Law. There was an understanding among the Rabbis that healings could take place on the Sabbath if it was a case of life and death, but in this instance the woman has had the condition for eighteen years; another day is not going to kill her. Why not wait a few hours until the Sabbath was over, then the healing could take place, the Sabbath would not be violated and everyone would be happy.

Or would they? It seems that Jesus has different ideas.

"You Hypocrites," Jesus replies. Now normally for us when we hear the word *hypocrite* we think of someone who says one thing and does something different, but in Greek *hypocrite* actually means an actor – someone who pretends to be someone else. Almost every time I've heard this passage preached, the charge made against the leader of the synagogue is that he is a legalist, someone more interested in keeping the rules than in keeping people. To some extent there is truth in that, but the heart of the issue runs much deeper.

Whatever else the leader of the synagogue may be mistaken about, he is correct in realizing what is at stake here. It is nothing short of the identity of Israel, the people God chose to be his reflection in the world – the people who would bear the image of God to the world and show the world what it means to be truly human. When the leader draws upon the Ten Commandments in Exodus to say Jesus should not be healing on the Sabbath, he doesn't do so simply as a proof text from scripture. He is saying, "...in six days the Lord made the heavens and the earth, the sea, and all that is in them, but he rested on the seventh day." *(Exodus 20:11)* If Israel is to bear God's reflection in the world then the seventh day must be a day of rest.

Sounds reasonable enough, but notice how Jesus responds. He makes a very commonsense argument –

"Doesn't each of you on the Sabbath untie his ox or donkey from the stall and lead it out to give it water? Then should not this woman, a daughter of Abraham, whom Satan has kept bound for eighteen long years, be set free on the Sabbath day from what bound her?"

The power of the analogy does not lie in its commonsense appeal, but in the imagery it evokes. A beast of burden, being released and being led out to water. Jesus is hinting at the exodus story, a different time when different children of Abraham were kept in bondage for many long years by another rival to God's authority.

In a subtle way Jesus reminds the leader of the Synagogue not of the command listed in the Book of Exodus, but the command contained in the Book of Deuteronomy. Both call for the people to keep the Sabbath holy, but they have very different reasons why the people should keep the Sabbath. In Deuteronomy it says:

"Remember that you were slaves in Egypt and the Lord your God brought you out of there with a mighty hand and an outstretched arm. Therefore, the Lord your God has commanded you to observe the Sabbath day." (Deuteronomy 5:15)

Israel, God's people, were delivered from the bondage of Pharaoh in Egypt, led by the mighty hand and outstretched arm of the Lord. And on what day of the week did that happen? The Sabbath, of course. After hundreds of years of slavery in Egypt, couldn't God have waited one more day before he delivered his people so he wouldn't have to perform this mighty deed on the Sabbath? Of course he could have, but the Sabbath is not about what God will not do; the Sabbath is a celebration

of what God has done,
of what God is doing, and
of what God will continue to do;

that is, it's a celebration of God being the God of deliverance, the God of salvation.

But why are all of the opponents of Jesus humiliated by this? Jesus has essentially shown them they have an incorrect understanding of what God is doing in the world and, if they don't understand what God is doing, how can they possibly claim to reflect God's image and likeness in the world?

It's a challenge that is as real for us in the church today as it was in that synagogue on that Sabbath day so many years ago. Jesus says to us that following him is not about memorizing a set of ideas about God. It's not about acting religious or going through the motions.

> We do not come here to listen to a story
> we wish was true.
>> We do not come here to be performers,
>> to put on a good show for the world.
>>> We do not come here to make believe
>>> we are a part of God's plan for the
>>> redemption of the world.

> We come here because we know Jesus is the real
> thing, the one who embodies the deliverance and
> salvation of God.
>> We come here knowing that practicing our faith
>> means being re-formed into the image and
>> likeness of God.
>>> We know it means reflecting God's
>>> love in the World.
>>>> We know what it means for a
>>>> human being to be a true reflection
>>>> of God

because we have seen Jesus, the love of God, revealed in his human flesh.

The question is, when the world looks at us as followers of Jesus, do they see God's love in our flesh? Do they see the love of God in our hearts? Do they see God's love in the way we offer ourselves for others?

It is fitting that our Gospel reading for today ends with parables of the Kingdom. They serve as a kind of reality check on what it is we think we are doing here.

The church is not the storehouse where the mustard seeds and leaven are kept safe and secure from the rest of the world. We are not intended to be a great big bag of yeast. Yeast does not reproduce itself. Only when the yeast is mixed with dough does it multiply. Only when a mustard seed is planted does it grow into a huge tree which can then accommodate all the birds in the sky.

One action in one synagogue on one Sabbath – what can this little event possibly achieve, we might ask. But when Jesus sows the seeds of the kingdom, anything can happen:
    healing where there had been only pain and suffering;
        freedom where there had been only bondage
        and slavery;
            life where there had been only sin
            and death.

One speck at a time, one small human being at a time, God's kingdom is being planted and is multiplying in our world.

Thanks be to Jesus Christ, the Lord of the Sabbath.

Amen.

Claiming Expenses

August 29, 2004

Luke 14:7-14

When we were planning our move out to Maple Ridge we expected our days of regular trips into Vancouver were coming to an end. But as it would turn out, the drive and the traffic have become somewhat routine over the past few months. All of the scenery has become familiar and nothing much seems to change. There is, of course, the odd traffic accident or construction delay, but for the most part the drive into the Children's Hospital is usually uneventful.

But one day, on one of our trips, I noticed something unusual. At the point where we would exit off the Trans-Canada Highway, there would always be a slow down in the traffic flow as vehicles waited for the light to change in order to cross Boundary Road. Quite often at this intersection I would see a man who walked down the centre of the street begging the people in the cars for spare change.

And then one day when I was traveling into Vancouver and stopped at the lights, it was immediately clear this man's begging had caused someone a great deal of grief. In large letters spray-painted on the fence where the man normally stood when traffic was moving, were the words, "Pay me not to work." Now I don't know if the message was intended to shame the man to the extent that he would stop begging there, or if the message was directed as a charge against the people who gave the man some money. Whatever the case, someone felt so strongly about the situation they had to get their message out.

You can be sure there was no shortage of people who agreed with that sentiment. After all, we live in a world where we are told you get what you deserve. If you're willing to put in a hard day's work, then you will be rewarded by receiving a fair day's pay. Not only that, but if you aren't happy with your lot in life, then you can always improve yourself with the proper work ethic, the right education and the right application of ingenuity. Getting ahead in life, we're told, is directly related to the effort you are willing to expend.

In Jesus' day people were equally wrapped up in getting ahead in life; only in that society, the one thing that was sought above all else was honour. Your status or your standing in society was determined not by how much money you had, or how big your house was, or what kind of car you drove, but by the honour that the people around you felt you deserved.

Seating assignments at a dinner party were one of the prime means of publicly advertising your standing in society. So we need to keep in mind that sharing a meal in Jesus' day was very different than what we today might expect out of a dinner party. In addition to the obvious need everyone had for food, meals were also pivotal social functions that often served to establish who was included and excluded from various groups. Invitations to meals were very serious business. If you were invited to a meal, it meant not only were you being included in the circle of the friends and relatives of the host, but at the same time it also obligated you at some point in the future to offer a similar invitation to the person who invited you. In essence you were expected to repay the invitation with an invitation of equal value. The social consequences for failing to do so were severe. It meant you would be excluded from the group, you would be an outcast with a poor reputation, someone who had low honour.

So when we hear that Jesus was watching how the guests at a meal were choosing the places of honour, we can be sure he is not simply interested in teaching a lesson about how to be humble. What Jesus says and does here has implications for the social structure not only of Israel, but of the entire Mediterranean world of that time.

At this meal Jesus is telling the people a parable, and parables are not simply a straight forward form of teaching. Parables are designed to draw people into a story or a situation in which they would expect a certain outcome or conclusion, but then a surprise twist is inserted at the end. The twist is meant to shake up their view of the world for a moment in order that they might see the world from a different perspective. In the case of Jesus' parables, we are intended to see the world from God's perspective.

So Jesus begins this parable by talking about a situation all of the guests could relate to. Imagine going to a dinner party, he says, and in the process of jockeying for the best seat you can get, you miscalculate by a few seats and the host is forced to come and put you in your place.

The consequences would be disastrous. While attempting to secure the most honour possible, you end up forced to sit in the seat with least honour, thus humiliating yourself in the eyes of everyone at the meal.

It was a scenario all the guests at the dinner party would have been aware of and concerned about, but Jesus appears to have a solution to the problem. He says, when you are invited to a dinner party, sit at the seat with the lowest honour and then when your host comes and sees you, not only will you be moved up to a better seat, but he may also call you his friend. To be called a friend of an honourable host would be an additional honour.

But keep in mind that in saying this, Jesus is not offering advice they never would have heard before. The Book of Proverbs offers very similar advice *(Proverbs 25:6-7)* and it certainly has some common sense appeal, but it is not without risk. What if you take the seat with the lowest honour and the host *doesn't* move you to a better seat? What if the host doesn't call you his friend? Then it would simply appear as if you knew you were less honourable than every one else at the meal.

So to the guests at the dinner party, it would have sounded as if Jesus was trying to encourage them to seek the most honourable seat by drawing upon the wisdom contained in the proverbs. It would have sounded as if Jesus was offering them advice for achieving their goal, advice for increasing their honour, but all of the advice Jesus has offered to this point begins to take on a much different meaning with what he says next.

Jesus says everyone who exalts himself will be humbled, and he who humbles himself will be exalted. Which may not sound particularly earth shattering to us. We are quite used to thinking of humility as a positive personality trait, but to the people Jesus was speaking to, the word '*humble*' meant nothing of the sort. To them '*humble*' meant

    someone of low birth,
        someone of low social standing,
            someone whose behaviour is considered shameful.

Clearly this is the point in the Parable where the twist comes. Where the guests might have expected Jesus to offer sage advice he essentially says, "If you think I am talking about how to improve your standing in society, think again." It would not have taken the guests at this dinner party long to figure out that Jesus was not offering them advice; there would have been no-one there who was of low birth, low social standing; certainly not anyone whose behaviour was considered shameful. If the humble were going to be exalted no one at this dinner party met the criteria. In fact, Jesus was standing in a room full of people who were anxious to exalt themselves, and according to his criteria they all should be prepared to be humbled.

Jesus' criticism falls not only on the guests, but on the host as well – the one who had drawn up the list of invitations. He says to the host, when you give a luncheon or a dinner banquet, do not invite your friends or your family or your wealthy neighbours, because they might in turn invite you and then you would have been repaid.

To most of us this sounds quite strange, because we tend to focus on whom we are not supposed to invite. Why, we ask, would Jesus be interested in preventing us from sharing a meal with friends, family, and neighbours, even if they are wealthy? Well, if we are asking that question then we are focusing our attention in the wrong place. The emphasis is not upon who we share a meal with; the emphasis is on the intent of the meal.

Jesus says if you *give* a meal – if your intent is to offer this meal as a gift – and the only people that you offer it to are people who are most likely going offer the same gift back to you at some later date, then there really isn't a lot of giving going on. If at Christmas time you give presents to your family, all the while knowing they are going to give you presents in return, there really isn't a whole lot of giving going on. Jesus says if you're going to *give* a banquet, then invite the poor, the crippled, the lame, and the blind.

Notice that Jesus does not simply say to invite those who cannot repay you. The list he gives is very specific in terms of what kind of people should be invited. The question is why?

Well, at this time in Israel's history there was a great deal of argument about who the true people of God were. Obviously, not everyone in the land was being faithful, so there must be some way of distinguishing between the truly elect people of God, and those who, even though they were residing in the Promised Land and were legitimate Jews by tribal blood lines, could be identified as being excluded from God's elect people. There were many, in Jesus' time, who believed the poor, the crippled, the lame, and the blind bore their infirmities as the result of God's judgment. Clearly, they thought, these people were the ones who should be excluded from any definition of God's elect people and therefore, most certainly, were not people who deserved an invitation to a meal given for honourable and ritually clean company.

So not only does Jesus shatter a concept of giving that is really nothing more than passing the same gift back and forth between a small and exclusive group of people, but he also shatters the notion that health and wellbeing are the markers that identify God's elect people.

If we are tempted here to think anyone who thought this was particularly hard hearted, we need to remember when God formed the covenant with the people on Mount Sinai, he promised faithfulness to the covenant would mean receiving blessings, and failure to keep the covenant would mean receiving curses.

It was not a great leap of logic for people to assume that physical infirmities and disease were the curses God had promised to visit upon the unfaithful. However early on in Luke's Gospel at the beginning of Jesus' ministry the very first thing he proclaims is good news for the poor, release from captivity, recovery of sight for the blind and freedom for those who have been oppressed. *(Luke 4:18)*

Infirmity, disease, poverty, and oppression are not the consequences of personal unfaithfulness, but nothing more than an indication that the world needs redemption. Humanity needs a second exodus.

When Jesus arrives on the scene he says if you think a gift is only given when you can be relatively certain you will be repaid, then you will certainly not understand the gift of redemption God is about to give the world through him. Only if you understand that giving a gift means there is no chance, no hope of being repaid will you understand what God is doing in Jesus Christ, and only then will you understand what it means to be God's people, what it means to be created in the image and likeness of God.

If we can give like God gives, if we can give without consideration of what we might receive in return, then Jesus says we will be blessed; and even though those to whom the gift was given cannot repay it, we will be repaid at the resurrection of the righteous.

Unfortunately, this verse often leaves the impression that while we shouldn't expect to be repaid from those who do not have the means to repay us, we can certainly expect to be repaid by God. But we need to be clear here that Jesus is *not* advising people to give so they may be repaid by God. Jesus is not saying we should keep our receipts for all the gifts we give so when the time comes we can stand before Jesus at the resurrection and submit our expense claim and be reimbursed for all the gifts we have made.

The point Jesus is trying to get across is that every act of human generosity, every gift we give, flows from an awareness of the generosity God has shown towards us. And the God who so generously and freely gives, is not about to withhold his grace and mercy from those who give as freely as God himself gives.

When we come to this passage today one of the difficulties we are faced with is that much of it has to with social practices that are so foreign to us that their application for our lives does not seem to be all that clear. But even though we may not face the same social situation of trying to improve our reputation and honour through our seat placement at banquets, the underlying points are as appropriate today as they were for guests at the meal Jesus attended.

Ours is a society that is quite happy to say to people on the margins that they are simply getting what they deserve. We tend to see everything we have and everything we are as flowing from our own hard work, our good decisions, our resourcefulness or prudence, and as such it is quite easy for us to say that people who have less than us

> must not have worked as hard,
>> must not have made as good decisions,
>>> must not have been as resourceful or
>> prudent as we have been.

It's tempting to say, if only they were more like us then things would be better for them.

But Jesus challenges us by saying it is the ones whom the world has pushed to the margins – the ones the world is quite happy to forget – they are the ones who will be exalted. If we find that offensive, chances are we are no different than the Pharisees jockeying for the seats of honour at the dinner banquet.

Whenever we look at another human being and feel we are superior, whenever we feel someone else is not up to our quality, our caliber, our pedigree, we are setting ourselves up to be humbled.

If we cannot recognize that every human being is at a fundamental level our equal, a brother or sister in the family of God, we will not see the world as God sees it.

If we do not see other human beings the way God sees them, then chances are we will not understand what he is doing in Jesus. We will not understand what it means that God left his seat of honour, that
> he humbled himself to take on human flesh,
>> he became the friend of outcasts, tax
> collectors and sinners, and
>>> he offered his life so we might be
>> set free from sin and death;
>>>> he offered us a gift that can never
>>> be repaid.

And he says to those who have eyes to see and ears to hear, "Follow me."

Amen and amen.

No Surrender

September 5, 2004

Luke 14:25-35

I remember the summer just before I went back to school to pursue my call to the ministry. Going back to school was going to require some lifestyle changes. I would not be able to afford the payments on my car, so there came a time when I had to sell my big silver Chevy Lumina with power everything and would have to settle instead for a used little blue Mazda 323 with standard everything – it didn't even have the optional clock. But I was so excited about what was ahead that none of the material things seemed all that important.

A bigger concern was the time I was going to lose with my wife and daughter. You see, Sheryl wasn't licensed to work in BC and at least one of us needed to be working. So we knew that during the school year I would get home to visit about three times before returning home for the summer. Losing that time with family ... that was going to be the most costly of anything we had to give up; but we had considered the cost. We knew ahead of time that it was going to be hard, but we were convinced this was what God was asking of us and that God would care for us. So we stepped out in faith.

As hard as that time was, and as long as it seemed, it *did* come to an end. After two years we were able to be together again as a family and it began to seem like the costly part was over. Then we discovered our daughter's heart problem and life as we knew it changed abruptly. We could not have foreseen it; we could not have planned for it; it just happened, and it caught not only my wife and I off guard, but everyone around us, our family and friends included.

I was surprised to hear some of our family saying things like, "How could God let this happen to a minister's daughter?" And I suppose I shouldn't have been all that surprised to hear comments like that. After all, I know first hand from meeting with people who have suddenly lost a loved one, how often the first thing to come under fire is their faith. "How could God have let this happen?"

For many, these moments are nothing more than an expression of the pain and grief they are feeling, but for others it can be the moment where they lose both their loved one and their relationship with God. It is faith challenges such as these that Jesus calls his followers to be prepared for in our Gospel reading this morning.

As Jesus is making his way up to Jerusalem he turns and sees a great crowd following him. Now, how we hear what Jesus has to say to the crowd has a great deal to do with what it is we think he has been doing on this journey to Jerusalem.

If we imagine Jesus is a young and charismatic religious leader looking to spread a new religious philosophy throughout Israel, then what Jesus says next is quite puzzling. It would be the equivalent of a political candidate stepping up on his soap box and saying if you vote for me, you're voting to lose your homes and families; you're asking for higher taxes and lower wages; you're deciding in favour of losing all you love best. So, come on, who's with me?

No one would even take the time to argue with someone like that, never mind follow him, but isn't that exactly what Jesus is saying in this passage: "So you want be my disciples, do you?

Well, in that case, you'll have to learn to hate your family, give up all your possessions and get ready for the worst kind of death imaginable." That's hardly the way to win friends and influence people. Keep in mind Jesus wasn't saying this only to his innermost followers – not just the twelve – but to the whole crowd that was following him, seekers and longtime companions alike.

So what is it that could possibly compel this group of people to continue following Jesus, particularly since what he was saying appears to directly contradict the commandment to honour your father and mother?

Jesus wasn't simply a young charismatic religious leader hoping to plant a new religious philosophy in Israel. Jesus wasn't the equivalent of a political candidate hoping to gather enough followers and contributions to make a successful run for the leadership of Israel, although for many who were following Jesus on the road to Jerusalem this might have seemed exactly like what he was he doing. Why else would this person be calling people to follow him? Why else would he be heading to Jerusalem where he could be certain he would be confronted by the religious authorities? What Jesus is trying to get across is that he is not going up to Jerusalem to bring about a coup that would see him expel Herod and Pilate and claim his dominion over the land and people of Israel.

When Jesus began his public ministry he proclaimed release of the captives. If the people are going to understand what Jesus is doing, they need to remember their defining moment as a people – the exodus. Jesus has not come to be a contender for the throne in Jerusalem, but as the one who will begin the new exodus. But if that is the case, then the people of Israel are in for a bit of a shock.

When Moses returned from the wilderness to set God's people free, he went up before Pharaoh and performed wonders that failed to move him. Now we see Jesus come out of the wilderness, but instead of going to Pilate's palace or going before the emperor in Rome to show God's wonders and convince him to take his troops out of the Holy Land, we see that Jesus is on an journey to Jerusalem. What's worse is that when Jesus works wonders, it is not Pilate or the Emperor who will not be moved by the wonders, it is the religious leaders – the Pharisees, the Scribes, and the priests – who harden their hearts. Having sight, they do not see and having hearing they do not listen. *(Luke 8:10)*

Jesus is preparing the crowds that follow him for the fact that unlike Egypt, this new exodus will not take them out of a foreign land, but will take them out of their idolatry into a renewal of their covenant faithfulness to God within the Land. He is also preparing the crowds for the fact that unlike Egypt not all the people will choose to participate in this new exodus; many will choose not to follow. And where that is the case there will be families who will be divided over the issue of whether or not to follow Jesus.

We need to remember when Jesus uses the word 'hate' he is not using it the way we normally do. For us today 'hate' describes an emotional state of extreme anger, but in Jesus' day, when every action was measured in terms of its honour or its shamefulness, the word 'hate' would have meant you had disavowed yourself. You had changed your allegiance from being loyal to your family to being loyal to Jesus.

To disavow your family was considered an act of hatred. When Jesus says you must hate your family members he is not saying you should go call them up and tell them that you hate them. He is saying if you are going to be his disciple, your primary loyalty must be to him.

Jesus is not denying the importance of a close family and the benefits of living in supportive harmony with them. That may make this passage somewhat easier for us to take in, but we need to remember it still would have seemed like an outrageous demand, not only because of the foundational role that family played in their lives, but also because calling someone to bear their cross was not simply a figure of speech to these people. Not only did everyone know being crucified was the worst kind of death imaginable, but they also knew it was reserved for the most shameful criminals, for the lowest of low.

Jesus is calling the people to reflect on whether or not they are prepared to pay this kind of price in order to be his disciples. The question is why? Why is Jesus being so demanding? Why is discipleship so costly? What Jesus has to say next gives us some direction. He gives two examples of the consequence for people who fail to plan adequately. The first is the builder of a tower who is mocked when he fails to calculate the resources needed to complete the project and the second is of a king going out to battle unprepared for the force he is about to meet and so is forced to surrender.

As this crowd is following Jesus up to Jerusalem there is a buzz of excitement. They have seen the wonders he has been performing, and there is quite a bit of speculation that this may be the one, the Messiah, the new King. So Jesus is trying to refocus the crowd – trying to get them to look past their expectations and to remember what it is he has been teaching.

In both examples, Jesus describes the person sitting down in order to consider his actions. Sitting is not simply a good posture to assume in order to reflect on whether or not they want to follow. It is also the posture of a student. Jesus reminds the crowd that being a disciple does not mean he is there to fulfill their expectations. If they want to be a disciple, they need to remember he is the master and they are the students; he is the teacher and they are there to learn from him, not dictate to him.

And if they understand that being his disciple means placing their trust and allegiance in him, then they must also understand he will have no part-time followers; no disciples who will give their loyalty to him only when it suits them. Disciples must be prepared to follow him until the work is complete and be prepared to never surrender. Just like their teacher.

Anyone who wants to be his disciple must be prepared to let go of everything. In the Greek it literally says that would-be disciples must say a formal farewell to every thing. Now to us that may sound a little too demanding, a little too extreme ... what ever happened to the tithe of ten percent? But here Jesus is not talking about making an offering. He's not talking about how much of our wealth we need to give in order to be a true disciple. He is talking about the disposition of our heart.

What is often overlooked in this passage is that if Jesus is asking those who are planning on following him to stop and count the cost, then we can be sure he has already done so. When Jesus gives these examples of being prepared to see a project through until it is finished it is because as he marches on to Jerusalem he has already decided nothing will keep him from finishing what God has called him to do –
    not his family,
        not his friends,
             not his disciples,
                not anything –
and those who are going to follow him need to be aware of that.

Similarly, when Jesus makes reference to a king planning to meet another king in battle we can be sure this is not some example he has just pulled out of the air. He knows people are expecting a military messiah, a king who will come and challenge the military might of Rome, but Rome is not the enemy that Jesus has come to conquer.

He has come to conquer idolatry, sin and death, and it is a battle where the odds do not appear to be in his favour. He knows he is outnumbered. He is facing a force that is double the size of his forces, not only facing the idolatry of the gentile world, but the idolatry of his own people, the ones who should have recognized who he was and what he was doing.

If Jesus has taken the time to consider whether or not he will finish what he has started, whether or not he is prepared to enter this battle shorthanded with no intention of surrendering, then his followers need to be prepared to do the same.

When the people were led out of Egypt it wasn't very long before they were complaining they had no food or water and they cried out that it would have been better if they had stayed as slaves in Egypt. Now Jesus is telling those who think they want to be his disciples that there is no going back. There will be times in this battle
> when the fighting gets fierce,
>> when the casualties grow high,
>>> when the supplies run low;

times when it will seem like the tide of the battle has turned against Jesus and all who follow him.

What will happen then to those who still have mixed loyalties for the families they left behind, who left stores of material goods to fall back on in the event this Jesus project didn't pan out? They will be the first to leave Jesus' side, the first to return to the security of family and fortune, the first ones to turn their backs on Jesus as he fights on, determined never to surrender.

If Jesus is marching in one direction while we are fleeing in the other direction we cannot claim to be his followers, his disciples. So Jesus tells the crowd in advance to say their farewells here and now, either to the things they are likely to run back to when the going gets tough, or else to say farewell to him.

That may sound a little overwhelming, but we need to be clear here that Jesus is not asking those who continue on with him to be perfect. He's not asking them

> never to have questions,
> > never to have doubts,
> > > never to look over their shoulder
> > > at what they left behind.

Jesus knows in the heat of battle some will fall back only to regroup and press forward again. He knows when he arrives in Jerusalem, when he bears his cross, the crowd is going to disintegrate and disperse. He knows even his closest disciples, the twelve, will abandon him for a time. But remember Jesus sat down and considered whether he would be prepared and able to meet his enemy, even outnumbered two to one, and Jesus answered 'yes'.

He looks into the hearts of his would-be followers and sees not what they used to be, not even what they are now. Instead, Jesus sees what they have the potential to be, and seeing that potential, with no thought of surrender he presses on, determined to finish the work that has been given to him.

The moments of crisis, grief, heartache and suffering are often the times when we are most likely to feel we have been abandoned by God, times when we feel God is distant, impersonal, and arbitrary. It is times such as these for which Jesus was preparing his disciples, times when it seems like despair, warfare, disease, and death are about to overtake us, times when it seems the tide of the battle has shifted against Jesus and his followers, but through it all Jesus reminds and assures us he will finish what he has started. He will not quit until the good news being proclaimed by his disciples is brought to its completion. He will press on
> until the poor have been lifted up,
> > until the blind receive sight,
> > > until the captives are released, and
> > > > until the oppressed are set free.

Jesus will continue to lead his followers out to meet the enemy in battle, not armed with swords, or guns, not with chariots or tanks, but armed with the cross – armed with a love that transcends anything within the enemy's arsenal.

Although there will be times when the fighting is fierce and we are tempted to look over our shoulder at the world we left behind, if we keep our eyes fixed on Jesus we will see him pressing on to the world that lies in front of us. It is the new creation, where death will be swallowed up in victory, where God will wipe away every tear.

That is not to trivialize or take away from the reality of the world's suffering. The battle is very real. We see it in the broken hearts and broken lives of the people around us each and every day. We see it in the bloodshed, warfare and disease all around the world. The battle rages on, and the question for us is not what we need to give up in order to be classified as true disciples of Jesus, but whether or not we have given up, whether we are engaged in the battle or whether we have surrendered.

Jesus remains on the front lines meeting the enemy in all times and places and for those of us who count ourselves among his followers, who include ourselves as his disciples, there can be no surrender.

May God grant us ears to hear him calling to us today.

Amen.

Lost Causes

September 12, 2004

Jeremiah 4:11-12, 22-28; Luke 15:1-10

When I was ordained, my father was asked if he was surprised I had become a minister. It was a fair question given that my father has never really been a church going kind of person and someone who was always more comfortable questioning the faith than practicing it. So it caught me a little off guard to hear him say he wasn't surprised that I had become a minister.

He recalled when I was a child he and my mother never had to worry about any of the children getting lost, because I was always keeping track of my older sister and younger brother, making sure I knew where they were at all times and never letting them get out sight. And so while he may not have understood much of the faith that was behind my call, he had no problem seeing me in a role where I was charged with making sure people wouldn't be lost.

I appreciated the sentiment. I understood my father's comments as being complimentary as I am sure he intended them to be, but at the same time when I look back and recall those times when I would watch out for my sister and brother, I remember it was not out of some sense of benevolence and kindheartedness that I was doing it. I was the middle child and I was anything but benevolent.

When I look back, I remember the primary motivation for keeping tabs on my brother and sister was my own fear. I didn't want to be lost. So if I always knew were they were, then I knew I would never be lost and alone. I went to great lengths to ensure I never ended up that way. And to the best of my recollection I never did get lost. I never did wind up alone, but I was also a pretty anxious little kid, not because I didn't think my parents would keep track of me, but because I didn't trust anyone but myself to handle the responsibility.

I never got lost and it was thanks to my own efforts, thanks to my own care and self-responsibility; I was sure of it. So you can imagine what I thought when I heard of other kids who had gotten lost. Obviously, they were careless, foolish, or irresponsible. They got what they deserved.

I know I wasn't alone in thinking like that. In fact, people have been thinking like that for as long as we have written evidence. Even in our Gospel lesson for today we find Jesus being confronted by a group of Pharisees who are taking exception with Jesus for associating and eating with people who were quite clearly lost causes – those who, at best, existed on the fringe of God's elect people, and who, at worst, were considered to be damned, and beyond the reach of God's salvation. It is to these Pharisees that Jesus tells the twin parables of the lost sheep and the lost coin.

Keep in mind that sharing a meal in Jesus' day meant something quite different than it does for us today. We may see a meal as an opportunity to socialize and to entertain our guests, but for them it really was much more about establishing kinship ties. You only shared a meal with those whom you considered in some respects to be like family.

So when Jesus shares meals with both Pharisees and the lost causes, or the "sinners" in their society, there is a serious problem. The Pharisees are essentially reminding Jesus he is either one of them, or he is one of the sinners, and as such Jesus needs to make up his mind which group he belongs to. So Jesus responds by drawing the Pharisees into a story.

Suppose one of you has a hundred sheep and loses one of them. Wouldn't you leave the ninety-nine in the wilderness and go after the lost sheep until you find it? We know the image of a shepherd caring for his sheep is often used both of Kings and, very frequently in the Old Testament, used as an image of God caring for his people. That image was also applied more generally to leaders of God's people.

In some respects, the Pharisees had an obligation as the religious leaders, and were responsible for caring for God's people. So in one sense the role in which Jesus has placed them within this story is nothing out of the ordinary; but in another sense, comparing Pharisees to shepherds would have been something of an insult.

You see, shepherds tended to be young boys who had very little in the way of social standing. Having a flock attacked by wild animals was a very real danger and as such it was too risky for people of high status. Shepherds tended to be people who were considered expendable, certainly not people the Pharisees would have been sharing meals with. They were simply too low on the social ladder.

Jesus structures the question so the expected answer to whether you would leave the flock of ninety-nine to go and search for the one lost sheep is, "Yes, of course," but is that really what the Pharisees would have been thinking? If we were shepherds and had a flock of one hundred sheep, would we really leave the flock in the wilderness and go looking for the lost one? Chances are, we would want a little more information, such as whether or not the flock was premium breeding stock or if the missing one was diseased. Was it continually getting lost or was this the first time it had wandered off? Because the reality is that so long as we have the ninety-nine, we can always make more sheep, and going off to search for one lost sheep exposes us to the risk of losing the entire flock to the dangers of the wilderness.

If we think this reasoning sounds a little harsh, chances are it's because we have made the leap from seeing ourselves as the shepherd in the story, to seeing ourselves as the lost sheep. If Jesus had asked, "What if *you* were a lost sheep, wouldn't you want the shepherd to leave the ninety-nine to come and search for you?" then we might expect the answer to be, "Yes, of course," but that is not what Jesus asked. Jesus asks us to look from the perspective of the shepherd. Then would you leave the ninety-nine?

Well, if we were to follow the proverbial wisdom of the world, we might say a bird in hand is better than two in the bush, and most certainly ninety-nine in hand must be better than one in the bush. But obviously the proverbial wisdom of the world is not the wisdom upon which Jesus is drawing.

In a similar fashion, Jesus asks, "If once you find the lost sheep wouldn't you put it up on your shoulders, carry it home and call your friends and neighbours to come and celebrate the recovery of your lost sheep?" Again Jesus assumes the answer is, "Yes, of course," but is that what we would do when we found a sheep that had caused us to put our entire flock at risk? Would we carry it home and throw a party to celebrate? Or would the sheep be the main course at your next dinner party? Again the wisdom of Jesus does not seem to line up with what we might expect a shepherd to do under these circumstances.

So, not only are the Pharisees being confronted by the fact that as shepherds they have not answered, "Yes, of course" and gone out in search of the lost sheep of God's flock, but they are also confronted by the fact that the celebration meal accompanying the restoration of the lost sheep is a dinner party that they have already said they are not interested in attending. It's not until the next verse that we really begin to feel the full force of what Jesus is driving at. He says there will be more rejoicing in heaven over one sinner who repents than over ninety-nine righteous people who do not need to repent.

The thrust of the parable centres on the Jewish belief that the two halves of God's creation, heaven and earth, were meant to fit together and be in harmony with each other. If you understand what is going on in heaven, you'll understand how things were meant to be on earth. That, after all, is the point of praying that God's kingdom will come on earth as it is in heaven.

As far as the legal experts and Pharisees were concerned, the closest you could get to heaven was in the Temple, and the temple required a strict code of purity from the priests. The closest non-priests could get to copying heaven was to maintain a similarly strict code of purity in every aspect of life. But now Jesus was declaring that heaven was having a great celebration every time a single sinner saw the light and turned to follow God's way.

The irony of the situation is that by refusing to join in on the celebration, the Pharisees show they are actually the ones out of step with the reality in heaven. Once they begin to realize that, any notion they might have had that suggested they did not need to repent is shattered. Every person in Israel, every last one, is lost and is in need of repentance. Just as the psalmist said,

"The Lord looks down from heaven on humankind to see if there are any who understand, any who seek God. All have turned aside, they have together become corrupt; there is no one who does good, not even one." (Psalm 14:2-3)

It is at this point our reading from Jeremiah is helpful. We hear the prophet proclaiming the exile is about to take place, that God's unrelenting judgment is about to come upon Jerusalem and the people Israel. We need to keep in mind that God's judgment is not a matter of simple cause and effect. God does not act like a mechanical switch doling out blessings for good behaviour and judgment for bad behaviour. A full reading of the Book of

Jeremiah reveals it is only after much debate and anguish that God finally is left with no alternative but to bring this disaster upon his people.

Even when God acts in this fashion, we need to be clear that God's intent is much more than punishment. God is trying to discipline his people, trying to bring about repentance. Remember, during the time Jeremiah was proclaiming the Word of God it was not as if the people believed they were on shaky ground with God. Life was proceeding pretty much as it always had. People carried on with their daily routines and dealt as best as they could with the concerns of their day.

To many people, prophets like Jeremiah would have seemed like one of those people you encounter now and then wandering the streets proclaiming the end is near. The reality is, there were many who claimed to be prophets, who were prophesying precisely the opposite of Jeremiah – where he proclaimed destruction and exile, others proclaimed peace, no warfare and no hunger – and the people were quite happy to listen to these false prophets. They were a people who were charting their own course in life, making political deals with other nations and pretty much convinced they were in control and God was with them to ensure things turned out the way they expected.

The people did not think they were lost; they didn't think they needed to repent. Yet all the while they were failing to be what they had been called to be. So what will it take for the people to listen, to turn back to God? What will it take to shake them out of the delusion they are calling reality? Nothing short of shaking the foundations of creation.

The words Jeremiah speaks are reminiscent of the creation account, only in reverse. Then God's Spirit hovers over the formless void and when God speaks he brings forth light, he forms the earth, and land, and vegetation.

The word God speaks is judgment, and hot wind is coming that will make the earth formless and empty and lights from the heavens will be gone. The mountains will quake and the hills will sway, there will be no people, and no birds of the air. Destruction is coming ... but not total destruction. Remember that God had promised Noah never again to wipe humanity off the face of the earth. God's action is intended to be enough to remind Israel what is at stake here. He formed Israel to be a light to the nations and if they were determined to abandon their calling, they would no longer be a people formed by God, no longer a people set apart from the other idolatrous people.

It's not God's plan to wipe out humanity, but God knows it will take drastic action, nothing short of a national crisis, to remind Israel what they were intended to be. It's not that God needs to force the people to be lost in order that they may be found, but to shake them into realizing they have been lost the entire time. By and large, the people never even realized they were lost. All the while God was
    seeking,
        searching,
            calling,
but they didn't hear, and they didn't see. They didn't answer.

But thanks be to God, judgment is not the final word. Salvation is the final word. By the unshakable faithfulness and immeasurable grace of the Lord, God's plan was for restoration, for redemption. Indeed, the people returned to the land, and rebuilt the temple; yet at the same time the underlying problems persisted.

The people who had recognized God's amazing grace in his searching them out – lost as they were in exile in a foreign land, and in bringing them back home – attempted to control and ration that grace, extending it only to those few who could measure up to the standards of ritual purity set by the religious authorities. And in the process, God's grace was treated as the possession of the religious elite.

In telling the parables of the lost sheep and the lost coin, not only does Jesus challenge the Pharisees by saying the expansive grace of God reaches far beyond the grip of their fingers. It extends to every nook and cranny, to every lost cause, inviting all who repent to be carried home on the shoulders of our Shepherd. Jesus also issues a rather disturbing warning. It's not the lost causes who will be excluded from God's salvation, rather it is the ones who refuse to celebrate when the lost return home; they are the ones who exclude themselves.

It is easy enough for us to talk about God's amazing grace. Most here will have had the experience of being sought out and found by the grace of God in Jesus. But things can quickly change when we begin to imagine God's grace being extended to others, particularly others that we do not like. How willing do you suppose a Russian Christian would be to celebrate with a Chechnyan terrorist who was found by the Lord and had repented?

At times, God's grace can be much more than amazing; at times, God's grace can be downright scandalous ... particularly in our world that is filled with its own solutions for how to restore yourself when you are feeling lost.

Whether it be the right diet, the right herbal supplement, the right exercise program or any number of pop psychology books promising either a cure or preventative treatment, our world believes God helps those who help themselves.

If we get caught up in that kind of thinking, there will quite likely be times when the grace that found us, that set us free, and that brought us home, when given to someone we consider to be a lost cause, will leave us in no mood for celebration.

Before long we are liable to find ourselves again lost and alone in the wilderness, but even then, even when we have run from the voice of our shepherd, when we have hidden and trapped ourselves amidst the thorns, Jesus comes searching for us, pressing into the thorns, piercing his head, his side, his hands, and his feet, that we might be set free.

Jesus came for the lost causes; not for some, but for all of them.

Hear again these words from the Apostle Paul:
"Here is a trustworthy saying that deserves full acceptance: Christ Jesus came into the world to save sinners-- of whom I am the worst. But for that very reason I was shown mercy so that in me, the worst of sinners, Christ Jesus might display his unlimited patience as an example for those who would believe on him and receive eternal life. Now to the King eternal, immortal, invisible, the only God (wise), be honour and glory for ever and ever. Amen." (1 Timothy 1:14-17)

God's Bottom Line

September 19, 2004

Jeremiah 8:18 - 9:1; 1 Timothy 2:1-7; Luke 16:1-13

Every time I go to the grocery store and line up to pay for my food, I can't help but notice some of the sensational headlines of the tabloids that are strategically located right at eye level. Every once in a while I will see some headline about a two-headed baby or about how the world is about to come to an end. But mostly I have realized the tabloids are interested in finding and reporting on the alleged scandals among the rich and famous.

So far in my life, I have only met one person who admitted to buying and reading tabloids, but last I heard none of these publications were in any danger of going out of business, which should not be a surprise judging by the amount of celebrity news covered on television talk shows on any given day.

Clearly, there is a significant number of people in our society who are intrigued by hearing the tales of how the rich, the powerful, and the famous have fallen off their pedestals. This is nothing new. So long as there have been people distinguished and separated by wealth into the 'haves' and the 'have nots', into the 'rich' and 'poor', 'noble' and 'peasant', people who see themselves as having received the short end of the stick have been interested in hearing stories not only of how the rich have fallen from grace, but how the clever and wily poor have outfoxed and outsmarted the rich and powerful.

The same was true of the people of Israel. In fact, their entire history was an epoch adventure of how a slave nation was led from the brick pits of Egypt to form their own nation – a people chosen by the one and only God Almighty. It was the ultimate "rags to riches" story. But over the course of time, these rags to riches people began to behave just like any other nation. Where once they had been twelve tribes, now they were divided into rich and poor, clean and unclean, sinner and righteous. No longer were they a brotherhood of tribes, each seeking to care for the needs of the other. Now they were like any other nation with a small and wealthy elite who were masters over the majority of the people who were heavily debt ridden and barely able to make ends meet.

You see, as a result of the demands of King Herod, most of the former rural property owners had lost their independence. The taxes he demanded meant nearly every property owner had to mortgage their property in order to pay the tax, and the repayment terms often included a substantial amount of interest.

It was a scenario that was supposed to be impossible under the Law. Jews were forbidden to lend money at interest to their brothers, but the rulers had managed to work their way around that little problem by taking part of the harvest as an annual payment on the debt. Instead of selling off the harvest at market and paying the debt off with the proceeds, the master demanded oil and wheat in amounts which, if sold, would have included a healthy chuck of interest. Not only that, but the amount demanded often amounted to more than half of the farmers' harvest. The former landowners were transformed to the point of being little more than slaves on their own land.

If that weren't enough, the situation was made even worse by the fact that the masters themselves did not collect the amounts directly from the farmers. Instead, there was a hierarchy of middlemen whose job it was to collect the debts. Not only were these men responsible for collecting the debts, but they were also the ones charged with keeping the records in order.

Now any accountant worth his salt will tell you that this situation is an invitation for embezzlement, which is exactly what happened. These middlemen extorted from the farmers arbitrary sums of goods amounting to far more than the amount of the debt and taxes which were really due. This allowed them to accumulate a great deal of wealth in very few years. But the poor farmers had no way to address the situation, no one who would listen to them. So long as the master received the amount due to him, he was happy. The master landowner was happy and the middlemen were happy. The only ones who would listen to the poor farmers were people in the same situation and no one really cared what they said anyway.

So when we hear Jesus begin to tell a story about a rich landowner and a dishonest manager in our Gospel lesson, we can be sure he wasn't just using it as a good tool for making his point. Many of the people he would have been speaking with would have personally been involved in a situation like this.

The parable tells how a certain rich landowner one day discovers the dishonesty of his manager and demands an accounting of his management before he fires him. The manager realizes not only has his embezzlement been found out, but he is also not in a position to pay back what he has taken. When the owner demands all of the dishonest gain that the manager has taken, he will be left without a home and without the ability to do anything other than to beg for handouts.

Keep in mind how the people listening to this parable would have been reacting – finally, one of these managers was going to face justice; finally, one of them was going to see what it was like to live at the bottom of society. You can be sure stories such as these were not uncommon.

There were quite a few stories about how there would come a day when all the abuse, all the dishonesty, would have to be accounted for and those who were found to be dishonest would be cast out to where there would be great weeping and gnashing of teeth. So when people listened to Jesus telling this story, they would have thought they knew what was coming: the master would return and the dishonest manager would be justly punished. But already the story Jesus is telling begins to take a different turn.

The manager knows what's coming. He knows he is about to face the judgment of his master, so he immediately acts to ensure he doesn't wind up being cast out into the streets begging for a living. He restores to the farmers the excess of the debt which he normally collected for himself. One by one he calls the farmers in and offers them deep discounts on how much they owe – fifty percent off on oil and twenty percent off on wheat.

Keep in mind that the farmers who are having their debt load relieved do not know the manager is about to be fired, and in that day and age when someone scratched your back you were expected to scratch their back in return. The manager would be welcome in any of the households where he made these deals regardless of whether or not the previous amount he had charged had been inflated. Even though the deep discounts were taken more or less from his own pocket and that would mean he would have even less to offer the master when he came, the manager could rest assured that when he lost his position he would not be cast out into the streets.

So when the master comes and discovers how the manager has acted in order to ensure his own future well being, the master commends or congratulates the manager for being shrewd or clever in his business dealings.

Now it may be true that the manager was shrewd or clever, but for the farmers who would have been listening to this story, and generally for us too, we find the commendation of the owner to be unacceptable. Most of the farmers would have expected to hear a story where the manager was punished, where the owner made amends for the wrongs the farmers suffered at the hands of the dishonest manager by canceling debts and restoring them to their rightful status as owners of the land they worked. To hear that the dishonest manger continues to do well, by pulling the wool over the eyes of the farmers and then having the owner come and congratulate the manager for being shrewd, would have been infuriating for them.

> Where is the justice?
>> Where is the accountability?
>>> Where is the concern for the poor farmers?

Just imagine Jesus telling us a story about a CEO who cooked the books in order to fill his own pockets at the expense of the shareholders and employees of a company. Then when the authorities came asking questions, and he was certain he was going to lose his job and his fortune, made arrangements to use his money to relieve large sums of debt owed to the company by some of its debtors so long as they promised to provide for his needs when he lost his job.

What would we think if the investigators said, "Hey, that was a really clever way of dealing with the situation"? The employees and shareholders would be furious. They would demand the CEO be brought to justice, demand that he be charged, convicted, and punished.

To make matters worse, Jesus seems to suggest that as God's people, as children of the light, we could stand to learn a thing or two from such a shady character. He says "…use worldly wealth to gain friends for yourselves, so that when it is gone, you will be welcomed into eternal dwellings." What can Jesus possibly mean by all of this?

For starters, we need to remember Jesus is not using the story of the dishonest steward as a moral object lesson. It is a parable; it is designed to challenge people. Remember how David schemed to have Uriah killed so he could take Bathsheba for his wife, and how the Prophet Nathan came to challenge him. Nathan did not come in condemning King David, but told him a story about a rich man who took and killed the only and beloved sheep of a poor man. When King David proclaimed that such a man deserved death, Nathan stepped in and said you are that man. In the end King David condemned himself.

In the same way, Jesus tells us a story about a dishonest manager that gets us demanding justice be done, that the man be punished, and then Jesus turns the tables on us and begins to talk about our stewardship, our management of the resources God has entrusted to our care.

Do you think it's only the wealthy who will be held accountable for how they managed God's resources? No, Jesus says, *"Whoever can be trusted with very little can also be trusted with much, and whoever is dishonest with very little will also be dishonest with much."* He says to all of the farmers who have gathered to hear this story, *"How honest are you being with the little that you have? Do you walk past the needy on your way to the temple, just like the wealthy landowners?"* He asks us, when we think of the rags to riches stories do we ever image anyone other than ourself in the starring role?

Out of all the people in North America who have imagined winning a big lottery, how many do you suppose have wished that their neighbour might win the lottery? In the same way, he asks when you think of the rich and powerful falling from their place of power and privilege, do you ever see yourself in that position, or is it always someone else who deserves punishment more than you do?

Jesus knew the heart of the issue was the question of whether or not the people understand what true wealth is. If we think that wealth means houses, cars, boats, home furnishings or electronics we are not going to recognize the kingdom of God.

In our reading from Jeremiah, God does not weep because his people have caused the destruction of his temple, he does not weep over the loss of the city of Jerusalem, not over lost houses. God is in agony because his people are being slaughtered. The ones who were intended to bring God's light to the neighbouring gentiles, instead brought deceit, death, and darkness to their own brothers and sisters.

As Paul says in our reading from 1 Timothy, Jesus gave himself as a ransom for all people, because it is God's desire that every human being should be drawn into his salvation. People, human beings, are what God considers to be true wealth, and if in this present age we do not recognize that, chances are when we pass from this age to the age to come and all worldly wealth is gone, we will not recognize the true riches in the kingdom.

When we see the eternal home that has been prepared for us, will we wish it had a big screen TV? Will we wish our eternal dwelling was in a better neighbourhood? Will we wish we had a better class of neighbours? Or worse will we say no thanks to the dwelling that Jesus has prepared for us, thinking we can find a better dwelling elsewhere?

What exactly is it that God's people, the children of light, can learn from a dishonest, yet shrewd manager? Chiefly this: that in acting as he did, he acquired genuine wealth, namely the gratitude and friendship of those who were his former victims and enemies.

Jesus declares to us, *"Practice the jubilee which I am announcing. Set people free from whatever holds them in bondage, whatever separates them from God and neighbour, and by liberating others from their burdens you will also be liberated from the shackles that bind you to your worldly wealth and you will be ready and prepared for the kingdom of God."*

Amen and amen.

Investing for the Future

September 26, 2004

Jeremiah 32:1-3a, 6-15; 1 Timothy 6:6-19; Luke 16:19-31

It wasn't so long ago that the decision to make an investment was based on whether or not you believed in a particular company, believed in what they were trying to produce or create, but investing in today is far different. We tend to be more interested in investing in the skill of a financial manager – someone who has the expertise, someone who we think can take our money and do whatever he has to do with it in order to grow it into a nice retirement nest egg.

Long gone are the days where people actually believed in what they were investing in. Most people today would be hard pressed to name two or three companies in which their mutual funds are invested and some I'm sure would even be hard pressed to give the names of the mutual funds themselves. We tend to place our trust in the mangers, the experts, so much so that even through the last several years of highly volatile stock markets most people are still willing to listen to the advice of their manager to stay in the market for the long term. As one mutual fund company proclaims: "Buy, Hold, and Prosper."

But not everyone has been willing to sit tight through the recent ups and downs of the market and many have opted instead for investing in land. After all, there is no more of it being made and with populations constantly on the rise, land is virtually guaranteed to increase in value. Land, it seems, is a good commonsense investment.

So when we hear that Jeremiah's cousin Hanamel has come offering to sell a portion of his family's inheritance in the Promised Land it might seem like a great investment opportunity for Jeremiah. That is, until we catch the circumstances of the sale. The land of Israel has been invaded by the armies of Babylon and the capital city of Israel, Jerusalem, is under siege. Not only that, but Jeremiah is currently in prison in the palace in Jerusalem. Not exactly ideal circumstances for making a sound real estate investment. Best to wait and see if King Zedekiah will come to terms with the invading forces. Best to wait and see if the Egyptian allies are going to come and rescue them. Best to wait and see if Jeremiah is going to be released from prison any time soon.

After all, there's no sense throwing away your wealth by purchasing land that is soon to be under the control of a foreign nation. No, the commonsense thing to do in times like these was to sell, not buy. So the shrewd businessmen Hanamel comes looking for any relative who might be interested in buying his parcel of the Promised Land – interested in buying a share in the promises of God in uncertain times. The Law required that you had to offer your share in the land first to your family as a kind of insurance against a family losing all claim upon the land, but you can be sure Jeremiah would have been among the last of the family relations to whom Hanamel would have offered to sell.

You see, Jeremiah was not imprisoned for telling the King everything was going to go well, that God was on their side in battle and the enemy would be quickly and soundly defeated. No, Jeremiah was imprisoned for telling the people to surrender to the Babylonians so their lives might be spared. He had already prophesied King Zedekiah would be carried off into exile and the bulk of the people with him, so commonsense would seem to suggest the one who appeared to be proclaiming the end for the nation of Israel would be the last one to be interested in buying a piece of the Promised Land. But before Hanamel can offer the land publicly for sale he is required to offer it to Jeremiah. So he meets his obligation, but to his surprise Jeremiah has been expecting him.

The arrival of Hanamel confirms the word the Lord has spoken to Jeremiah: he is to purchase the land that is offered, and he does just that.

We are not simply told the sale took place, we are told all of the details of the transaction. That may seem like a whole lot of information we simply didn't need to know, but it is very clear we are to understand that this sale actually took place following all of accepted practices of the day, down to the last detail. The sale is real. Real silver was used to purchase the land, a real bill of sale is drafted and real people witnessed the transaction. The sale is legal and it is binding.

At this point we might imagine Hanamel would be quite pleased with the transaction, but at the same time it is hard to escape the feeling that Jeremiah has been more or less taken advantage of by his own cousin. Sure, we might be sympathetic with Jeremiah; we might think we understand he is trying to remind the people that even in the midst of the destruction that's coming, God will not abandon his people.

But why couldn't he just say that? After all, isn't that the way prophets are supposed to work, proclaiming God's word? Why is it necessary to squander his wealth in this manner? To everyone around, and generally for us, too, Jeremiah's actions seem foolish and contradictory. If God is sending the people into exile, then spending real money on land was poor use of his resources – a waste of money – and what's worse, his actions in no way provide a solution to the crises he is proclaiming. Buying land does nothing to prevent the Babylonian hordes from ending their siege on Jerusalem. It just doesn't make sense.

Remember that this action was not Jeremiah's idea, but God's. Jeremiah was instructed to purchase the land despite the fact that it was contrary to all common sense. Jeremiah's actions were never intended to be an investment in land, but a reminder and a call to the people to act not in accordance with what is

happening around them at the moment, but to act in accordance with the promises God has made to his people. Through Jeremiah, God is calling his people
> to use *un*common sense,
>> to have a very real and concrete faith,
>>> to believe in his promises

not just with their minds, but with their whole being – everything they are, and everything they have. God is calling them to invest themselves in his promises and to invest themselves in his future.

Shortly thereafter, the Babylonian armies broke through the defenses at Jerusalem, destroyed the temple and carried off the King and the bulk of survivors into exile, just as Jeremiah had warned. The only reason this foolish purchase of land has any meaning at all is because God was faithful to his promises and restored the people Israel to the Promised Land. Houses, fields and vineyards were again bought in the land of Israel.

But the exile left a lasting impression upon the people. They knew they had been exiled for their unfaithfulness and were determined never to let it happen again. They were determined to ensure the Law was never again forgotten. The problem was that over time this determination to never again turn their backs on the commands of the Lord changed. It changed to the point where the Law was no longer a source of life, but a means of drawing boundaries between
> who was in and who was out,
>> who was clean and who was unclean,
>>> who was righteous and who was a sinner.

In Jesus' day one of the groups particularly interested in these distinguishing marks were the Pharisees. Often we hear the charge that the Pharisees believed they could earn their salvation through works of the Law, but that really isn't an accurate statement. Pharisees, along with others, believed God's salvation meant dwelling in the presence of the Lord. The problem was that God was ultimately holy and you could not expect to dwell with

God if you were not holy in his sight. For the Pharisees, achieving that kind of holiness meant strictly observing the commands of the Lord. In essence they believed you would not be welcomed into God's house if you were going to be tracking in dirt. So at all times you needed to maintain your ritual purity.

The problem is that when Jesus arrives on the scene, he is proclaiming God is less worried about the dirt on your hands and feet, than he is with the dirt in your heart – that holiness has less to do with your ritual purity than it does with how you treat your neighbour. So when we come to our Gospel reading for today, we need to remember when Jesus is telling this parable about Lazarus and the rich man, he is telling it to the Pharisees.

Just prior to our passage, Luke has told us the Pharisees were lovers of money, and we need to understand there is nothing we can point to historically that indicates the Pharisees were generally more concerned with money than any other group in Israel, particularly since they tended not to be as wealthy as the Sadducees. What Luke is trying to remind us is that the Pharisees were operating under the common sense notion of their day that proclaimed wealth was an indication that God was happy with you – that your material blessings were a reflection of your spiritual condition, a reflection of your holiness before God.

Likewise, if you were poor, or diseased, you had quite clearly done something to warrant the wrath of God – your miserable life reflected your spiritual poverty, your un-holiness before God.

So Jesus begins to tell them a parable about an extremely wealthy man who dressed in purple and fine linen. Within the Roman Empire, the color purple was restricted from use by everyone other than the most elite members of society. Anyone wearing purple was not simply well off, but was as rich and powerful as you could get. By stark contrast we see poor Lazarus dumped at the gate of the rich man and the only thing we're told is he is covered in sores. The rich man regularly feasts at banquets fit for a king and Lazarus lies outside the gate longing even for the bread that has fallen from the table. It was a common practice at feasts like this for the guests to use bread as a kind of napkin to wipe the grease off of their hands and then cast it on the ground where the dogs would scavenge it.

The dogs were not the domesticated house pets we are accustomed to. These dogs would have been the wild animals that lived off of the garbage generated by a city; so when we hear the dogs were licking the sores on Lazarus' body, we may be tempted to think they were almost ministering to him, but the hard reality is that they were more likely hanging around waiting for Lazarus to die.

It's at this point in the parable that commonsense of the day begins to fail. People believed there was a kind of continuity between this world and the next – that the wealthy who received material blessings now would continue to receive blessings throughout eternity. The poor on the other hand were cursed now and would continue to be cursed unless they turned back to God, which of course meant being included with the other social elites. But the first shock of the parable is that there will indeed be continuity, but what continues is not the apparent blessings or curses, but the chasm that is fixed between the two.

The rich man who wouldn't be caught dead associating with or even offering table scraps to Lazarus is similarly nowhere near Lazarus in the age to come. The distance that existed between Lazarus and the rich man in life remains intact, but everything else is reversed. Just as Mary had proclaimed when the angel Gabriel informed her she was to bear a son who would be the Messiah:

> *"He has brought down rulers from their thrones but has lifted up the humble. He has filled the hungry with good things but has sent the rich away empty. He has helped his servant Israel, remembering to be merciful to Abraham and his descendants forever, even as he said to our fathers."* (Luke 1:52-55)

As we listen again to Mary's words, what stands out is that Israel as a people were supposed to be the ones who would be raised up, while all the rich idolatrous gentiles would be humbled. We begin to see the second shock of this parable. Both Lazarus and the rich man are children of Abraham – both are a part of the people Israel – but only Lazarus is carried to the bosom of Abraham by angels (something held by Jews to be roughly the equivalent of paradise), while the rich man is in torment, dying of thirst and pleading with father Abraham to recognize him as a son, which Abraham does, but that alone will not bridge the chasm.

That may make us squirm a little, to think that ultimately there will come a point of no return; no going back. The rich man pleads with Abraham to send Lazarus back to warn his brothers. Apparently the rich man still sees Lazarus as someone who he can order around, but if the rich man's brothers have not listened to Moses and the prophets, why should they listen to one who rises from the dead?

Is that the point of the parable? That there will come a time of no return; a time when hope no longer exists? I don't think so.

Notice that although the rich man is very distraught about his condition there is very little in the way of guilt or remorse for his failure to help Lazarus. So far as I can tell, the rich man does not feel badly about anything except that his life of luxury has landed him on the wrong side of this chasm. But remember Jesus is not telling this parable to condemn the Pharisees or to condemn us. He is telling this parable because he could not and can not understand the way people love the things they can get for themselves more than they love the things that God wants to give them.

We are more satisfied with linen suits and sumptuous feasts, and all the while God wants to give us the kingdom. We are content to live in the world with beggars lying near death in our doorway, when all the while God wants to give us brothers and sisters.

What they did not seem to realize and what we still do not seem to realize is how easily we become the victims and prisoners of our own way of life. When we succeed in cutting ourselves off from each other, when we learn how to accept the misery of other people as nothing out of the ordinary by convincing ourselves they deserve it, or that it is simply the way the world works, when we defend our own good fortune as God's blessing and fail to see how our lives are intertwined with the lives of others, then we are the real losers. Not because God is waiting to punish us for our wrongdoing, but because we prefer a world and a life of our own design. And that world is on the opposite side of the chasm from the world and the life God offers. Who do you think fixed that chasm in the parable? Was it God or was it the rich man?

C. S. Lewis once described hell, not as a flaming inferno, but as a dark, shady, chilly, and above all boring place. Its inhabitants are free to leave whenever they so choose. But just as they did on earth, people
> choose separation from God,
>> choose misery over joy,
>>> choose hollowness over reality.

One ghost in Lewis' hell insists, "I don't want help. I want to be left alone." Why don't they leave hell for heaven if they are free to do so? "Because," he says, "there is always something they insist on keeping, even at the price of misery. There is always something they prefer to joy." Indeed, Lewis concludes, "There are only two kinds of people in the end, those who say to God, 'Thy will be done,' and those to whom God says, in the end, 'Thy will be done.' All that are in hell, chose it."

All too often talk of heaven and hell boils down to entrance requirements. What do I need to do to get into heaven or worse what do I need to do to keep out of hell? The problem is when we think in those terms we fail to think about what life will be like beyond the entrance. If we think the point of doing good deeds is that they can be stored up and cashed in for an entrance ticket when we retire from this life, then we are missing the point. The kingdom of God is a way of life – a life conformed to the will of God, a life conformed to the Way of Jesus Christ. When we hear Paul calling us to live a life rich with good works, he is not giving us hints for how to get into the kingdom, but a description of what it is like to live in the kingdom.

That is why Paul urges Timothy and urges us to fight the good fight – which in Greek actually has more to do with conditioning yourself for an athletic contest than it does with confrontation. Paul wants us not simply to be allowed into the kingdom, but to have conditioned ourselves so well in our present life, that we will feel at home living in the kingdom.

Those of you who have traveled to countries outside the influence of western society are likely to have experienced culture shock. Being suddenly immersed in a different culture shakes up our sense of comfort and stability, and if the experience is strong enough it leaves people with a feeling of homesickness, of wanting to return to the certainties of the way of life they left behind.

Well, just image arriving in the kingdom of God and instead of a family reunion, we see all of the people we were sure God would not allow into the kingdom, all of the people we didn't help, all of the people we turned our backs on. Imagine arriving in the Kingdom and discovering it looks nothing like the life we lived. Imagine arriving in the kingdom only to find it looks like a foreign land.

What Jesus is trying to tell us is unless we invest ourselves in his kingdom in this life – unless we believe in the kingdom not only with our minds, but also with our hearts, with everything we are and everything we have – we are likely to experience culture shock upon arriving in the kingdom, and what will we do then?

Which home will we choose? The one of God's design or one of our own design? The reality is, conforming our lives to God's will, investing ourselves in the way of the cross will often mean a conflict with the common sense of our day. But
> if we will invest ourselves in the *un*common sense of the cross,
>> if we will invest ourselves in God's plan for the future,
>>> if we will invest ourselves in extending the love of Jesus across the chasms that divide us from our neighbours in this life,

then our arrival in the kingdom of God will be nothing short of a joyous homecoming.

Having laid a firm foundation for the coming age, we may take hold of the life that is truly Life.

Amen and amen.

Mastering Faith

World Communion Sunday, October 3, 2004

Luke 17:3b-10

One part of my training for pastoral ministry was to do some work within a congregation under the supervision of a minister I would meet with on a regular basis for discussion and feedback. The minister I was assigned to was Tony Plomp, who at that time was the minister at Richmond Presbyterian Church.

During one of our meetings Tony told me a story about how, after he had been ordained, he was serving a congregation in Saskatchewan and was feeling quite frustrated by what he saw as a lack of faith on their part. So one Sunday morning he stood up in the pulpit and delivered a very heavy-handed sermon demanding more from the people of the congregation – demanding more commitment, more faithfulness to their calling to be disciples of Jesus Christ.

Tony recalls that after the service had ended he stood at the door to greet people as they left. They were much quieter than normal. Several hurried on their way by, barely making eye contact; but what stood out for Tony was one man who was anxiously waiting for everyone else to leave so he could have a word with the minister. Tony knew the man. He was a regular attendee at church and even sang in the choir, but the interesting thing about him was he was not really a believer. He was ethnically Jewish, but didn't practice Judaism and he had married a Christian woman who was a member of the congregation so he came to church because it was important to his wife.

After everyone had left the church this man came up to Tony and said to him, "Don't ever do that again." Then he continued, saying, "Do you have any idea what I would give to have the faith you have? Don't ever do that again."

Tony said those comments marked something of a turning point in his ministry. Never again in his forty years of ministry did he treat the faith of others as if it were simply a matter of will power, a matter of self-willed commitment.

I am sure many of you realize Tony wasn't the only one who has thought like this. Nearly every Christian leader I have spoken with has at one time or another been confronted by the frustration of a lack of enthusiasm or support
> for their ministry,
>> for their mission, or
>>> for their outreach.

It's a problem often most apparent in the first year of ministry, when newly-minted ministers and their ideal visions of the church and its mission come face to face with the realities of the human condition. So it was no surprise to me when a few months ago I received a call from one the classmates I had graduated with. He said, "Is this really what the church is supposed to be; Jesus died for this?"

I think in many respects our Gospel lesson for today touches on this issue. As we have been following the Gospel of Luke over the past several weeks, we have heard again and again the demands Jesus is making of his disciples. He will settle for nothing short of all they have and they are … nothing short of total commitment. But just prior to this morning's passage Jesus turns to his disciples and tells them there are bound to be stumbling blocks along the way. His disciples shouldn't kid themselves that it's all going to be smooth sailing from here on in.

Jesus is preparing the disciples for the fact there are going to be times when as disciples they will fall short of the demands he has made. So he instructs his disciples on how they should respond when this happens. He says if someone sins, rebuke them; if they repent, forgive them. Sounds simple enough, right? But then Jesus continues, "Even if they sin seven times in a day and come back to you seven times saying 'I repent', forgive them."

Now stop and think about that for a minute. We think we are being generous when we say three strikes and you're out – here Jesus is saying not even after seven strikes in a single day is it okay to tell them they're out of chances. And what's worse is that the number seven also has a particular symbolic value – it is the number of completeness, the number of perfection. In a sense, Jesus is telling us not that the limit on forgiveness is seven times, but
>to forgive as many times as is necessary,
>>to forgive completely,
>>>to forgive perfectly.

How easy it is for us to feel we are taking the higher moral ground in offering forgiveness – that we haven't done anything wrong, so if we choose to forgive, we do so from a position of moral superiority. If we choose to forgive them, then that makes us superior to them. But once we have enjoyed exercising that superiority once, twice, maybe even three times, then we start to feel it's time to draw back a little. It's time to prove we are not going to be taken advantage of; we will not allow them to walk all over us. After all, why should we continue to give them all that freedom? No, there comes a time when they will need to prove to us they are really interested in changing their behaviour if we are going to continue to offer our forgiveness.

But as we see, that is not the approach Jesus takes. When we forgive someone, we are making ourselves their servant, not setting ourselves up to be their master. Forgiving someone again and again should not get harder and harder. It should not be a matter of restraining our anger for a longer and longer period of time like someone trying to hold their breath under water for ten seconds, then twenty seconds, and so on. If that's what we think it's like to forgive someone over and over again then we are missing the point. The point is not to keep score of our good behavior. The point of forgiveness is to offer the other person the generous and welcoming forgiveness that God has shown to us.

But forgiveness of that kind does not tend to come naturally to us any more than it did to the first disciples who quickly came to the realization that all this will require more faith than they think they have. Increase our faith, they cry; give us more, we cry –
    give us more members,
        give us more committed disciples,
            give us more money in our bank accounts,
                give us more youth in Sunday
        school.
If only we had more, then we could really do what Jesus has called us to do. Then we could really be the people God wants us to be. Faith too easily becomes one more commodity in scarce supply, something we feel we simply do not have enough of to do what Jesus is asking of us. But Jesus is quick to respond: you don't need more. You don't need a great amount faith. What you need is faith in a great God.

Faith is like a window through which you can see something. It doesn't matter whether the window is six inches or six feet high. What matters is the God that your faith is looking out on. If it is the Creator God, the God revealed in Jesus and active in the Holy Spirit, then even the tiniest peep hole, even a hole the size of a mustard seed, will give you access to power like you never dreamed of – power enough to say to a mulberry tree, be uprooted and be planted in the sea, and it would obey.

Now you can bet there have been more than a few who have put this saying to the test, hoping to verify Jesus' claim. Then after the tree has remained firmly fixed in the ground and indeed has not been planted in the sea, they conclude either that Jesus was mistaken, or that they simply did not have enough faith, and they quickly find themselves back where they started, crying, "Increase my faith." But nothing could be further from what Jesus is trying to say here.

He is not telling his disciples they all now possess the power to operate their own miracle forestry business, cutting out the middlemen – the trucks and the chainsaws – and allowing us to simply tell the cedars to pop out of the ground and fly on over to the booms in the Fraser River.

Jesus does not say we will have the strength to uproot the tree and cast it into the sea. What is important here is that the only thing required is to speak to the tree. Jesus it trying to remind us there is only One whom, when he speaks, creation answers.
God spoke and formed the earth.
    God spoke and separated water from the dry land.
        God spoke and vegetation formed on the
        land.
When God speaks, Creation responds. Our faith does not give us superpowers. Our faith offers an opportunity for the power of God to work through us.

Remember earlier on in Luke's Gospel there was a raging storm upon the Galilean sea. This time Jesus spoke and the sea listened, the storm subsided. Do you remember what Jesus said to his disciples? Not "Why don't you have more faith?" but, "Where is your faith?" *(8:25)* When they cried out, "Master, Master, we are perishing" does their fear and distress offer a window out upon a God who can still the storm, or does it offer a window into the fear and distress that results from placing all of our faith in our own strength and abilities?

Jesus knows exactly what's coming. He can see it brewing already in the midst of the crowd following him. He has made serious and costly demands upon the lives of those who would number themselves among his disciples, yet at the same time Jesus has made a concerted effort to reach out and offer forgiveness to those whom the rest of the world was quite happy to treat as garbage. So what's going to happen when this very different and diverse group of disciples tries to live this new Kingdom life? What's going to happen when they try to live together as the new creation?

What will the disciples who are able to fulfill the commands Jesus has given going to say to those who seem to continually fall short? Are they going to say:
- they simply need to make better choices,
- they need to have more will power,
- they need to be more committed,
- maybe their faith is insufficient.
- they aren't real disciples after all, or maybe
- they are a lower order, a lower class of Christian?

Jesus says, "Not a chance!" To every disciple that has followed his commands to the fullest, Jesus says, "Suppose one of you had a servant plowing or looking after the sheep. Would you say to the servant when he comes in from the field, 'Come along now and sit down to eat'?"

It's a question no one even needs to respond to; they all know the answer: "Of course not." The servant never eats with the master, the servant prepares the food, the servant serves the food, the servant cleans up the mess, and if there is time left over the servant can wolf down a quick bite to eat before he has to get on with his other work. There's not the slightest chance the master would invite the servant to share a meal with him, and there's never any thought the master should thank the servant for carrying out his duties.

To every disciple that rigorously seeks to live in accordance with the commands of God, all that we do, even the hard work we do for God, never for a moment puts God in our debt, never puts God in the position that he owes us something.

How often have you heard it said and how many more times is it thought, "I've done all this; I've given all that money, I've worked so hard, surely God must be satisfied?" Or worse, "I've done so much more than my brother, I've given so much more money than my sister, I've worked so much harder than my neighbour, surely God must be more satisfied with me."

The answer we hear back is the same one Jesus gave his first disciples: that all genuine service to God is done out of gratitude, not to earn anything at all. Saying we are unworthy servants doesn't mean that we lack a proper sense of self-worth or self-esteem. It simply means we must constantly remind ourselves that nothing we do can or will ever put God in a position where he will owe us something.

And so Jesus leaves us with a double challenge. On the one hand he asks those who feel inadequate and ill equipped, "What does your faith point to?" Do we come here to worship and talk about the God who offers steadfast love, abundant mercy and endless forgiveness, only to go into the world offering haphazard love, being stingy in extending mercy, and being quick to place limits on our forgiveness? Do we believe in a God who demands us to do things we have not been equipped for? If we do not see the power of God almighty working in our midst, it is not a question of a lack of faith. The question is: *where is our faith*? Is our faith pointing to the God who formed the heavens and the earth, or is it pointing to our own skill and ability?

On the other hand, the second challenge comes to those who feel they are among the few Christians who truly get it –
    those who are committed,
        those who are devoted,
            those who have counted the cost, born the cross and followed wherever Jesus has led them through good and bad, through high and low, and who, looking around the room, seeing not brothers and sisters but disciples of varying degrees – those who are committed, partially committed, and uncommitted.

Again Jesus asks to what does our faith point? Do we come here to worship and talk about the God who offers grace as a free and unmerited gift, only to go out into the world convinced of our spiritual superiority? Is our faith pointing to the God who freely offers his life for sinners, or is it pointing to our own will power?

In the end, both challenges are meant to confront us with the fact that mastering faith has nothing to do with how much faith we have. Mastering faith means remembering who the Master is.

So as we prepare to come to this, our Master's table, let us come not asking for more for ourselves, and not demanding more from our brothers and sisters. Let us come to this table in gratitude and thanksgiving for the faith we have been given and the grace we have received – not according to anything we have done, but according only to the steadfast love of God, revealed in our Lord, Jesus Christ.

Amen and amen.

Food for Life

Thanksgiving Sunday, October 10, 2004

John 6:24-35

A little over two months ago, I was asked to preside at a funeral for a woman who was not a member of our congregation, someone who I really didn't know much about. I soon discovered her death had taken a heavy toll on both her husband and her son. It was clear even after the funeral service that neither of them had found much comfort in the hope of the Gospel.

Recently I discovered one of the people who had attended the funeral lives just down the street from us and one day while our daughters were playing together, we spoke briefly. He mentioned he was a friend of the son of the woman who had passed away and he told me his friend was still having a real difficult time coming to terms with her death. The son felt he simply could not believe in a God who would let something like this happen.

It used to be that when I would hear people say things like that, I would feel almost a duty as a believer to come up with some reasons to convince them to hold on to their belief in God. I felt I should try to convince them to hold on, that sooner or later they would come to see that God was faithful and just – that their belief would be justified if they would just hang on. But when I heard this man had more or less stopped believing, instead of having a rush of thoughts on how I could prevent this from happening, one single question came into my mind. Does it make a difference? Now that he can no longer believe in God, what difference does it make to him? How has his life changed?

And I want to be clear. In no way am I saying that grief, sorrow, or anger are inappropriate responses when faced with the loss of a loved one. The point I am trying to make is that somehow we tend to think believing has primarily to do with what goes on inside our heads. We think believing is an intellectual or philosophical process, that we only believe something when we have good reasons to do so.

When it comes to belief in God, people are often prepared to believe so long as life works out pretty much as they expect it should. We are relatively prepared to live with the fact that bad things happen so long as they happen to bad people. But when bad things start happening to good people, which essentially means people like you and me or the people that we like, then we start demanding answers.

We cry out to God, "I'll believe in you, if you will just show me how this fits into the master plan. I'll believe if you will let me take a glimpse at the blueprints ... if you will just allow me a brief tour of the mind of God. I'll believe if you will just tell me why." But every time we say that or even something like that, we have lost sight of the fact that God has already given us not simply a glimpse of his plan, but has revealed his will and his way in Jesus Christ. The only problem is, as we see over and over throughout the history of Israel, God's revelation is often not recognized or not accepted.

Psalm 78 recollects many of the key events in which God revealed himself to the people:
- how he divided the sea and led them through;
- how he made the water stand firm like a wall;
- how he guided them with the cloud by day and with light from the fire all night;
- how he split the rocks in the desert and gave them water as abundant as the seas.

But, despite these signs and wonders, the people continued to sin against God, rebelling in the desert against him. The psalmists say they willfully put God to the test by demanding the food they craved, saying, *"Can God spread a table in the desert? Sure he gave us water, but can he also give us food? Can he supply meat for his people?"* Despite all the wonders, despite all the signs that God was right there dwelling in their midst and providing for their needs, they still did not believe in God and did not trust in his deliverance. *(Psalm 78:13-22)*

We may be tempted to ask why.
Why were the people so blind?
Why couldn't they see?
Why couldn't they believe despite all God was doing in front of their very eyes? And the answer is they thought they were being realistic. In the real world if you do not look out for your own well being, if you don't make provision for the necessities of life, for food and water, then you are likely going to die. They were just trying to do what any reasonable person would have done being lost in the wilderness: to provide for their own survival or face the fact that they would likely perish. Then and now it is easier to trust in our own provision than it is to trust that God will provide. It's more reasonable to believe in ourselves than it is to believe in God.

Not much had changed when Jesus arrived on the scene. In the Gospel of John, we hear that after Jesus had fed the five thousand in the wilderness and left to meet his disciples in Capernaum, the crowd that had just been fed was anxious to find Jesus, so they set off and discovered him on the other side of the sea. When we stop and think about this – a crowd of five thousand people following after Jesus – we might be tempted to think this is what Jesus was calling for … calling people to come to him. But the problem is, when this crowd finally catches up with Jesus, instead of receiving a warm welcome and congratulations for following after him, Jesus confronts and challenges their motives. *"I tell you the truth, you are looking for me, not because you saw*

miraculous signs but because you ate the loaves and had your fill."
(John 6:26)

For the most part it's hard to fault the crowd for wanting more food. These would not have been some kind of middle class people who generally had all the food they needed. They were those who lived on the edge of subsistence, those for whom a whole day's manual labour earned just enough money for one day's food and no more. The feeding in the wilderness must have seemed to them like a dream come true ... to be relieved of the constant struggle just to make ends meet. It's hard to blame them for chasing after Jesus even if it's simply for another free meal. But we need to keep in mind that large scale feedings were not unknown in Jesus' time. Roman troops and local leaders occasionally handed out bread to the multitudes in order to win the hearts of the people for their own political purposes.

To the crowd, it would have appeared Jesus was simply another leader trying to secure their loyalty and support by providing their daily bread. This is why the first question we hear from the crowd is, "When did you get here?" If they are going to be around when Jesus needs them to lend their support, to cheer when he says witty things, and to boo when his opponents speak, then he needs to keep them informed of when and where he is going. The crowd of people is trying to keep tabs on their patron, trying to keep tabs on their supply of food, but with what follows, Jesus makes it quite clear he is not simply another patron seeking to gather a mob of support for his plans and his agenda.

Jesus says:
"Do not work for food that spoils, but for food that endures to eternal life, which the Son of Man will give you. On him God the Father has placed his seal of approval." (John 6:27)

Jesus is reminding the people of the appropriate criteria for following someone who is claiming to represent God. Jesus says don't follow someone just because you think they can give you what you want. Don't support someone for a crust of bread and piece of fish. The only appropriate reason for following someone, the only appropriate reason to offer to support someone, is because they legitimately represent the will of God.

Jesus is not interested in a crowd who will follow him so long as his food holds out because Jesus knows what's coming. He knows there will come a time when he will be handed over to the authorities. He will be condemned, and then crucified. Then what will happen to this mob of people who followed him because they though it was an easy way to get the food they needed? Well, they will quickly find the next patron, the next person willing to offer bread for their support. Jesus knows
    only the followers who believed he was the one
    sent by the Father,
        only the followers who believed he was
        the Son of Man,
            only the followers who believed he was
            the one of whom the scriptures spoke,
would be able to recognize him as the King when he was enthroned upon the cross.

At this point the crowd immediately understands what Jesus is asking. He doesn't want a crowd of mercenary followers – those who will support his bid to be the messiah so long as he is able to provide their food. Jesus wants his followers to actually believe he is the Messiah – not based on what they get out of the deal, but simply because they believe it to be the truth.

Jesus is not interested in bargaining with his followers, agreeing to meet our demands, to fulfill our expectations if we will agree to follow him. Jesus is not interested in buying our support for his agenda by giving us whatever we want. Jesus wants us to know that when we are looking at him we are seeing not simply the one who has things to teach us about God, but the one in whom God is present.

It's not as if Jesus was the only one claiming to be the messiah. We know of several other historical figures who claimed to be the messiah, who, just like Jesus, were calling the people to follow them. The crowd would have heard calls like this before. Why should they believe in Jesus any more than any of the other messianic pretenders?

So they ask Jesus to show them his credentials. You say God has set his seal upon you, let's see your marks. Show us the signs and wonders just like Moses did for our ancestors in the wilderness. Now to us that may sound a little ridiculous. After all, Jesus just miraculously fed them in the wilderness. How can they possibly miss the connection? But if we look back we will see that after they had been fed none of the crowd gave any indication that anything out of the ordinary had taken place at the meal they shared.

To them it just seemed like Jesus had somehow found enough food to go around. Surely if Jesus was working signs and wonders, then they would have known it. Surely Jesus would have given them some indication he was about to do something amazing … maybe say some fancy words, or do some fancy actions, something to indicate he was performing a sign. But that's the problem. They were convinced a person who could do signs was trustworthy, but Jesus responds by saying if you think Moses worked all these signs and wonders, then you've missed the point. God works the signs and wonders through his servants.

Was it Moses who parted the Red Sea? Was it Moses who commanded the pillar of cloud and the pillar of fire? Was it really Moses who called forth water from the rock? Was it really Moses who made manna appear in the wilderness? No, Jesus says, it is not Moses who has given you the bread from heaven, but none other than the Father who gives the true bread of God which comes down from heaven and gives life to the world.

Jesus speaks here of the hope of Israel, of
> a time when God would once again dwell with his people,
>> a time when heaven and earth would be reconciled,
>>> a time when the whole creation would be redeemed,

and you can almost hear the longing in their request, hear that their real hunger is for redemption. Sir, they say, from now on give us this bread. And Jesus responds by saying, *"I am the bread of life."* The bread of life has already been given by God. It is present in their midst, standing right in front of them. The question is, will the gift be recognized and received?

On this weekend in particular, we give thanks for every good gift from God. Not only that, but we usually also celebrate the occasion with a substantial meal. Thanksgiving and food seem to go hand in hand. We can be sure all the work, all the preparation that goes into this meal, will result in many a full belly and maybe even leftovers for the better part of a week. But soon the food will perish and all the work that went into the meal will be gone and forgotten. The question is, will we have spent anywhere near as much time feeding on the Bread of life, on the food that endures?

When we offer our thanks to God for all of the good gifts of the harvest, the food that nourishes our bodies, we do so by hosting a feast of sorts. But when we offer our thanks for the gift of Jesus Christ, the food for life, will it result in anything more than a thirty-second prayer before the meal and an hour at church on Sunday?

There are bound to be realists who will say, sure we need to feed on Jesus, but if we don't work at all for perishable food, for food we eat, then we are going to starve to death. Just imagine what would happen to your body if you didn't feed it:

>decline,
>>decay, and eventually
>>>death.

It's at this moment Jesus turns the tables on us by saying that is precisely the point. Imagine what happens to the body of Christ when we as its members rarely feed on the bread of life. We come to the realization that all the emptiness we feel, all the hunger that cannot be satisfied by food, possessions, and money, are really nothing more than indications we are suffering from starvation.

This thanksgiving we need to ask ourselves, will the gift of Jesus Christ simply be abstract and philosophical, something we think about, something we talk about? Or will the gift of Jesus Christ be food for a malnourished life, something that will leave a lasting and imperishable mark upon us? Will it be something that defines who we are as human beings? Will it shape the way we live our lives? Does our belief in God, our belief in Jesus Christ, make a difference in our lives?

Think about Paul for a minute. A staunch Pharisee and a rigorous persecutor of the church until he was confronted by the fact that Jesus was not the latest in a long line of messianic pretenders. In fact, Jesus was nothing short of the revelation and reality of God's will for the world. And believing in Jesus and working for the food that endures, he produced a collection of letters through which the Holy Spirit has continued to feed the church for nearly two thousand years.

>It wasn't because he had super human powers;
>>it wasn't because he had the best philosophical ideas or even the most rational reasons;
>>>it was simply because his belief in Jesus was the foundation of every aspect of his life.

So even when Paul sat in prison with a death sentence hanging over his head, he could proclaim, *"Rejoice in the Lord always. I will say it again: Rejoice!"* (Philippians 4:4)

And later in the same letter Paul goes on to say, *"I know what it is to be in need, and I know what it is to have plenty. I have learned the secret of being content in any and every situation, whether well fed or hungry, whether living in plenty or in want. ... I can do everything through him who gives me strength."* (Philippians 4:12-13)

As we prepare to feast this weekend, let us also take time to reflect on where our strength comes from. Does it come from the perishable food on our table, or does it come from the imperishable food on the Lord's table? As we give thanks for all our blessings, let us, above all else, give thanks for the bread of God who comes down from heaven and gives life to the world.

Thanks be to God for the gift of Jesus Christ.

Amen.

Praying for Faith

October 17, 2004

Luke 18:1-8

Being someone who did not grow up with the benefit of Sunday School or any real connection with a church, praying was never something I did as a child ... or as a youth; not even as a young adult for the most part. Until one day when I was seventeen years old.

You see, like most other seventeen-year-old boys, I knew life consisted primarily of having fun with friends and trying to impress girls. Well, I never really had any problem with finding friends, but girls, on the other hand, now that was something I struggled with. But eventually there came a time when I met a girl I knew was special. I couldn't stop thinking about her. I desperately wanted her to be my girlfriend, but despite all the efforts and charm I could muster, she just was not interested in being anything more than a friend.

I knew there were people who believed in God. I knew they talked about praying to God and how they said that sometimes God answered prayer in miraculous ways. Mostly I was suspicious of those people, thinking they were primarily out to take away my freedom and fun, but I was desperate, and desperate times call for desperate measures.

I decided I was going to test out this God hypothesis. I was going to do a little experiment. I would try praying that God would give me this girl as my girlfriend, and I was determined to not try it only once. I was determined to try it for as long as necessary – maybe even for two weeks – just to see what would happen. I mean, I had nothing to lose. I didn't really expect anything would happen, but then again, nothing else seemed to be working either so there was no harm in giving it a try.

The first prayer I ever said went something like, "Um, God, please, if you let me have this girl as my girlfriend I won't ever ask for anything again. Amen." I was pretty sure I had all the necessary components. I addressed the prayer to God; I said 'please'; and I ended with 'Amen'. It seemed pretty complete to me. The next day I waited and nothing happened. So I prayed again, and again, and again, and still nothing happened.

Well, I shouldn't say nothing happened. You see, as I prayed night after night, I noticed my prayers began to grow. I found myself giving thanks for the good things that had happened to me, and later on I began to pray that good things would happen for my friends and family. I was finding I actually enjoyed my prayer time, and one day I was really quite shocked to hear myself say, "I love you, God."

Then one day, after more than eight months of nightly prayers, this girl suddenly had a change of heart and wanted to be more than just friends.

I was reminded of that story when I read our Gospel lesson from Luke. Often I have heard this parable interpreted as if Jesus is simply telling us if we don't get what we prayed for, keep praying, keep at it and don't give up or lose heart – God's delays are not God's denials. If at first you don't succeed, try, try, again. But is that really what Jesus is saying,
    to be persistent in prayer until we reach our Goal?
        to pray as long as it takes to get what we want?

Let's take another look at it. Jesus begins by telling us about a judge, but not your average judge. No, this judge was one who didn't fear God and who also didn't care about people. This may not sound all that unusual to us. Many of us have likely heard stories of corrupt officials in our own judicial system, and why should we expect things to be all that different in Jesus' day? But we need to remember that anytime the Jewish people would have heard a story about a judge they would not have been thinking about a separate and secular court of law. They would have been thinking about the ultimate Judge ... thinking about God.

If you remember back to the Book of Exodus, it was Moses who was first charged with being a judge over the people. The people came to Moses to resolve their disputes because he was God's representative. Moses was the one
>who would hear the disputes,
>>who would inform the people of God's decrees and laws, and
>>>who would then make a decision between the two parties.

But it didn't take long before it was clear this work was too great for one man, so Moses delegated the task of judging to others as well, to
>those who were capable,
>>those who feared God,
>>>those who were trustworthy and hated dishonest gain,
>>>>those who showed no partiality.
>>>>>*(Deuteronomy 16:18-21)*

Judges were not merely appointed to keep good order, they were charged with resolving disputes according to the will of God. So when we hear Jesus say there was a certain judge who had no fear of God, who had no sense that he needed to act in accordance with the will of God, who had no sense that he would be held accountable for his rulings, then we know this is anything but a good reflection of the justice of God. Yet the fact remains, this man is a judge in Israel. He does have the power to make binding decisions, and whether he deserves it or not, he is someone who commands respect in society.

The judge is unlike the widow Jesus tells us about. She is at the opposite end of the social ladder. Where he is someone with position and privilege in society, she is one who is among the most vulnerable, someone left to fend for herself. Where the judge feels no need to uphold God's will, the widow comes time and time again to remind him of God's commands to protect the vulnerable, to protect the widows, the orphans and the outsiders. The fact that she is bringing this case in person indicates how alone in the world this widow really is.

In that society when the husband died, his property would transfer either to his sons or to his brothers, which meant the widow would be left without any property or wealth – left to the care and mercy of others. There were provisions in the Law that required the inheritors to care for the widows, to ensure they would not be left destitute without a means for survival. But
    if the judge wasn't interested in enforcing the Law,
        if he wasn't interested in pursuing God's will
           and God's justice,
                if he wasn't interested in vindicating the widows,
then there was no higher court that would hear an appeal. The widows were simply left to fend for themselves.

Normally, women were not allowed to bring a dispute before a judge. That task would usually be taken up by the nearest male relative, but clearly this widow had no one else to speak on her behalf and so she was forced to plead her own case.

At this point it is clear an injustice is being perpetrated, but the question is, what does this have to do with prayer? Luke introduced this parable by telling us Jesus told it so we might always pray and never give up. But so far we haven't heard anything about prayer.

We know the judge who doesn't fear God and doesn't care about people certainly isn't praying, and all we know about the widow is that she continues to come before the judge asking that she be justified against her adversary. In fact, she is so persistent, so aggressive she affects a change in the mind of the unjust judge. He says, "...because this widow keeps bothering me, I will see she gets justice, so she won't eventually wear me out with her coming!"

That may not sound all that impressive to us, but in the Greek it literally says the judge is worried that the widow is going strike him under the eye ... give him a black eye so to speak. So in order to keep this aggressively persistent widow off his back he is going to give in to her demands. He is going to give her justice. It's not until Jesus speaks that we begin to understand that this story is in some ways symbolic of how we are to take our pleas, our requests, before God in prayer.

Almost without exception, whenever I have heard someone talk about this passage they turn to the widow and say, see, we need to be like her, we need to be persistent like she was, even aggressively persistent in our prayer life. But stop for a minute and notice who it is that Jesus talks about.

Jesus does not say, "Look at the widow and how she got exactly what she wanted." It is the unjust judge that Jesus points to. Jesus says, "Listen to what the unjust judge says." And what was it that the unjust judge had said? Was it, "I will give her whatever she wants – I will give her whatever she asks for'? No, the unjust judge says, "I will see that she gets justice. I will see that she is treated in accordance with the commands and decrees of God." Jesus points to the fact that even an unjust judge motivated entirely by self interest is capable of making the right decision.

Surely now that Jesus has made his point about the unjust judge he will turn to the widow and congratulate her for her perseverance. But again the answer is no. Jesus points to God, the real Judge, the ultimate Judge. He says if it is possible for this unjust judge with all the wrong motivation to arrive at a just and righteous verdict, how much more certain is it that God, the one who is in his very being justice and righteousness, will arrive at the just and righteous verdict. How much more certain is it that God will grant justice to his chosen ones?

Jesus never congratulates the widow for her perseverance; he never says they are supposed to act like the widow. Instead, Jesus turns to his disciples and says to them, you are the widow. You, God's chosen ones, followers of Jesus, you are the widow. The disciples will be the vulnerable ones crying out in the midst of an unjust world.

That may be a bit hard for us to understand. How are we like the widow? Most of us have friends and family who care for us. Most of us have enough wealth and material possessions to care for ourselves. The first disciples were likely thinking along the same lines. We have homes. We have families. How can we possibly be vulnerable like a widow?

Sure, Jesus says, you are full of faith now, ready and willing to be disciples, ready to follow wherever I lead, but what you do not know is that you are not following me up to the palace in Jerusalem, but to the cross. There his followers will be widowed – the bridegroom will be taken from them.

In the crisis that follows, when it appears as if all hope has died with Jesus on the cross, will they remember who God is? Will they remember what Jesus has been teaching, preaching, revealing with signs and wonders? Will they fall into their old habits and routines? Will they forget the kingdom?

As many of you are no doubt aware, every age seems to have its moments of crisis –

moments which seem to drain the hope out of us,
moments that challenge our faith as followers,
moments that leave us feeling very vulnerable and alone.

And not only in the large scale events that forever altered the lives of people who lived through them, but even in our own lives, any number of other personal crises – perhaps a failed marriage, a serious illness, a battle with substance abuse – also have life altering consequences.

In times like these when all the promises of God seem to fade into the background, when it appears as if God has abandoned us, the question we are left with is will our faith endure?

In this parable Jesus tells us the answer to that question depends on who it is we have faith in, who it is we are praying to. If we think God is like the unjust judge – that he is arbitrary, that he only listens now and then when he feels like it or when he isn't too busy, if we think God grants justice because he is tired of hearing us whine and complain, or worse, that he is something like a slot machine producing a jackpot if we persevere and pull the handle enough times – if that is who we are praying to, chances are our faith is not going to hold up when we are confronted with a crisis.

I started this sermon with the story of my earliest experience of prayer, of how I received an answer after spending eight months praying for what I wanted, but what I didn't tell you was that after my prayer was answered, after I had received what I wanted, I didn't pray again for about five years.

Why? Because, basically, I saw God as someone who could pull a few strings for me, someone who had it in his power to give me what I wanted. After I got what I wanted there wasn't really any reason to keep on praying. That is, until about five years later when gripped by despair and feeling as if the world was falling in on me, I turned to God again, this time not even knowing what to pray for.

All I could muster were the words, "God help me". The answer came immediately and clearly, "Don't be afraid, I'm right here with you" – words that transformed my despair into peace in an instant. And for the first time I knew who God was: compassionate and gracious, slow to anger, abounding in steadfast love, truth and faithfulness, offering his love, and forgiving wickedness, rebellion and sin. *(Exodus 34:6-7)*

When we are confronted by crises in our lives, in our cities, or in our world, when it seems to us that we have been abandoned and left to fend for ourselves, we need to look back on the definitive moment of crisis within the faith and ask ourselves what we see when we look at the cross. Do we see death, the end of hope? Or do we see the end of death that gives us hope?

If we believe God is the ultimate judge, that his justice rules supreme, then we, like the widow, will never be content or comfortable with the injustice of the world. We will never be willing to settle for any vision of reality that discounts, diminishes or falls short of God's kingdom. We will constantly be coming before our judge crying out for justice.

That is, after all, why Jesus taught us to pray. Not that we might have everything we want, but that God's kingdom would come, that his will would be done on earth as it is in heaven.

If we will remain firmly fixed, and focused on who God is, on his steadfast love, justice, and compassion revealed in Jesus Christ, if our prayer is constantly that God's will be done, then we will find

        our weakness transformed into strength,
            our grief transformed into joy,
                our despair transformed into hope,
despite any trial or crisis we may face.

    And finally, when the Son of Man comes, he will not find the church endlessly praying for what we do not have or for what we wish we had. Instead, the Son of Man will find the church praying day and night because we have faith –
    faith in him who vindicated Jesus,
    who raised him from the dead,
        faith in him who sent his Holy Spirit to equip and
        empower us, and
            faith that he will bring to fulfillment all
            he has promised.

    So it is wholeheartedly that we pray, "Come, Lord Jesus, come."

    Amen and amen.

Seeing Through the Crowd

October 24, 2004

Luke 19:1-10

Imagine hearing about a nearby preacher – one who was proclaiming a message with such authority that people were coming from all over the countryside to see him in person and hear what he had to say. Some came hoping to hear an uplifting message, others looking for a sign from God or an answer to prayer. Imagine what a shock it would have been for those who had traveled to see this preacher when the first words out of his mouth were, "You brood of vipers!"

Many had heard that John was proclaiming a baptism of repentance for the forgiveness of sins ... that he was calling out in the wilderness, "Prepare the way of the Lord, make straight paths for him." *(Luke 3:4)* They had also heard he was proclaiming that all humankind would see the salvation of God. *(Luke 3:6)* Perhaps it was that which drew the crowds down to the Jordan River from the surrounding areas including the city of Jericho.

It must have been somewhat unsettling for the crowds who had come to hear about the salvation of God, instead to hear John accuse them of trying to flee the coming wrath of God. But he certainly caught their attention. Those who came looking for inspiration or perhaps simply for entertainment were suddenly concerned for their own well being. "What should we do then?" they cried out. John was quick to respond, saying those who have two tunics should share with those who have none and the same

281

goes for food – those who have more than enough should share half of what they have with those who have none.

Well now, that might be fine for farmers and craftsmen, but what about those who made a living off the tolls and taxes of all the trade that flowed through Jericho? It was a city known for its export trade; it was the gateway out of Israel, the doorway for all exports moving inland, so it was also a city that had more than its fair share of tax collectors. They, too, have a pressing question for John: "What about us tax collectors? What should we do?"

Most people believed tax collectors were among those guaranteed to face the wrath of God. It's fine to talk about repentance and the fruits of repentance, but the tax collectors want to know if there is any hope for them. Is there any chance they could experience God's salvation? Much to everyone's surprise, John does not tell them to find a new line of work. Instead, he proclaims that salvation is possible for tax collectors also, but they must not collect more tax than had been ordered by the chief tax collector.

Just imagine what that day must have been like for Zacchaeus, the chief tax collector of Jericho, having some of his tax collectors return from the Jordan saying there was hope for them, that they had been baptized by John, and from now on they were going to collect only the appointed tax and no more.

Imagine what must have been going through the mind of Zacchaeus when he heard these claims. Could it be true? Was there hope for tax collectors, hope for people like him? Certainly no one else in Jericho seemed to think so. He would have been despised by the people. They would have seen him as someone who had betrayed his own countrymen for profit. He would have been looked down upon not only because he was short, but because he was a sinner, someone beyond the reach of God's salvation.

Whatever hope he may have had in John's message likely began to fade away when John was imprisoned by Herod and later beheaded. It must have seemed like all hope for redemption had died with John. Then again, there had been a lot of talk about this Jesus fellow. Some were saying he was John raised from the dead, *(Luke 9:7)* and others thought he might even be the Messiah. Last Zacchaeus had heard, Jesus was coming this way, passing through Jericho on his way up to Jerusalem. If he could just see Jesus maybe there would be something that would stand out, maybe there would still be a reason to hope, if he could just see him. The problem is, when Jesus arrives in town, the crowd around him prevents Zacchaeus from seeing him.

But the question here is, what does this have to do with us?

So often when we come to the story of Zacchaeus we hear about how he wants to see Jesus – we hear about how short he is, about how he is not able to see Jesus, and we assume that in some way we are supposed to fill the shoes of Zacchaeus, that we are supposed to see his experience as somehow related to our faith in Jesus. But the reality is, most of us have very little in common with Zacchaeus. Most of us are not extremely wealthy thanks to shady or downright illegal business practices. So we tend to spiritualize the story.

We assume the story is about all those times when we have felt as if Jesus is not near us, or times when some obstacle seemed to stand between us and our Saviour. Then we hear about how Zacchaeus risks humiliating himself by running and climbing the nearest tree so he can overcome this obstacle, only to learn Jesus was seeking him the whole time. In the end, we say this story is simply meant to point to the fact that God's grace in Jesus continues to seek us out even when obstacles present themselves.

Now it's not that I think this is a bad or a wrong conclusion to draw, but doesn't it seem strange to you that we, the people who come here week after week claiming to be disciples of Jesus, do not associate ourselves with the disciples in this story? Don't you find it strange that we choose instead to associate ourselves with the one who has amassed a great deal of wealth by dishonest means? With one who doesn't know Jesus?

To be fair, it's not all that easy to single out the disciples in this story. They are not mentioned specifically as a separate group, but it's not as if they took the day off either. The disciples are there, mixed in with the crowd that's around Jesus following him through Jericho. Probably one of the reasons we tend not to associate with them is because the disciples are a part of the crowd that is preventing Zacchaeus from seeing Jesus.

At this point it's easy for us to defend the crowd. After all, if Zacchaeus was so short that he couldn't see Jesus, then maybe the disciples simply couldn't see him either and thus weren't aware he was trying to see Jesus. But one of the things that stands out when we read the story in Greek is there is the sense that the crowd is not simply neutral – that they are not simply unaware that Zacchaeus is trying to see Jesus. In fact, it suggests the crowd is willfully preventing him from seeing Jesus.

That may sound a little strange to us, even if he was a tax collector. Why would anyone want to prevent him from seeing Jesus?

The thing we need to keep in mind is that in Jesus' day someone who had a fair amount of honour, someone who had a good reputation, or position in society, would have been shown respect in the way people acted around them. When they walked down the street, people would have stood to one side to show their respect. Had it been any other wealthy ruler who approached Jesus, the crowd would have made room for him. It was simply the socially acceptable thing to do – but not for one wealthy ruler in particular, not for a ruler of tax collectors. People would have taken every opportunity they could get to show their disrespect to him.

And the disciples would not have been any different in this regard. We might expect that after the parable Jesus told about the tax collector and the Pharisee the disciples would have had a different disposition toward tax collectors, but in reality it will take a great deal more than one parable to change the attitudes that have been reinforced over the course of their lifetime.

You see, the disciples, like anyone else, would have known tax collectors in their own home towns. They would have known what it was like to be a neighbour to someone like Zacchaeus, watching
> as his house became more lavishly decorated,
>> as the number of his servants increased,
>>> as his clothes became finer and his
>>> food richer.

And the worst part of all was that everyone knew it was their money paying for it – money that rightfully belonged to them, money that Zacchaeus had no right to. Despite everyone knowing it was dishonest wealth, there was nothing anyone could do about it.

It was simply the way the taxation system worked. Zacchaeus may have been rich, may have had fine clothes, but that didn't mean the people had to treat him with respect. If he wanted to see Jesus, he could go humiliate himself by running on ahead and climbing a tree. After all, he didn't deserve any better.

Now just imagine what the crowd must have been thinking as they were approaching the tree where Zacchaeus was perched. Imagine what they were expecting Jesus to say to him. You can bet they remember what Jesus had said to the last rich ruler that had come to him asking what he needed to do to inherit eternal life. Jesus had responded by telling him to sell everything he owned and to give the money to the poor, then come and follow him, and by saying it is easier for a camel to go through the eye of a needle than for a rich man to enter the kingdom of God. How much harder was Jesus going to be on this man, who was not only a rich ruler, but the bulk of his wealth was essentially stolen?

Imagine the shock of the disciples who are awaiting the booming judgment of the Lord, as they hear Jesus say, "Zacchaeus, come down immediately. I must stay at your house today." Not only is there no judgment, but Jesus says he **must** stay with him. It's not a matter of choice or even a matter of desire, it is a divine necessity that Jesus stay with Zacchaeus. It is nothing short of the will of God that Jesus be a guest in the home of this man that everyone considers to be a thief!

Understandably, the people respond with murmurs, grumblings and complaints. How could this one who holds himself out to be the messiah not only defile himself by eating and staying with a chief tax collector, but how could he possibly suggest he was a representative of God's justice?

Would we consider someone to be on the side of God's justice if they sided with a known criminal rather than with the victims? Not likely. We, along with the crowd, along with all of the disciples, murmur and complain that Jesus has sided with sinners – not simply the sinners who have tried to live according to God's commands and have fallen short, but with those sinners who reject outright the commands of God. After all, if they had any regard for God's will and God's commands then they wouldn't be criminals in the first place.

But just as quickly as the complaints arise, so does the response from Zacchaeus. "Look, Lord!" he says, "Here and now I give half my possessions to the poor, and if I have cheated anybody out of anything, I will pay back four times the amount." In public, Zacchaeus makes a promise to give half of his possessions – exactly what John the Baptist had said was required as fruits of repentance – in addition to repaying anyone four times the amount that he had cheated them. Certainly an amount that would satisfy the strictest application of the Law even by the standards of the Pharisees.

The crowd, the disciples of Jesus, are confronted with the immediate and extravagant repentance of Zacchaeus which is much more than a simple change of heart. His repentance has substance. It involves restoration and making amends. The crowd is left with the problem that if Jesus had acted the way they wanted him to, then the victims would have remained victims, the tax collectors would remain numbered among the lost with no hope of being found, and the poor would have been denied the support of half of Zacchaeus' possessions.

Likely the most stunning part for the disciples is that Zacchaues should not have responded as he did. We all know what to expect from thieves – when you offer them something for free they are going to take it run; they are going to take advantage wherever they can. But Jesus seems to be able to see through the layers of greed and deception to something deeper.

He'd met enough tax collectors to know exactly what life was like for them, and how, even though they couldn't seem to resist the chance to take more for themselves than they should, it was a sickness of the heart for which he had the cure.

Somehow the crowd, and we along with them, fail to see what Jesus sees. Extending God's grace always seems to us like something that should be reserved for those who deserve it, for those who have not turned their back on God but who are trying to live according to God's will.

Extending God's grace to those who have turned away from God always seems to us to be throwing the good in with the bad. It seems contrary to good common sense and human nature, but what we find in the story of Zacchaeus is precisely the opposite.

When God's grace is extended without condition, particularly when it is extended to those whom the rest of the world has written off as lost causes fully worthy of condemnation, it ignites a need to repent and a desire to conform to the will of God.

That's not to say that when Jesus extends grace in this way it guarantees a response like the one we see in Zacchaeus. Rather, if grace is never extended in this way, then we can guarantee we will never see a response like we see in Zacchaeus.

Ultimately the story of Zacchaeus is a reminder for those of us who crowd around Jesus, that he is on a mission, a mission that extends far beyond our small definition of grace.

At the beginning of the story of Zacchaeus we were told Jesus was passing through on his way to Jerusalem. We know what to expect there. The Prophets have spoken of the fate that awaits the son of man, but we also know his mission is not simply to suffer and die, but rather through that fate, through his death, he rescues all the lost sheep. Soon the charge we heard from the crowd in Jericho that Jesus has gone in to be the guest of a sinner will change in Jerusalem to the charge that He has gone out to die with criminals. And the same mission, the same motivation, stands behind both actions. Jesus the Son of Man has come to seek and save the lost.

So the question remains for us – for those who crowd around Jesus and claim to be followers of Jesus –
- Will we remember the voice of the one crying the wilderness?
- Will we prepare the way of the Lord?
- Will we make straight paths for him?
- Will we be agents of his grace reaching out to the lost, or will we be obstacles pushing them further away?

Will we follow in his way or will we get in his way?

If we will be agents of God's grace, then we will see our Lord Jesus raise up children, raise up heirs for Abraham, and if we will share in his mission of seeking out the lost, we will see the salvation of God.

Amen and amen.

Honest to God

October 31, 2004

Luke 18:9-14

You saw for yourself in the children's time this morning just how obvious the point of Jesus' parable is. The appropriate way to approach God in prayer is with humility rather than pride, with self-examination rather than self-promotion. It was obvious to the children and it was obvious to all of us, so that leaves us with the question, if the point is so clear – if it is so self-evident – then why is Jesus even talking about it? Why teach something that everyone already knows? Why tell a parable when common sense seems to make the same point?

Perhaps there is more going on in this parable than a simple lesson in humility.

Two men are on their way to the temple to pray, Jesus tells us. One is a tax collector, the other is a Pharisee. Now, as we have been following the Gospel of Luke we have heard that Jesus is the friend of the outcasts, a friend to tax collectors and sinners. We have also seen several instances where Jesus has taken the Pharisees to task for their behavior, challenged them on the way they act and the way they treat other people. So as soon as we hear Jesus telling a story about a tax collector and a Pharisee we know who we should be cheering for. In fact, as Jesus tells this story, we may even begin to put ourselves in the shoes of the tax collector. After all, we come here to worship because we believe we have been befriended by Jesus, right?

So, in many respects when we hear Jesus tell the story of self-righteous Pharisee praying and giving thanks for the fact that he is such a good person, in our minds we may begin to imagine the times when something similar happened to us – times when we have had run-ins with people convinced of their moral, financial, or spiritual superiority. When we look at the broken tax collector crying out to God, we tend to see in him our own reflection, but who is this tax collector anyway? Jesus never really gave us any history on this individual. Maybe we should do a bit of a background check before we so willingly throw in our lot with him.

People didn't go school to learn how to be a tax collector. The way you became a tax collector was by bidding on how much tax you were going to collect. The ones who were awarded the job of collecting the tax were those who had promised to collect the highest amount from their fellow citizens. However, even the amount they bid was not the full amount of the tax that would be demanded. After all, the tax collectors had to make a living, and they usually made a very good living. Tax collectors were normally dishonest and betrayers of their fellow citizens.

Just imagine being audited by Revenue Canada and discovering that the Auditor assigned to go over your tax return didn't get paid unless he got more taxes out of you. Imagine discovering that Revenue Canada didn't care whether or not auditors were dishonest. What kind of people do you think would apply for that kind of job? Would you apply for that job?

Of course not. We aren't liars. We aren't thieves. Compared to most other people we are good people.... Wait a minute! Whose side are we supposed to be on again? Who are we supposed to look like in this parable?

If these two men were to show up in most churches it would be the Pharisee who would be given a hero's welcome. Just imagine a well connected, rich, self-employed business man who knew the scriptures inside and out, who gave ten percent of his income to the church, and offered his time on nearly every project the church engaged in. I mean, sure, he might be a little judgmental. He tends to let other people know that they are not living up to their duty as disciples, and he is also quite willing to stop talking to people who he thinks are living inappropriately; but overall he's not so bad.

But that other guy, the one who only shows up when we are celebrating the Lord's supper, and usually late, the one whom everyone knows is running a string of 'grow-ops', but who seems always to be able to evade the justice system? Who would we rather associate ourselves with?

We are far more likely to be comfortable with the Pharisee's faults than with the tax collector's. We would rather be good. We would rather be respected. We would rather be honourable. But in the end it is not the Pharisee who is justified by God, it is the tax collector. The question is why?

Earlier, when the parable seemed to be so clear and straightforward, we would have argued that the tax collector was justified because his prayer was not self-righteous like the Pharisee's; that his prayer was humble. Yet that leaves us with something of problem. In this case God has justified the one whom everyone would have considered to be bad, while at the same time, the one whom everyone would have seen as good goes home unjustified. Is Jesus trying to tell us that our actions do not matter as much as our prayers? No, of course not.

What we need to keep in mind is that for us the word 'justification' is religious language. Many of us have grown up hearing the phrase *'justified by grace through faith'* as an article of faith, a dogma to be memorized. For the people who were first hearing this parable, however, the word *'justified'* was not primarily religious language; it was legal language.

When two parties came before a judge, the one who received the favourable decision was justified, and, as we saw last week with the parable of the unjust judge and the persistent widow, Jesus presents prayer as bringing our petitions before the ultimate Judge, God. So when we see these two people, the tax collector and the Pharisee, come into the courts of the temple and begin to pray, we are in some respects meant to think of them in terms of petitioners before a judge ... and their petitions are in no way complimentary to one another.

The Pharisee holds himself to be superior in every way to the tax collector. In every way the Pharisee points to his actions and says he is deserving of God's favourable rule. Meanwhile, the tax collector can only point to his actions and say to God, "Have mercy on me – make atonement for me – a sinner." Only one of these two men can be justified. The judge cannot rule in favour of the Pharisee who is petitioning against the sins of the tax collector and rule in favour of the tax collector who is petitioning God to have his sins forgiven. If God were to do that, he would be an unjust judge. So the question is, how will God arrive at his decision?

Imagine that you were a judge trying a case between two people. How would you decide who to justify? Would you rule in favour of the nice one and against the mean one? Would you rule in favour of the clean one and against the dirty one? Perhaps the place to start is by remembering what it is that witnesses are asked before they offer testimony – something like, "I swear to tell the truth, the whole truth, and nothing but the truth, so help me God."

Wouldn't we decide in favour of the witness, the petitioner who is telling the truth? Wouldn't God justify the petitioner who is telling the truth?

Let's take another look at who it is who is being honest before God. The Pharisee is standing in the temple away from the crowd of common people because as a strictly observant Jew he knows that one of the commoners might be ritually unclean, and if they so much as brush against his clothing it will mean he will have to ritually purify himself. What's worse is that he sees in the temple with him someone whom he knows to be unclean, a tax collector – a swindler and thief, someone who he thinks deserves no place in the temple. So the Pharisee prays, most likely aloud, in order to instruct the people around him about what it means to be righteous, as well as to point out the fact that he himself is so righteous that he is doing even more than what the scriptures demand.

Keep in mind what is happening in the temple while he is making this prayer. Twice a day the priest made sin offerings to atone for the sin of the people. Clearly that is why the tax collector is there. While the sin offering is burning and the smoke is rising up to God, the Pharisee stands in the temple congratulating himself for being better than the rest of the God's people. He can look around the temple filled with God's people and give thanks that he is better than the rest. Nothing in his prayer indicates he thinks he needs the sin offering. He has deceived himself; he's offering false witness.

At the same time, the tax collector comes before God, eyes downcast and beating his chest. The accepted posture for prayer was to cross your hands over your chest and keep your eyes looking down, but the tax collector's arms do not remain motionless. He beats on his chest.

It is a dramatic gesture that is still used in many Middle Eastern villages to express extreme anguish or intense anger, and normally is used only by women. For a man to behave in this manner would not have been an act or some kind of ceremonial ritual. It would have been a genuine gesture of extreme sorrow – the recognition of the truth that out of the heart come evil thoughts, false witness, slander.

While the priests in the temple offer the sin offering, the tax collector beats his chest, pounding on his heart as if to say, "Put within me a new and clean heart," and he prays, "God have mercy upon me," or, more accurately, "God, make atonement for me, a sinner." (It's worth noting the only other time we are told of people beating their chests in the whole of the bible, is on Golgotha following the crucifixion of Jesus.) It is the tax collector who has offered an honest witness before God; he will go home justified.

The idea that our prayers are seen to be petitions before a judge may not sit all that well with us. The last thing we want is to be judged on our prayers, but the issue Jesus is driving at with this parable is not that we will be judged on the quality of our prayer. Rather, what will be judged is the quality of our witness. Can we be honest witnesses, particularly when it comes to what it means to be righteous? Often when we use a word like *righteous* it sounds like some kind of religious lingo, but it simply points to
    what is good,
        what is fair,
            what is just,
                what is right in the eyes of God.

Clearly, for the Pharisee, righteousness can be measured in terms of how well you observe the Law. It can be measured in terms of how much willpower you exert. But we see in rather dramatic fashion where that leads us.

It leads us to a place where righteousness has nothing to do with the atoning work of God. Righteousness has nothing to do with God's desire that all should be reconciled to him. Instead of seeking out the lost in order that they may be reconciled to God, the Pharisee finds himself in the position of condemning a lost sheep who desperately wants to be found. In the end, self-righteousness, dishonesty and false witness drive us away from God, and God's intention is to seek out the lost and draw them back into his salvation.

It is no coincidence that Jesus ends the parable with the same words he spoke to the Pharisees who were seeking the places of honour at the dinner banquet by using their own skill and resources to elevate their reputation in society. Here Jesus, in a much broader sense, indicates these same tactics are being employed to win God's favour, and he rejects them, saying that righteousness – being reconciled; being made right with God – is always and only a gift of God. It is God alone who makes righteousness possible through the atoning sacrifice, first in the temple and finally on the cross.

The only way to receive this gift is through the honest recognition that we have not and cannot make ourselves right in God's eyes. Righteousness is not a function of our will, but the effect of God's grace upon our lives. The tax collector, broken, humble, and repentant, comes before God honestly crying out for atonement, crying out to be made right, and goes home justified. The Pharisee also goes home, but he is not justified.

Jesus wants us to stop and think. How will we go home? Will we go the way of the Pharisee, deceiving ourselves
    about our spiritual superiority,
        about our place of honour in the presence of God,
            about how little need we have for God's grace,
                about how little need we have for the atoning act of Jesus?

Do we come before God clothed in self-righteousness, with hearts wrapped in layer upon layer of self-justification, or will we go a different way? Will we go the way of the honest witness, pounding upon our hardened hearts, crying out for a new and clean heart? Will we go
    searching for God's atonement,
        searching for the cross,
            searching for Jesus?

One of the most difficult parts of this parable to come to terms with may well be the fact that we never learn what becomes of these two people. What was the effect of grace upon the life of the tax collector? Did he really repent? Did he give up his job as tax collector? Did he follow Jesus? Did he go on to be a strong member of the church?

Or on the other hand, what about the Pharisee? What happened to him and his self-righteous attitude? Did he learn that the search for the faults and failures of others does the greatest harm of all to the critic himself? Did he continue to tear up the fabric of his own spirituality?

Well, if we really want to know, all we have to do when we get home today is look in the mirror and take a close look at who is looking back.

And may God grant eyes to see.

Amen.

Remember the Way

November 7, 2004

Luke 6:20-31

Remembering is not always easy. Often the most memorable times in our lives are moments that are also the most painful. Particularly as we approach Remembrance Day, we remember the impact that the two world wars as well as the Korean wars have had upon the lives of those who lived through and died in them.

Yet even those of us who have never known firsthand the terrors of war know that remembering carries with it a cost. We remember our tragedies, the loss of loved ones, particularly in times of great suffering. And even in the church, the heart of our faith, the heart of our identity flows out of remembering one dark day – Good Friday, the day the Son of man was betrayed and killed by those whom he came to save.

Remembering is not always easy because it is not simply an exercise of the brain ... not just bringing to mind something that happened a long time ago. In many respects remembering involves re-living the experience. As Remembrance Day draws nearer I suspect the dreams of Veterans are growing clearer. The faces of friends and perhaps even enemies long gone suddenly seem close enough to touch. The memories flood back, both the good and the bad times, yet in the end even the good is outweighed and overruled by the fact that all they have left of their friends is their memories.

So we might be tempted to think if remembering brings with it such discomfort, then perhaps we would be better off forgetting, but we know when we forget, we lose something, not only the memories of our loved ones and comrades, but also hope–
hope for a time and place when things that separate us from them will be removed,
hope for a time when wrongs will be made right.

If we forget the pain of good Friday, we lose the joy of Resurrection Sunday. If we forget the horror of war, we lose our hope for peace. If we forget the tragedy of death, we lose our hope for life.

The problem for us is that we are charged with living faithfully in between our memory and our hope. If spend too much time on the memory side of the equation, we find ourselves living in the past – seeking, but never finding those elusive good old days. Yet if we spend too much time living on the hope side of the equation, we find ourselves constantly living for tomorrow, casting aside the old in favour of those things claiming to be new and improved. As Christians we are called to live between the memory of the promises of God and their fulfillment, but what will that look like?

In many respects Jesus addresses that question in our Gospel lesson this morning. We find Jesus preaching a sermon to his disciples, to people like you and me, on the life filled with blessings versus the life filled with woes. But when we hear Jesus preaching about the blessed life it doesn't really come across like anything we might consider to be a blessed life. Instead it appears to be the exact opposite of what we expect blessings to look like.

Jesus says to his disciples, *"Blessed are you who are poor; Blessed are you who are hungry now; blessed are you who weep now; blessed are you when you are excluded, insulted, and rejected because of the Son of Man."* If we were to go out in the streets and ask anyone we met what the recipe for happiness is, I suspect the answer we would hear would be, "Why, prosperity, comfort, peace of mind, and popularity, of course. That's the recipe for happiness, the recipe for a blessed life."

> After all, they say, the poor are those people
> who didn't plan their lives properly,
> who did not get the proper education,
> who do not have a good work ethic.

The poor are the ones they use as an object lesson for our children, pointing to them and saying, "You see, if you don't work hard and get a good education you'll wind up just like one of them." And the same goes for the hungry. If you don't have food, it's because you don't have money. It's because you are poor that you have no food.

Weeping may be a little bit of a different story. After all, we all experience moments of heartache and sorrow, but the blessed ones are those who can get through it without weeping – those who are strong enough, who can keep their emotions in check. Weeping looks too much like weakness and if there is one thing we cannot show it is weakness. Even before we get to the part about the blessedness of being excluded, insulted, and rejected, it's quite clear that according to the wisdom of our world, Jesus' sermon does not make a great deal of sense. His words don't seem to line up very well with what we know of '*the real world*'.

The question is, what do we do with these 'un-real' blessings? Well, for the most part we tend to idealize them. We think Jesus is using hyperbole – that he is exaggerating, setting up an unattainable goal so that by shooting for the stars we might land on the moon. We think he knows we'll accomplish far more than we think is possible by chasing after an impossible goal. Any of you who have tried that tactic yourselves know it isn't all that effective. Those of you who are parents know if you set standards that your children cannot attain they may achieve more in the short run, but in the long run they are far more likely to see themselves as failures.

So do we really think Jesus is setting us up? Is he setting up the Children of God for failure? It might appear that way when we hear Jesus describing the woeful life:
woe to you who are rich;
> woe to you who are well fed;
>> woe to you who laugh; and
>>> woe to you when people speak well of you.

To some it may appear Jesus is saying it is only by becoming failures that we are able to receive the blessings of God, but that misses the thrust of what Jesus is getting at.

Jesus pronounces his blessing on those who have failed to find their satisfaction in the worldly goals of fame, fortune, and self sufficiency. He is not suggesting that everyone who suffers misfortune is somehow automatically living the blessed life. He is not suggesting poverty, hunger, grief, and public resentment are somehow the keys that unlock the door to eternal blessing. If we want to understand what Jesus is getting at here, imagine a huge banquet filled with every kind of food imaginable. Who do you suppose will appreciate the banquet more – the one who is hungry or the one who is well fed?

Jesus has come proclaiming that the kingdom of God is breaking into the world and the ones who are most likely to recognize the blessing of this announcement are those who have the greatest need, the greatest longing for its inexhaustible riches.

On the other hand, those who have been sidetracked and distracted by the false promises and comforts of the world around them will be the ones who are least likely to recognize this blessing of the Kingdom. What Jesus wants for his disciples, what Jesus wants for us, is an emptiness that only God can fill – a discontent with the ways of the world that will leave us hungry and searching for the wealth, the satisfaction, the consolation, and the fellowship of the Kingdom of God. In its most basic terms, Jesus is calling his disciples to remember the ways of the world are not God's ways. But more than that, Jesus is calling his disciples to present themselves as a living reminder to the way of God despite the fact the world around them stands in opposition to God.

Living according to God's way in a world that is opposed to God and his reign means, as Jesus disciples, we also will face opposition and so it no surprise at this point to find Jesus turning to address the issue of how we are to live amidst conflict – how we are meant to live in the midst of our enemies.

"Love your enemies," Jesus tells us, but not in the sense of passionate devotion or warm affection. We are not called to fall in love with our enemies or feel the same feelings toward them that we feel towards our family and friends. Jesus wants us to demonstrate a gracious, determined, and active interest in the true welfare of others, a welfare that will not fail in the face of hatred, cursing, or even abuse.

We often forget when Jesus spoke these words to his disciples, Israel was under the occupation of the military might of the Roman Empire. The call to love your enemy is difficult enough when we think of our enemies as those whom we don't get along with, but it is even more difficult to accept when we remember Jesus was calling the people who were regularly being provoked by their Roman overlords to respond with love – not simply to submit to the aggression of the enemy, but to rob the aggression of its sting by voluntarily going far beyond its demands.

Now here, even more so than with the blessings, we are likely to feel Jesus has simply gone too far – that he has finally taken a full step outside of the real world into a world of idealistic fantasy. Just imagine what would happen if you never stood up for yourself – if you constantly allowed people to beat you up without any kind of response. How much good would we be to God if we were beaten to a pulp? The same goes for giving to everyone who asks. If we did that, then we would soon be the ones who were begging for money.

Not only does it seem idealistic, but in a very genuine way it also seems to us to be somewhat immoral. If someone strikes us without any reason, shouldn't we seek justice? Shouldn't we seek to ensure the perpetrator of this evil deed is brought to justice, punished for their wrongdoing, or at least reprimanded? If we don't resist, are we not simply turning a blind eye to sin? Aren't we promoting evil? I think this is one of the few moments in the scriptures where we can get a sense of just how slippery and subtle that serpent in the Garden of Eden really was. In our zeal to do the right thing, in our noble intentions to seek justice and uphold the righteousness of God, we actually become a force for evil.

If any of you have seen the movie *The Untouchables* you will remember it is the story of an FBI agent named Elliot Ness who has been given the task of bringing the notorious Mafia boss, Al Capone, to justice. Ness teams up with a streetwise police officer who gives him the surefire strategy for bringing Capone down: "If Capone brings a knife to a fight, you bring a gun. If Capone puts one of your men in the hospital, you put one of his in the morgue." A surefire strategy for dealing with evil. If someone strikes you on the cheek you respond with a well placed kick. If someone takes your coat, you take it back along with their shirt so they won't make the same mistake twice.

How do we respond to evil? Quite clearly the wisdom of the world says you respond to evil with more evil. The irony is that those who retaliate believe they are vigorously resisting evil, when, in fact, they have made an unconditional surrender to evil. Where before there was one person whose actions were dictated by evil, now there are two.

And so we begin to see that evil spreads like a virus. It infects nearly everyone with whom it comes in contact. The only way evil can be contained, the only way evil can be defeated, is when hatred, insult, and injury are absorbed by love – when evil is consumed rather than being reflected back upon the perpetrator.

The Book of Revelation is filled with vivid images. One of the most exceptional of these is of the Beast. The one who is ravaging the earth and God's people is finally defeated not by an even bigger beast, but by none other than the slain lamb. The hideous and terrifying beast is ultimately and eternally defeated by the sacrificial love of God in Jesus Christ. In our passage, Jesus confronts us with the fact that the call to love our enemies is not idealism of the highest degree. It is, in fact, nothing short of the only real antidote for evil. Love is the only thing that can turn an enemy into a friend.

Our passage ends with one of the most well known sayings of Jesus: "Do to others as you would have them do to you." After everything that has come before, it may sound to us as something of a reprieve from the challenge that has preceded it, but what we need to keep in mind here is that Jesus is not simply calling us to treat others by our own standards.

Most of us have a rough and ready system of morality, based on common sense, measured self-interest. It may be some balance of give and take that gives us a degree of confidence that we are as good as our neighbours. But here Jesus is not pointing to our own way. He is urging his disciples to choose a higher standard than that. He is urging us to look beyond our sense of duty.

> Duty obeys rules, but love grasps opportunities.
> > Duty acts under constraint, but love
> > is spontaneous and gracious.
> > > Duty expects to be repaid, or at least
> > > recognized, but love expects nothing
> > > in return.

To love is to be children of God, not in some abstract sense, but in the most basic and foundational sense. When we love, we look like God. When we love, we bear God's image and likeness in the world.

The question that remains for us is, what is our vision of the blessed life? Do we follow our own way of blessing, satisfying and comforting ourselves however and wherever we are able? Or do we choose the higher standard? Will we remember the way of the Lord? Will we line ourselves up to follow in the footsteps of the saints who came before us – those who followed the way of Jesus, who loved the world when it would not love him back and remained faithful to God unto death, even death on a cross?

Indeed, faithfulness has a cost. Remembering and living the way of God will place us in situations where the world around takes offence, but through it all, the blessing of God in Jesus Christ will remain with us. Even though it may appear easier to forget than to remember the way, we will not forget, and neither will we lose our hope.

Amen.

Can You See It?

November 14, 2004

Isaiah 65:17-25

New – new heavens, new earth, new everything. We can be sure these words of the Prophet Isaiah take on a very different ring in our society than they would have when they were first spoken and written down. To us 'new' most often refers to new stuff, new cars, new houses, new toys, and most often 'new' means better. Most times the word 'new' in our world is found along side of the word 'improved.'

In recent years I have found it difficult to watch the retail industry gear up for the annual Christmas rush. I look at all the products on shelves and can't help but wonder how long it will be until all those things find their way into the landfill. Part of the problem is that things are just not built to last anymore. Products are built under the mindset of planned obsolescence – a philosophy that ensures future sales and future profits. But it is not the manufacturers alone who are responsible for this decreased emphasis on durability; it's also the buyers – those constantly hunting for the cutting edge, hunting for something newer or better than what they already have. It's an attitude present not only in merchandizing, but also in religion and spirituality.

Those things which at one time were foreign or perhaps even forbidden are now seen as the cutting edge of spirituality and are embraced by so called open minds looking for new paths to experience the "divine". At the same time there is a general disdain and contempt for what is seen as the outdated and obsolete institution of the church. Where once the church was an essential part of the fabric of our society, now it continues to be pushed more and more to the fringe. Where once it had enjoyed a place of honour and respect, now it's regularly treated with suspicion and skepticism ... sometimes with good cause, many times without.

The world around us continues to change faster and move in directions which are often difficult to cope with. So we might expect the words that would bring us the most comfort would be those offering us a sense of stability and safety. Instead the hopeful word we hear seems to be one of change; we hear a word of newness. It's not a newness that replaces the old, but a newness that fulfills the old. Perhaps one of the reasons why these words are hopeful for us is that our own sense of insecurity and instability in a complex and confusing world is, in some respects, a much milder form of the challenges that faced the people Israel when they were given this vision of hope.

You see, the people who originally found hope in this word from the Lord were not dwelling safe and secure in the Promised Land. They were living in exile in Babylon. Their faith was the object of scorn, mocked and scoffed at by their overlords. They were regularly taunted for having faith in their God. After all, if the God of the Jews was indeed the Lord of all, then why had he allowed Jerusalem to burn and why had he allowed his chosen people to be carried off as the spoils of war?

Beyond the ridicule the people faced, there were other significant challenges. For those of us who are used to the idea of being able to worship God anywhere, the problem of the exile seems to be primarily one of lost homes and lost possessions. We tend to think of the exile as primarily a geographic displacement, but for the Jews at this point in history, we need to remember the only appropriate place to worship was the temple in Jerusalem. The temple and it alone was the place where the presence of the Lord dwelled.

So being dislocated from Jerusalem meant the exiles experienced not simply a loss of land, homes and possessions, but also a loss of the things that gave meaning and structure to their lives. They were in very real danger of losing their identity. And that was precisely what the Babylonian rulers wanted. The way to get rid of your enemies was not simply to defeat them in battle, because that could ignite an even greater resistance. No, the point of the exile was to assimilate your enemies, to turn the Jews into Babylonians by taking away all the symbols and structures that stood at the centre of their identity, and surrounding them instead with the symbols and structures that were at the heart of Babylonian life and identity. The exile was intended and designed to be the end of the Jews' way of life and worship. So any talk of return, any talk of a restoration, would have seemed like pure foolishness ... nothing more than wishful thinking.

But what the Babylonians failed to realize was even though the temple in Jerusalem was the centre of Jewish religious life, it was not the defining symbol for the people Israel. What was at the heart of the identity of the Jews was not a building, or even a city, but a moment in history – a moment when God had delivered them from bondage in Egypt, a time when God acted to set the captives free and called them to be a covenant people, called them into the family of God.

The great irony of the exile is that while the Babylonians were systematically trying to tear down the identity of Israel, they were actually putting God's people back in the situation in which their identity was forged and founded. And rather than forgetting how to be Jewish, the people remembered who they were and whose they were. They remembered who their God was – the God of the exodus.

Then the prophecies of Isaiah began to make sense to them. God had sent them into exile to reform them, to call them back into covenant faithfulness. God had not abandoned them, but would be faithful to the covenant and lead them on a new exodus, a new journey into a renewed promised land where the former things –

their idolatry and rebellion, their failure to be faithful to the covenant – would be left behind and forgotten. The new exodus would begin with a clean slate.

The question is, is there really anything new in what God is promising here? If we look back at the book Deuteronomy we will find all of these promises – long life, dwelling in their land, living off the fruits of their labour – are all blessings Moses had indicated would flow from keeping God's commands. They are the blessings that flow from being faithful to the covenant.

So we are left with the fact that the description of new life in the new creation is focused not on something different, but primarily on the renewal of human faithfulness to the will of God. Where, before, the people had not lived according to the covenant – where they had grown rich at the expense of the most vulnerable in their midst, where they had been the cause of much pain and suffering not only to the people around them, but also to God – God promises to re-create Jerusalem to be a delight, and re-create the people to be a joy through the same power that created the covenant people out of a slave nation.

The defining characteristic of the new heavens and the new earth centres upon God's people finally becoming what God intended them to be – a source of joy for the rest of the world, a people that God the Father can look upon with delight and say, "Yes, those are my children."

It's at this point we gain some insight into why, at Jesus' baptism, the voice of the Father spoke saying, "This is my Son with whom I am well pleased." Not simply pointing to Jesus' divinity, but also pointing out that in Jesus we see what faithfulness looks like; we see what it means to live God's intention for us, what it means to be truly human.

Now let's return to the vision of the new heaven and the new earth. Even though what is being said here has been said before by Moses, what should stand out for us, and what would have most certainly stood out for the people hearing this vision, is that something rather big is missing from this picture of a new Jerusalem.

Nowhere is there any mention of a new temple in Jerusalem. Instead we are told that when the people call, God will answer them and before they are finished speaking, God will hear them. There will be nothing that stands between God and his people – no priests, no religious authorities. God will not be kept behind the curtain in the temple's holy of holies; instead he will dwell in the midst of the people.

But at this point we begin to see that with this description of the accessibility of God, the vision points even further back than the formation of the covenant at Mount Sinai. There the people were so afraid of the presence of God they demanded Moses intercede between them and God, that Moses keep them apart from God.

This vision of God being so near to his people that he answers before they call, points all the way back to the account of the Garden of Eden where no intermediary or obstacle stood between God and human beings. So here we begin to get the sense that this new creation, the new Jerusalem, is not simply limited to the restoration of those who have been sent into exile in Babylon, but in many respects the vision of the new Jerusalem points back to the intentions of God at the dawn of the creation, where humanity was meant to live in harmony with the natural world as well as to have dominion over the creatures of the earth.

We often understand the language of the wolf grazing with the sheep and the lion eating straw with the ox as an indication that the natural predator versus prey instinct is overcome by an instinct for peace and harmony. There is nothing wrong with seeing that here, but we often forget when we see wolves grazing with sheep, and the lion penned up with the ox, it's an indication that they are no longer wild. The wolves and lions are no longer creatures that threaten and kill human beings, but have instead become farm animals just like the sheep and the ox.

God's intent that humanity should rule all creatures that move along the ground is being fulfilled in this vision of the new creation. The question is, what are we to do with this vision of the new creation, especially since, by and large, we have lived in our homes and have long enjoyed the fruits of our own labour? We have not geographically dislocated and do not see Jerusalem as the only place where the presence of God dwells.

For the most part, the Christian response has been to suggest this is a vision of the age to come. After all, in the Revelation of John this passage in particular is used to point to the hope for the fulfillment of God's promises. John says:

> *"Then I saw a new heaven and a new earth, for the first heaven and the first earth had passed away, and there was no longer any sea. I saw the Holy City, the new Jerusalem, coming down out of heaven from God, prepared as a bride beautifully dressed for her husband. And I heard a loud voice from the throne saying, "Now the dwelling of God is with men, and he will live with them. They will be his people, and God himself will be with them and be their God. He will wipe every tear from their eyes. There will be no more death or mourning or crying or pain, for the old order of things has passed away.""* (Revelation 21:1-4)

Indeed, there is a very significant part of the vision of Isaiah that points to the hope for fulfillment of God's purposes at the dawning of the age to come, but there is also a potential problem in placing too much emphasis upon the future aspects of the vision. This is the problem Paul is addressing in our reading from his second letter to the Thessalonians.

As it turns out, some of the members of the church in Thessalonica were so convinced Jesus would bring his promises to fulfillment very soon they simply quit their jobs, kicked up their heels, and lived off the wealthier members of the church while they waited for the Christ to return. Paul wants to ensure members of the church do not use the future hope we have in Jesus as an excuse to live idle and disorderly lives – to get so caught up in the future that we forget the present.

Yet on the other hand there is also a potential for problems with spending too much time focusing on fulfilling God's promises in the present. Fulfilling God's promises can quickly become an exercise in fulfilling our own dreams, our own visions. As we see in Isaiah, no sooner has the vision of the new heaven and the new earth been given without a temple in the new Jerusalem, when God is forced to respond to those who cannot envision Jerusalem without a temple. The people who are meant to be a joy have instead chosen their own way, their own nationalistic dream. They get so caught up in the present that they cannot see the goal.

We are called to get caught up in God's vision. The word from the Lord begins with a call for his people to 'behold'; he calls them to look, to see what he is doing. So the question is, can we see it? Do we get caught up in his vision? Do we see God at work in our lives and in our world renewing us, recreating us to be the people we were intended to be?

Does this vision call us to action? Does it remind us we are meant to be a source of joy in a world filled with sadness, violence, and separation? Or do we think this vision calls us to sit back and wait for the new and improved version of the heaven and the earth? Is the vision that drives our lives the vision that God has called us to see – the vision that God has called us to participate in – or is it simply
  our own dreams,
    our own agenda,
      our own wishful thinking?

When we envision our heavenly Father commenting on our lives, is he saying, *"When I called, no one answered and when I spoke, no one listened,"* (Isaiah 66:4) or is he delighted in saying, *"These are my children with whom I am well pleased"*?

May God grant eyes to see and ears to hear.

Amen.

The Last Word

November 21, 2004

Luke 23:33-43

I am sure there are some here today who can remember the occasion of the coronation of Queen Elizabeth II. It was something of an historic moment not simply because a new monarch was being crowned, but because this was the first time a coronation ceremony had been shown on television. People from all over the world watched as she was crowned Queen. I have no memory of that day. It was well before my time, but I understand there was no shortage of pomp and ceremony – horse drawn carriages, regal robes, a full house at Westminster Abbey, and of course, the reception of royal jewels, crowns, scepters and a sphere. It was a ceremony fit for a queen.

In the church today we acknowledge something of a coronation. It's the last Sunday in the Christian year, Christ the King Sunday, the day we recognize the sovereignty of Jesus. So it may strike us as somewhat unusual that our Gospel lesson for today is taken from the account of Good Friday – from the day Jesus was crucified. Wouldn't it have been better to read of our Lord's resurrection and his ascension into heaven? To remember Jesus in all his glory? Good Friday and crucifixion just doesn't seem fit for a king.

In place of a lavish procession of carriages, Jesus carries his own cross. Instead of receiving the assent of archbishops, Jesus is mocked by the religious authorities. Instead of receiving the crown jewels, Jesus is given a crown of thorns. In place of the anointing oil, he is given a cup of the wine suitable only for the poorest of the poor. And instead of the throne his ancestors have sat upon for generations, he is enthroned upon the cross. In every respect we are confronted by the fact that Jesus is not what we expect a king to look like. The question is, what makes a king?

We heard in our reading from Jeremiah what it was that the people were expecting from the coming king – they were expecting one
> who would save them,
>> who would allow them to live in safety,
>>> who would reign wisely with justice and
>>> righteousness.

This new king would not simply be a descendant of David, but would rule like David, the most faithful king Israel had ever known. However, the people had a somewhat selective memory. They remembered David as a military genius who led the people in battle, conquering all their enemies. But they seem to have forgotten that in the beginning David did not exactly fit the mold of a king. He did not stand head and shoulders above all the other fighting men the way King Saul did. In fact, David was a small shepherd boy who had no skill with a sword, although he did know plenty about keeping his flock safe from harm ... about keeping his sheep out of reach of the vicious beasts in the world.

David had no royal blood, no pedigree, only his absolute faith in the Lord – faith enough to stand between Goliath and the people Israel with nothing more than a staff, a sling, and five smooth stones. He was confident enough in the Lord to proclaim that he was going to give Goliath's flesh to the birds of the air and the beasts of the field. Goliath was not only the biggest and the fiercest warrior the enemy had to offer, he was the very symbol of the apparently insurmountable power and strength of the enemy. We might expect the one to meet him in battle would be none other than the representative of the people of Israel, King Saul, but this not what happens.

Instead, we find David, a little shepherd boy – too small to fit into the king's armour, too small to wield the king's sword. This is the one who goes out to what must have seemed to many to be his certain death. Yet as it would turn out, David was more than adequately armed. It took only one smooth stone and an unwavering trust in God to take down Goliath. After having slain the enemy, David took the sword of Goliath – the weapon of the enemy – and cut off his head and took it to Jerusalem.

It might sound rather gruesome to us that the head of an enemy was used as a trophy, but it was much more than that. David took the head to show that the symbol of the enemy's power and strength had become instead a symbol of the Lord's victory, a symbol of the Lord's ability to overcome the worst enemy.

We are never told what happened to the head after that, but I suspect it wasn't simply thrown in the trash heap. I suspect it served as a monument – perhaps buried in a public place where everyone could remember what God had done; perhaps in the very place that was referred to in the time of Jesus as the *Place of the Skull*.

This is the place where we find Jesus in our Gospel reading, being crucified alongside two criminals. The worst instrument of torture the Roman Empire had in its arsenal, the cross, was being employed against the enemies of Rome. The Place of the Skull continued to be used as a place of remembering. Only now it is used to remind the people under occupation of just how far the iron fist of Rome stretches. This is the place where the general population is reminded of the cost of opposing the emperor. So as Jesus is being crucified, we might expect him
 to lash out at his executioners,
  to curse them for their failure to recognize him
  for who he was,
   to condemn them for opposing the will
   of God.

After all, he was not raising an army; he had no intention of starting an armed resistance. Instead of cursing and condemnation, what we hear from Jesus is a prayer: "Father, forgive them for they do not know what they are doing."

For us who have heard this prayer over and over, it simply seems that Jesus is acting according to his gracious nature. We know Jesus to be the one who offers us forgiveness, and here he seems to be asking the Father to forgive even those who have failed to see that he was the Messiah. But if we pause for a moment and consider what Jesus is saying, we are confronted with a problem. Jesus is not being crucified because of a misunderstanding or a miscommunication. It is no accident that has landed him on the cross.

All the people involved in his arrest and trial knew exactly what they were doing. The religious authorities had been actively seeking ways to have Jesus arrested for a crime that would result in his being crucified. Even though Pilate may have understood Jesus was not interested in leading a military revolt, he still believed it was better that Jesus should be crucified since keeping him around might be enough to ignite the swell of messianic expectations and create all kinds of trouble for him and his ability to keep the people under control.

You see, everyone – the religious authorities, the roman rulers and military, even the condemned criminal – all think they have the world pretty much figured out ... that they have a good grip on reality. Jesus is nothing more than a problem and an expendable one at that. The sooner they get rid of him the sooner things can get back to normal, back to the way they should be. Somehow their grasp of the real world and the way it works allows them to justify their plans to condemn and execute an innocent man.

In their attempt to eliminate Jesus, they succeed in showing their actions are out of line with God's reality, out of line with

God's righteousness and justice. When Jesus says they don't know what they are doing he is really saying that they do not know what God is doing. Not only that, but it seems everyone, even those who would normally not be caught dead claiming to have anything in common with one another, suddenly find themselves united in opposition to Jesus. The religious authorities and the Roman military hated one another and neither one of these groups would ever have chosen to associate themselves with a justly condemned criminal, yet all of these stand in solidarity, sneering, mocking, humiliating and insulting Jesus.

Just like King David, Jesus does not fit the mold of what anyone is expecting a king to look like. Notice what it is that all of these people want Jesus to do in order to prove he is the Messiah, the king of the Jews. "Save yourself if you're the Chosen One," sneer the Jewish rulers. "Save yourself," the military cohort calls out as they mock Jesus with wine fit for a slave. Amid the insults he is heaping upon Jesus, one of the criminals calls out, "Save yourself and us." The one thing all of them expect out of a king is
> someone who has the power to crush anyone who opposes him,
>> someone who can put down any threat to his rule,
>>> someone who has staying power.

After all, everyone knows how the real world works. The strong survive and the weak perish, and if Jesus cannot even take care of himself, how can he possibly take of his people? What kind of saviour could he possibly be?

At the Place of the Skull, the sign placed over the head of Jesus is intended to leave no doubt about the answer to that question. Jesus is no saviour at all, no king at all. His crucified body is intended to stand as a warning ... a deterrent to
> anyone who has visions of grandeur;
>> anyone who has hopes of leading a revolt or a rebellion;
>>> anyone who wants to challenge the rule of the emperor.

The cross was the most horrendous, and effective, means of maintaining Roman power and control. But keep in mind that being crucified did not come as a shock or a surprise to Jesus. He had told his disciples three times that this was precisely what awaited him in Jerusalem. Jesus knew he was on a collision course with the cross, that he was heading to do battle with enemies of God. But unlike the majority of Jews, Jesus did not see this battle as being waged against Rome.

No, Jesus had been sent to tackle a much larger enemy, an enemy of enormous proportions. The enemy – the Goliath Jesus set out to meet in battle – was none other than sin and death. And like David, Jesus would not go into battle armed with horses and chariots, clad in armour and wielding a mighty sword. Instead, he would be stripped naked and armed only with obedience – armed only with faithfulness to the will of the Father.

It's often at this point that we are eager to jump ahead a few days to Easter, to the moment of the resurrection, the moment of Jesus' vindication and victory over death. But that leaves us with the problem of what to do with the second criminal who was crucified with Jesus – the one
> who rebuked the first criminal,
> > who declared that Jesus had been unjustly executed, and
> > > who asked Jesus to remember him.

What are we to make of the fact that at this moment of humiliation, rejection, pain, and suffering, a confessed criminal sees Jesus for who he really is? Chiefly this: the worst kind of death that Rome had to offer – death on a cross – failed to do what the Romans intended it to do. Death failed to convince everyone that Jesus was not the king of the Jews, that he was not the Messiah. In the case of this criminal, death had no power.

Now this may seem like a small victory. One justly convicted criminal who will soon be dead sees Jesus for who he really is. But if a single criminal can look at Jesus crucified and see
> that death does not have the power to take away his kingdom,
>> that death cannot keep God from fulfilling his promises,
>>> that death has no power,

then how many more will see when Jesus is resurrected? How many more will see when the Spirit is poured out upon the church at Pentecost? How many more will see when they look at the church and see God's love in action.

On that Friday, at the Place of the Skull, Jesus took the symbol of the enemy's power and strength and transformed it into a symbol of his victory. For many people that will simply sound too much like a delusion. Just imagine standing by and listening in on the discussion of these crucified men – one dead man calling another dead man a king who then responds by promising him paradise. At the very minimum it should cause us to realize that calling Jesus Christ our king will set us at odds with much that the world calls 'reality'.

The world is continually telling Christians to 'be realistic'… to 'face facts'. All too often such expressions are little more than an invitation to settle into present arrangements, to accept the mold that Jesus shattered, to be content with the world as it is rather than to lean forward into the world as God intends it to be.

We have problems in our society with violence, with the plight of the poor, with sickness and with death, and it is quite easy to become discouraged, feeling there is nothing we can do.

But to believe Jesus Christ is our Sovereign Lord is to be convinced he has created the world and he is determined to reclaim his creation, and that is powerful motivation to work not simply for a better world, but for a world which is more nearly and more clearly his world.

In our daily skirmishes with evil, we can live with hope and confidence. We can act faithfully and live with courage. Although the battles may be tough, we already know who has won the war. We know the fullness of God dwelling in Jesus Christ upon the cross has had the final word, and it is
> a word of forgiveness,
>> a word of salvation,
>>> a word of victory.

This knowledge, the knowledge that we have been transferred to the kingdom of God's beloved Son, the knowledge that the powers of death and sin no longer hold us in their tight grip, enables us to live our lives with courage. The war has been won. Now it's time to live like it.

Amen and amen.

Resting Secure

November 28, 2004

Matthew 24:36-44

Some time ago there was a significant psychological experiment conducted. People were given a puzzle to solve. While they were solving the puzzle, loud, distracting music was piped into the area where they were working. Some of the subjects were put in rooms where they were given a control knob that allowed them to turn down the music if they wanted to. The others were forced to sit in rooms where there was no control knob.

It should come as no surprise to anyone the group that had volume control knobs did significantly better on the test than those with no way to turn down the music. But what may come as something of a surprise is the majority of those in the rooms that had control knobs *never used the knobs.* Just knowing they had some control, even if they did not choose to exercise it, was enough to keep them at the task – enough to enable them to do significantly better at completing the puzzle. It seems the psychologists have proven what we had already learned from the account of Adam and Eve in the Garden – as human beings we really want to be in control.

It would not be an exaggeration to say the modern world is very much concerned with *control.* Through science and technology, through our expanding knowledge of the way the world works, we have learned to control our environment; or at least it appears that way. We have population control, birth control, climate control. Many of us wouldn't know how to turn on a

television without a remote control. We have been so successful – we have learned to control so many aspects of our daily life and to control so much of the world around us – that we quite naturally tend to think,
    given enough time,
        given enough research,
            given enough effort,
we will eventually be in control of everything.

So when September 11th struck, and the security of the western world was shaken, the leader of the most powerful nation in the world acted. He sent ships out to sea and put planes in the air, not simply in an attempt to catch those responsible for the deed, but rather, in the words of one commentator, "because it was important for the president to prove to the American people that he is in control." And it wasn't just the United States whose people needed to be reassured of their security. Around the western world airports were shut down while more intensive security precautions were implemented. All kinds of resources were poured into making people feel their nations were secure.

I think if we are being honest, the real reason why so many people had a sense of insecurity after the events of September 11, 2001, was because they were confronted by the realization that we are *not* in control. A strong and powerful nation, with the highest technological defenses, and the best security, suddenly found themselves out of control. They felt ripped off, as if some thief had snuck in and stolen the safe, secure world in which they thought they lived.

Of course, much of the time we are in control. Most of our days go exactly the way we plan them. Even most of the problems we can expect to face can be somewhat foreseen and plans can put in place to reduce their harmful effects upon our lives. We have our burglar proof locks, home security systems, even insurance policies to protect against accidents and disasters. But what about that late night phone call, that flat voice on the other end, or the news flash interrupting "our regularly scheduled programming" – then what? We find ourselves in the midst of crisis ... one over which we have no control.

Today's first lesson, from the prophet Isaiah, comes from a time during Israel's exile. For long periods of time, Israel enjoyed great prosperity and relative peace. They really had it made. When Solomon was king, they had a strong army and great security. That is, until the Babylonians and the Assyrians came from the north and laid waste Israel's cities, killed many of their people, and carted off everyone else as slaves in exile, all while believing they were in control, that God was a weapon they could wield against their enemies to ensure their security.

Out of exile, out of the dust, rubble, ruin, and hopelessness, we hear the words of a people who had lost control. These tend to be the words in the bible that we would rather skip. We don't like hearing that kind of biblical truth. We desperately want to believe we have at last found some means to insulate ourselves from such instability and insecurity.

We try desperately to insulate ourselves from the hard truth that, for much of human history, most of humanity has lived from one crisis to the next, jerked around by forces over which they had little control, pushed toward some future they did not want. The hard truth is *we are not in control*. At any moment any one of us is only a heartbeat away from crisis. This world, our world that today seems so together, so safe and secure, is not as tangible and solid as it appears.

This is the point Jesus wants to get across to his disciples. In times of crisis we reach for those things that offer us comfort and a sense of security – things that help to give us a sense of still being in control – but as Jesus prepares his disciples for a crisis of epic proportions, what seems strange to us is that Jesus doesn't seem to offer them anything other than the advice to stay alert.

Jesus has just informed his followers the temple was going to be destroyed. Not one stone would be left on another; it was going to be thrown down. Keep in mind that in Jesus' day the temple in Jerusalem was not only the largest building in the city, it was also the most beautiful building that most Jews had ever seen. It had been adorned and decorated with skill and love over hundreds of years and it held a central place in the national life, religion and imagination of nearly every Jew.

News of its destruction would have been as unthinkable for a Jew as it would be for an American to imagine the destruction of the White House, the Washington Memorial, or the Statue of Liberty only much more so, because the temple also signified a thousand years of God's dealings with the fledgling kingdom of Israel. It would have most certainly come as bad news to the disciples. Jesus was essentially telling them the world as they knew it and understood it was coming to an end. For the disciples, a crisis of this magnitude could only mean one thing: the end of the age.

So they want to be prepared. They want to know what to watch for, and when it will all happen so they can take the appropriate action. If the disciples know what to watch for and when to watch, then they can make plans for their safety. They can make provisions for their security. Since Jesus seems to have some inside information about the destruction of the temple, then surely he could give them some inside information about the timing of the end of the age so they can rest secure knowing they will be prepared for the crisis.

But instead of offering signs and times, instead of offering the disciples some comfort and security, Jesus tells them the signs they can expect are persecution, hatred, deception, an increase in wickedness, and an absence of love. Jesus says no one – not the leaders, not the people, not his disciples, not the angels, not even the Son – will know the hour in which this crisis is coming.

There will be no one with insider information about the timing of the end of the age and the crisis that accompanies it. Just as it was in the days of Noah, where life proceeded just as it had on any other day – nothing different, nothing out of the ordinary – that is, until the rain began to fall and didn't stop. But Jesus is not simply pointing to the story of Noah to show that the coming of the Son of Man will be unexpected. He is pointing to something much larger than that.

The story of Noah not only tells us about God's justice but also how God deals with the wickedness of the world. It also tells us a great deal about who God is, about God's nature.

What we see, despite the near total failure of humanity to live according to the will of God, is that he shows an incredible amount of restraint and mercy. He does not bring an abrupt end to his rebellious creation. In the end, the way God chooses to deal with the wickedness of the world is by purging it, removing it, taking it away and leaving behind a faithful remnant to make a new beginning, a new creation.

In the time of Noah, we are told the world had become so godless and corrupt that of the human race only Noah stood out as someone who was righteous, faithful and obedient.

Stop for a minute and think about what it must have been like to be the only morally responsible person in the world. Don't you think there would come a time when Noah would have said, "This is too hard. It's too much for me. After all, I am only one human being. What difference can I possibly make in the face of so much wickedness?" Can you image what it would be like to live as a faithful person in a world filled with unfaithfulness? Can you imagine how little security you would have? Can you image how little control you would have over the events in the world around you? Maybe it would just be easier to fit in with everyone else… settle for a world of wickedness, and forget there was ever a promise of something better.

But that's not what Noah did. He remained faithful to the Lord and he did whatever the Lord asked of him. Noah knew the Lord was just and righteous and that he would set things right. So Noah was able to live in the midst of great tribulation because he knew who God was and knew God would act. In every respect Noah knew who was in control.

If you have any doubt about it, go back and read the details of the construction of the ark and pay close attention to what the ark did not have –

    the ark had no oars;

        the ark had no sails;

            the ark had no rudder.

It was not a ship that required a crew of knowledgeable sailors. In fact, it was nothing more than a huge box that would float on the water. Everyone who entered into it was purely and totally in the hands and at the mercy of God.

That's what Jesus wants his disciples to come to terms with. It's easy enough to follow when everything is going your way, when you seem to be fully in control of your own destiny, charting your own course in life, but what about when the crisis strikes? Will his disciples still be interested in following him into the new creation when they see the gateway is a cross? Will we have any interest in learning to pray like Jesus, "Father ... may your will be done"?

The prophet Isaiah speaks out of the rubble of a dashed world, the dust of failed dreams. Yet he has the audacity to proclaim the vision of a new world being born – a world re-created by God to resemble the world God had originally intended, the world God wants.

This is a large, powerful God who moves, creates, and makes new. How different is this God who comes to us at the very point when we recognize we have no power of our own. When we are not in charge, he comes to take charge. How different this God is from the empathetic but mostly ineffective God whom most of us know. In our modern world, where we are allegedly in control, we don't want too much of a God. Most of us don't get much of a God. Until Advent, when the skies turn dark, and the earth heaves "signs in the sun, the moon, and the stars, and on earth distress among nations confused by the roaring of the sea and the waves," as one of the other Advent texts puts it. *(Luke 21)*

It's rather frightening to those of us who want to be in control, who want to be masters of our fate, captains of our souls. It's at this point we begin to understand something of what Jesus means when he talks about coming like a thief in the night. What is being stolen from us is all our sources of false security. What's being ripped off is our delusion – the illusion that we are, that we were ever, in control. The 'thief in the night' robs us of our lies.

Jesus tells us to be awake, to wake up, so this 'thief in the night' does not catch us sleeping.

Advent is not only an invitation to wake up to our true insecurity, but also an invitation to rest securely in the Lord, the only source of true security. This news, this dark, difficult news, is our good news, the sign of our deliverance. A world is shaking, being dismantled, but a new world is being born. Perhaps an old, false world – a world built upon the shaky foundation of our pride and our smug, modern self-deceit – must give way to a new world.

As Paul tells us, time is marching on. Our salvation is nearer than when we first believed. All the darkness – pain, suffering and death – is coming to end, drawing to a close, and the light of the new creation is near. It will be a time when the nations will say, *"Come, let us go up to the mountain of the Lord, to the house of the God of Jacob. He will teach us his ways, so that we may walk in his paths."* It will be a time when *"... they will hammer their swords into plowshares and their spears into pruning hooks."* And nation will not lift up sword against nation, and never again will they learn war. Even though the world around us is filled with darkness, let us remain awake and alert, clothing ourselves in Christ Jesus.

"Come ... let us walk in the light of the Lord."

Amen.

Nothing to Lose

December 5, 2004

Matthew 3:1-12

A few months ago I had a dream. There was nothing really special about it; it wasn't a vision from God or anything like that, but I remember it quite clearly. I dreamt I was coming in the church doors in the middle of the week and was surprised to find so many people in the sanctuary milling around the hallways. Just as I was about to ask someone what was going on, it dawned on me that it was a funeral service – a funeral service I was supposed to be leading, a funeral service I was not prepared for.

As the dream continued, I quickly put on my robe, grabbed my bible and walked to the front of the church. Now, you might expect that being a dream, I might have dreamt I came up with exactly the right words, prayed from the heart, preached with passion ... but that's not what happened. As it would turn out, this dream was a nightmare. I stammered and stumbled, grasping for words and ideas, but found none. Thankfully, I awoke before I could get to the end of the service, but just the same, I woke up feeling anxious, my heart pounding. Just imagining being caught unprepared was enough to get me physically worked up.

Dreams like this are not all that uncommon. I have had many people tell me about similar dreams – dreams about when they were in school, showing up to class only to discover they had an exam they hadn't prepared for. Maybe there are some students here today who have had similar dreams lately, with exams and term papers coming up quicker than they would like. Being caught unprepared is a nightmare.

If we get anxious about being unprepared for the ordinary events in our lives, just imagine what it must have been like to live in Judea two thousand years ago, to hear John the Baptist proclaiming the King, God himself, was coming back. Imagine hearing him calling Israel to get ready for God's kingdom. In some respects, it would have come as wonderful news.

Finally, Isaiah's great message of hope, forgiveness, and healing for the nation after the horrors of exile was becoming a reality. But at the same time the people knew the coming of the Lord was also a time of God's judgment, and even the devout Jews who worshipped in the Temple, knew deep down inside that they weren't ready for God to come back.

The prophet Malachi had proclaimed God would send his messenger who would prepare the way before him and, suddenly, the Lord they were seeking would come to his temple. The messenger of the covenant, whom they desired, would come, but the coming of the Lord would not be all comfort and joy. It would also be like a refiner's fire, bringing quick judgment against the wicked, the unjust, and those who had no fear of the Lord. *(Malachi 3:1-5)*

If the people didn't want to get caught unprepared for the coming of the Lord – if they wanted to enjoy the deliverance of the day of the Lord – then they needed to ensure they lived in accordance with commands of the covenant.

Not only that, but the people would be given something of a sign that all of this was about to take place. Malachi prophesied that before the coming of the great and terrible day of the Lord, God would send the prophet Elijah to turn the hearts of the people.

So you can imagine what the people would have been thinking when they heard there was:
- a man dressed in a coat of camel's hair and wearing a leather belt;
- a man dressed the same way as Elijah is described in the second Book of Kings;
- a man who is proclaiming the Kingdom is near and calling the people to a baptism of repentance.

They would have been thinking the King was coming and they needed to get ready, so they came out to John in droves. They came not simply for a symbolic cleansing of their individual sins, but as a sign of the new thing God was doing in history for Israel and for the world.

More than a thousand years earlier the people had crossed the Jordan River when they first entered and conquered the Promised Land. Now they had to go through the river again, as a sign they were getting ready for a greater conquest – getting ready for God's defeat of every evil and the establishment of his kingdom on earth as it is in heaven. But John knew not everyone who came was genuinely interested in repentance. He knew full well the social landscape of the day … how the leaders were interested in making a good showing and his baptism was a great opportunity for the religious leaders to demonstrate their personal piety in the sight of a large number of people. It was good 'P.R.' – the equivalent of what we today might call a photo opportunity.

But John would have none of it. When he saw the Pharisees and the Sadducees coming for baptism, he scoffed at them, calling them a brood of vipers, a bunch of snakes. You can be sure it is no coincidence John chooses to compare these men to the same creature that led humanity astray – led humanity out of the garden and out of the presence of God. There would be no confusion on the point. John's baptism did not produce repentance. It was only the sign, a symbol of the conviction of the people to turn back to

God. Going through the motions was not enough. Real repentance, a lasting change of heart and of life, was required.

That may sound straightforward to us, but it's clear from John's reaction to the presence of the Pharisees and Sadducees that they had not come to demonstrate their conviction to repent – that even after being called a brood of vipers they did not leave. They still saw some potential in what John was doing. What were they interested in?

Keep in mind the Pharisees and Sadducees did not see eye to eye on most issues, but the one thing they were united about was that the Roman occupation of the holy land was contrary to God's promises. Any talk of the fulfillment of God's Kingdom had to involve the cleansing of the land from its pagan overlords. When they heard John was preaching about the coming kingdom, they must have seen in John an opportunity to galvanize the people of Israel into a united front against the Roman oppressors. Sure, there would be judgment, judgment for the pagans, for the Romans, for those who oppressed God's people. Surely not for Israel, not for the sons of Abraham, the heirs of the covenant promises of God.

But John leaves no room for this kind of thinking. He has not come proclaiming that God was about to purge the land of gentile influence, but that God was about to purge the covenant people of their disobedience and unfaithfulness.

If the people of God are not prepared to bear the fruit of repentance, then God is no way obliged to save them simply because they are the descendants of Abraham. God, the Sovereign Lord of the cosmos, the Creator of the world, will have no problem finding heirs for Abraham even if the whole of humanity is found to be unworthy. God could simply start from scratch. The one who breathed life into dust to create humanity could just as easily create descendants for Abraham from the inert stones that lay at their feet. John reminds them there is no technicality in the tradition or in the scriptures that will allow them to justify their failure to bear good fruit. Even now, John tells them, the axe is at the roots of the tree and every tree that does not bear fruit will be cut down and cast into the fire.

Words like this are bound to get attention, not only for those who first heard them but also for us. What's worse, John is not all that specific about what he means by bearing fruit. He does not give us a list of things to do so we can to be sure we will not be caught unprepared. He does not give the key to ensuring the axe will not swing at our roots. John wants to be clear that he has not come with some new program, some new philosophy, to institute a new religious sect.

He is purposely vague so people will need to turn to the Law and the prophets to fill in the content. He is not preaching his own word. He is insistent that we should not focus on him. He is, after all, only the messenger – the one preparing straight paths for the Lord.

The one who is coming will be more powerful – one who will not baptize the people with water, but instead will immerse them in the Holy Spirit and in fire. The coming one has his winnowing fork in hand to clear the threshing floor, to gather the grain into the barn and burn up the chaff with an unquenchable fire.

Before we have even had a chance to fully come to terms with his first image of judgment John moves on to a second image. Unfruitful trees will be cut down and cast into the fire and the grain will be separated from the chaff which will also be consumed in an unquenchable fire. The question is, why are we getting a double dose of judgment? Has John simply become fixated on the coming wrath of God? Is he determined to pound the concept into the minds of his listeners? Or is there more to it?

For the most part, the first image of judgment John gives us is pretty clear. If we had planted a tree in order to harvest its fruit and it never yielded any fruit, of course we would cut it down. The point is, as God's people, we have been called to order our lives in accordance with God's intention for creation ... specifically, God's intention for humanity.

But the second image John uses is not a call to bear fruit. It presumes fruitfulness – it presumes there is something to be harvested – but in order to get at the grain, the wheat must undergo a process of removing the grain from the head.

The way the process worked in Jesus' day was that the wheat heads would be gathered together on a threshing floor, a hard surface, and then farm animals trampled the wheat and pulled a large block of wood with nails embedded in it over top of the wheat.

While this process resulted in the grain being removed from the heads, it didn't separate them. Both the grain and the chaff were still mixed together on the threshing floor. So in order to separate the wheat from the chaff you would need to wait for a windy day, take your winnowing fork and throw the grain and chaff into the air. The lighter chaff would blow away and the grain would fall to the ground. When you were finished, you would be left with two piles ... one pile of grain and another pile of chaff.

So often when we hear talk of separating the wheat from the chaff we imagine two groups of people –
> the good are being separated from the bad;
>> the faithful are being separated from
>> the disobedient;
>>> the righteous are being separated
>>> from the wicked,

but that does not take seriously the example John has used here. He is saying there is no such thing as wheat that grows without chaff. Every stalk of wheat, every kernel of grain, comes packaged in chaff. Every person, even those who are bearing fruit, is a mixture of both grain and chaff. Every life must undergo the process of being threshed and winnowed – a process of transformation whereby all our evil, all our disobedience, all our wickedness is separated and burnt in the unquenchable fire ... destroyed with no possibility of return.

The one who is coming does not baptize with the Holy Spirit to prove who is grain and who is chaff, who is in and who is out. Instead, he baptizes with the Holy Spirit to transform humanity – to transform us into the people we are intended to be, the people that we truly are when we are not encased, enclosed, and imprisoned by our chaff, trapped in our sin.

But in the Pharisees and Sadducees, John is coming up against people who believe their election as God's people means they have no chaff; they have nothing they need to lose, nothing in their lives that needs to be consumed by the holy fire of God. John is coming up against people who believe they do not need transformation; all they need to do is to wait for the right leader, wait for the coming king, and then they can take their God-given place of honour in his kingdom.

Both then and now, one of the hardest things to come to terms with in John's preaching is not that there will be judgment, but that when the kingdom comes in its fullness we will not be the same people we are at this moment ... that we will need to pass through the refining fire of the Lord.

That's a concept quite foreign to us. Mostly we are happy with who we are so long as things more or less go the way we expect them to. Mostly we are happy so long as we measure up when we compare ourselves with our neighbour. So long as we can convince ourselves that we are not so bad, then we feel reasonably assured we will be among the wheat gathered into the barn – that we will be among those who are gathered into the Kingdom of God. If you want to test that out, go back to our first reading from the Prophet Isaiah, and look again at this vision of the kingdom of God:

> *"The wolf will live with the lamb, the leopard will lie down with the goat, the calf and the lion and the yearling together; and a little child will lead them. The cow will feed with the bear, their young will lie down together, and the lion will eat straw like the ox. The infant will play near the hole of the cobra, and the young child put his hand into the viper's nest. They will neither harm nor destroy on all my holy mountain, for the earth will be full of the knowledge of the Lord as the waters cover the sea.*
> *(Isaiah 11:6-9)*

Can you imagine a world like that, where the most vulnerable human beings – children – are safe even in the presence of the most dangerous beasts? For many people in our world, this vision is nothing more than a pipe dream.

The reality is that we would be willing to settle for much less. We don't want vicious animals to be docile. We would settle for being able to kill them when they got too close for comfort. We don't want snakes that are safe for children to handle. We would settle for the sure-fire cure for snakebites. We don't want a world filled with the knowledge of the Lord. We would settle for a world filled with the knowledge of how to prevent pain, suffering, and death. Getting from the vision of the kingdom we would settle for to the vision of the kingdom God has promised will take nothing short of
> a transformation of our hearts,
> a transformation of our minds,
> a transformation of our lives.

In the end, John's call to prepare the way of the Lord is not so much about doing whatever we can to avoid judgment as it is about allowing ourselves to be prepared by Christ through his baptism of the Holy Spirit and fire

that transforms us from the inside out,
    that burns away our chaff,
        that makes our hearts and minds clean by washing away our sin and filling us with grace.

When he comes to bring his kingdom in its fullness, there will be no anxiety about being caught unprepared, for we will have been refined and re-formed by his own hand back into the image and likeness of God.

Thanks be to God.

Amen.

What Are You Looking For?

Communion Sunday, December 12, 2004

Matthew 11:2-11

One of my daughter's favourite television shows is *America's Funniest Videos*. I have to admit I enjoy watching it with her. Usually at this time of year a group of videos dedicated to Christmas mishaps and embarrassing moments is included. Some of them have even become classics, making it onto the show year after year. There is one of these 'classics' that stands out in my memory. It features a young boy – probably five or six years old – opening a gift Christmas morning.

The video captures him tearing open the wrapping paper until at last he gets the gift. In a moment of unguarded spontaneous reaction, the boy yells out, "Socks! I don't want no stinking socks!" He proceeds to throw the gift down on the floor and cross his arms in thorough disgust. Apparently socks were not very high up on his Christmas list.

Despite my concern for the feelings of the person who gave the gift to the boy, I couldn't help but laugh. I remember being a young boy at Christmas time and how my brother and I would rummage around under the Christmas tree to find out which presents were for us. I also remember the disappointed look we would give each other when we found a 'soft one'. A soft present could mean only one thing: clothes.

It's not that socks and clothes are bad gifts. In fact, socks regularly make it onto my Christmas wish list these days. The real problem lies with the expectations. When you are expecting a new toy or some electronic gadget, socks simply do not measure up. Often it's hard to cover up the disappointment when our expectations have not been met – when we realize all the things we most hoped that gift would be, are simply not going to materialize. It is this kind of disappointment and unfulfilled expectation that we find in our gospel lesson for this morning.

Last week we got a taste of John the Baptist's fiery preaching. This week we catch up with John again, but under much different circumstances. John's preaching had been so clear, so direct – get ready, the Messiah is coming; the kingdom of God is upon us. The coming one is greater than I. He is a man of fire, unquenchable fire, coming to burn away all of the impurities in Israel.

Preaching with that kind of zeal and that kind of courage attracted all kinds of people. They came out from the cities, from all over the countryside, to hear his strong words. But the voice of John who had proclaimed so fearlessly has very quickly fallen silent. Our scripture today begins by telling us John was in prison. King Herod had taken exception to John's fiery preaching, particularly to his announcement that God's kingdom and the true king were on the way. That, of course, meant Herod was not the real king, that God would soon replace him.

It should come as no surprise to us that Herod would want to imprison someone for saying such things. I'm sure it wasn't much of a surprise to John either, but surprise or not, what was certain was that life in prison was a dramatic change for John. He who had spent most of his life living in the open wilderness was now living in a cage. He who had the multitudes coming out to listen to his preaching and responding in droves with acts of repentance, now suddenly finds himself with only his disciples to keep him company. He who had proclaimed the coming judgment of the Lord, is now a prisoner by the judgment of Herod. It must have been a severe disappointment to John.

Trapped in prison, he could only hear about what Jesus was doing, and what he heard didn't sound a great deal like the fireworks for which he had been preparing Israel. John was expecting Jesus to be a man of fire, someone like Elijah, who could call down the fire of the Lord and sweep the impurities of Israel away just as Elijah had done with the prophets of Baal. Undoubtedly, John eagerly looked forward to the day in the not-so-distant future, when Jesus would confront Herod, overthrow his kingdom, and replace him as King. Then not only would the newly inaugurated King throw open the prison doors and set his cousin, John, free, but he would also give him the place of honour he deserved in the new kingdom. John must have been wondering what was taking Jesus so long. When was he going to make his move?

It's fairly easy for us to sympathize with John. After all, he has done what was asked of him. He played the part of the forerunner, preparing the way of the Lord, and he did it faithfully. He did not snuggle up to the powerful and flatter them in order to win friends and influence people. No, John called it as he saw it. He called a spade a spade. He condemned Herod, and as a result he was wasting away in prison.

We have a word for that kind of situation. It's called injustice – when the one who tells the truth goes to prison at the hands of an incestuous adulterer there is no way of getting around the fact that an injustice has been perpetrated. And if Jesus is the true king, how can he stand by while a faithful servant of the Lord is treated so unjustly without acting to correct it? How could Jesus simply let this injustice stand?

It's a question that most certainly would have been on the mind of John, but one that seems to confront not only him, but almost every believer at one time or another, either by

circumstances in their own life or by someone else demanding an accounting of our faith. If Jesus is who he claims to be, then
    why is there so much injustice;
        why is there so much suffering in the world;
            why do bad things happen to good
        people?
This is the issue that lies at the heart of what John is asking when he sends his disciples with the question for Jesus: "Are you the one who was to come, or should we expect someone else?"

It should be abundantly clear to us that this is not simply some philosophical question John is pondering and needs Jesus' help to sort out. We should hear this question for what it really is ... a challenge. It's somewhat of a shocking question given that it's coming from John. Normally questions like this would be asked by Jesus' worst critics – those anxious to discredit him. It's one thing for Jesus' enemies to ask such a question, but now the question has been asked by Jesus' own cousin. Are you the Messiah?

Had things really changed that much for John? Was he really finding it difficult to look at Jesus and see the Messiah? His ministry began with great power and prominence. Sure, there was some resistance, but Jesus seemed to overcome it. John had said there would be one who would come preaching with fire, with mighty deeds, and he had been right ... but now things must have seemed to John to have levelled off. Much remained unchanged by the advent of Jesus and his ministry, particularly his imprisonment.

It must have been a hard pill to swallow for the one who had preached that change was necessary ... that repentance was necessary. John's whole ministry had been pointing to Jesus, saying he was the one, the coming Messiah. Now he himself is asking Jesus, "Are you the one?" Has John somehow forgotten his own sermons? Has he forgotten how, when Jesus had come to him for baptism, he had originally refused, saying, "If anybody ought to baptize anybody, you ought to be baptizing me!" It seems almost unbelievable that someone who had been there at the baptism of

Jesus, who had witnessed the appearance of the Holy Spirit, could now be demanding an answer to the question of who Jesus is.

It was no easier for John than it is for us to deal with the realization that things often do not to turn out the way we hoped or expected, and often it's not too long afterward that we are throwing our gifts on the floor in an angry temper tantrum. We like to think faith would have been easier to accept, or to live, if we had been there with Jesus, but as we see here with John, it seems almost inevitable that even the most dramatic religious experiences are followed by some kind of let-down – that our spiritual mountaintop experiences are quickly followed by spiritual valleys.

When I think back to the time I was first becoming aware of my calling, I can remember feeling so near to God that I could almost reach and touch him. It was a wonderful experience, but looking back on it, I also remember God never told me one day that wonderful call experience would lead me to the bedside of a twenty-one-year-old girl dying of Cancer. Over the past several weeks as I have struggled in prayer, pleading with God to do something – to intervene, to right this wrong – I realized that in my earnest desire to bring healing to this young girl I was trying to grab hold of God's power. I was trying to harness and control his Spirit, to do what I thought God should do. Until finally I heard the voice of the Lord saying, "Don't you trust me?"

Don't you trust me? I think that's very much what's at the heart of Jesus' response to John. He tells John's disciples to report back what they have seen and heard – the blind receive sight, the lame walk, those who have leprosy are cured, the deaf hear, the dead are raised, and the good news is preached to the poor.

It may sound to us as if Jesus is trying to prove he is living up to the title of Messiah, but keep in mind John has already heard all this. Remember from the first verse of our reading that it was **because** John had heard what Jesus was doing that he sent his disciples to question Jesus in the first place. As a child of a temple priest, John would have been well versed in the scriptures. It's not as if Jesus is instructing John on the prophesies and the promises he is claiming to be fulfilling. Jesus is not offering him anything new in the way of proof. If anything, Jesus answers back with something of a challenge of his own.

Throughout the prophecies of Isaiah, we hear the same promises – sight to the blind, hearing to the deaf, healing for the lame – but notice which promise is conspicuous by its absence. Jesus does not even mention release for the captives in his response to John who sits imprisoned. Jesus has a much larger prison break in mind. He is interested in much more than the dungeon in Herod's palace. Jesus has in mind setting humanity free from the captivity of sin and death. If John is to grasp what Jesus is doing, he will need to re-evaluate his commitment to his own expectations.

At this point Jesus pronounces God's blessing upon those who are able to trust him, to recognize that God is at work in him, and upon those who are not offended, who will not fall away because Jesus' words and deeds do not line up with the common expectations about the Messiah. This is what lies behind the questions Jesus asks the crowd about John. Three times Jesus asks what it was they were looking for when they went out in the wilderness to see John. He wants them to take the time to think through who John is, because once they come to terms with who John is, then they will be far more likely to understand who Jesus must be.

Did they go out looking for a king like Herod, whose emblem on his coins was a Galilean reed waving in the wind? Did they go out to see someone rich or famous, someone who dressed in fine clothes?

No, John was nothing like either of those kinds of people. The only way to explain who John was and what John was doing was to call him a prophet, and not just any prophet. John was the prophet that the previous prophets had spoken about. He was the one destined to get the path ready for the Messiah, whether Jesus was the kind of messiah John expected or not.

In telling the crowds about John, Jesus is really interested in pressing them to think about who he is, but in such a way that the people have to work it out for themselves. That may sound strange to us. We would prefer if he were more straightforward about his identity, so there would be no confusion. But Jesus knew being straightforward would not work because, just like John, everyone had certain expectations about what the messiah would do when he came, and none of those expectations involved the messiah coming to die on a cross. If the people were going to look at Jesus on the cross and see hanging there their King – their Messiah – no amount of straightforward teaching, convincing, or persuading would have been enough. Jesus knew the people would have to work it out for themselves, otherwise the cross would have served simply to prove he was not who he claimed to be, he was not the Messiah.

Now all of that may seem somewhat removed from us. After all, we are here today because we profess we are those who haven't taken offense at Jesus. We are those who look at Jesus on the cross and see there our King, but at the same time we are very much in a similar position as John. We have some insider information. We know Jesus is coming again – we know he is coming to bring the kingdom in its fullness – and like John, we are bound to have certain expectations about how that will happen and what it will look like when it happens.

But we need to be very conscious of the fact that if the kingdom had come exactly as John had expected, there would have been no cross, no outstretched arms to embrace a lost world. The light to the nations would have been a blazing fire.

That is in no way a slight against John. As Jesus said himself, *"Among those born of women there has not risen anyone greater than John the Baptist."* But it should serve as a warning to us as we await the coming of the Lord, as we await his coming kingdom. What are we looking for? What are we expecting? Is our vision of the kingdom of God limited to our expectations? Is our vision of the kingdom of God big enough, not simply to accommodate our hopes and dreams, but to accommodate the covenant promise that all the families of the earth will be blessed through Abraham's seed?

How we answer that question will have a great deal to do with who it is we expect to meet at this table. As we gather around this table are we still expecting someone else – a Lord who will fulfill all our dreams – or do we come face to face with the Lord who fulfills all his promises in ways we never expected – the Lord who is so much more than anything we could ever expect?

As we break bread together may we rejoice in the grace and mercy of the Lord that surpasses all understanding.

Amen and amen.

APPENDIX A

Memorial Minute

THE REVEREND KRISTIAN ROBERT DAVIDSON
January 6, 1969- January 7, 2005

The Reverend Kristian Robert Davidson, Minister of Haney Presbyterian Church, Maple Ridge, B.C., died on January 7, 2005, in a tragic car accident near Salmon Arm, B.C. while returning from a post-Christmas holiday in Calgary. His wife Sheryl, and nine-year old daughter, Lauren, were also killed. Their twenty-three-month old daughter, Katherine, survived the crash.

The Reverend Davidson, known to all and sundry as "Kris", was born in Burnaby, B.C., on January 6, 1969, but grew up in Calgary, Alberta, where he received his elementary and secondary education, graduating from Central Memorial High School in 1987 with an Advanced Diploma.

From 1987 to 1992 Kris found employment in various entry-level positions as a commissioned sales person. He enjoyed interacting with people but left the field because, as he said, "I was not prepared to employ what I considered to be pressure tactics in order to secure more sales...."

From 1992 to 1994 Kris attended the Southern Alberta Institute of Technology in Calgary receiving the Accounting Diploma in Business Administration (with Honours) together with various significant academic awards.

From 1994-1996 Kris worked as Staff Accountant with the accounting firm KPMG and then from 1996-1998 became Financial Analyst for the Canadian Red Cross Society where he assisted in the implementation of new financial software. In 1998 Kris became Controller (Alberta/NWT Division) for the Canadian Cancer Society, ending his career in the business world as Financial Analyst in 1999 for PIC Canada Ltd.

In 2000 Kris completed one year of full time studies, primarily in the Humanities, at the University of Calgary.

Among the most significant events in Kris' life was his coming to faith in Christ as a young adult. He had become disillusioned with the quest for material and social success and came to recognize that "a man's life does not consist in the abundance of things." He began attending church with his future wife, Sheryl, and in 1993 Southwood United Church in Calgary received both him and Sheryl as members of Christ's Church through adult baptism.

Kris has spoken highly of the Christian nurture he received at Southwood United Church where he participated in the Bethel Bible Studies, Levels 1 and 2, served on the Worship Committee, eventually as its chairperson, and became involved in other congregational activities.

As Kris grew in faith he noted how his perceptions about worship changed. "No longer was I coming to fill up my spiritual gas tank for the week that lay ahead, rather I was seeking a better understanding of how I might be the blessing I was intended to be."

During this time Kris also began to experience a call to the ministry of Word and Sacrament. A process of discernment began in 1999 and this led him eventually to make the decision, supported by Sheryl, to move to Vancouver and attend the Vancouver School of Theology under the auspices of the United Church of Canada. Kris graduated from VST in May of 2003.

Prior to his last year at the Vancouver School of Theology, Kris found himself increasingly ill at ease with some of the theological positions that seemed to gain influence both within the United Church and VST and after much soul-searching decided to seek ordination within The Presbyterian Church in Canada.

In October, 2002, the family joined Richmond Presbyterian Church where Kris spent the required six months under the supervision of its Minister and Session. The congregation so much respected and admired Kris that it rallied to support him and the family financially and by extending his "internship" into a full year. The Presbytery of Westminster certified Kris as a candidate for ordination in November, 2003.

He was then called to Haney Presbyterian Church where he was ordained and inducted in March, 2004. It proved to be a very good "match" and both Kris and his family as well as the congregation looked toward to the future with great optimism. It thus was heart rending for the congregation when the tragic news reached them that Kris, Sheryl and Lauren had died so tragically as they returned to resume their life and ministry within the congregation in the New Year.

A funeral service was held at Southwood United Church on Monday, January 17, 2005, attended by family and a large congregation of friends. The Presbytery of Westminster conducted a Memorial Service on Saturday, January 22, 2005, within Haney Presbyterian Church, attended by an overflow crowd from both Haney and Richmond congregations as well as family and many colleagues and friends.

The Rev. Kris Davidson, a humble man with a keen insight into Scripture and a truly pastoral heart would want to be remembered as one who saw the work of ministry as not about himself, or even about the church, but all about the good news of "the God who has called us out of darkness into his marvelous light."

As he lived out a gospel-shaped life, he did indeed become to many the blessing God intended him to be.

~ ~ ~

Excerpted from the Official Minutes - February 1, 2005
Presbytery of Westminster

and included in

The Acts and Proceedings of the
131st General Assembly
of The Presbyterian Church in Canada

www.ingramcontent.com/pod-product-compliance
Lightning Source LLC
Chambersburg PA
CBHW061629040426

42446CB00010B/1339